TORAH
24/7

A Timely Guide for the Modern Spirit

STEVEN ETTINGER

DEVORA
PUBLISHING
JERUSALEM ◆ NEW YORK

TORAH 24/7
A Timely Guide For The Modern Spirit

Published by Devora Publishing Company

Text Copyright © 2003 by Steven Ettinger
Cover and Book Design: David Yaphe
Editor: Shalom Kaplan

ISBN: 1-930143-73-7

Email: publisher@devorapublishing.com
Web Site: www.pitspopany.com

Printed in Israel

Table of Contents

TORAH
24/7

Chosen or Choosing?

What are the frames of reference for your life? Milestone and life events are easy choices — Bar/Bat Mitzvah, weddings, graduations, the birth of children, the loss of loved ones — and most of us can recall the textures of those days. But there are many events, big and small, that propel and direct us through daily life — and often even exert control over it.

Some are as trivial as when the television show or ballgame you wish to watch will start (unless you know how to electronically record it). The pace of an entire day in your life may be effected by that start time. Just imagine that because of that one event you may arrive at work a little earlier so that you can leave timely, you may take dinner out rather than worrying about cleaning up the kitchen, you may regiment the kids more tightly into their home-work/cleanup routine so that they will not disturb you, and you may pass on a conflicting social or communal obligation.

Of course other events, like those of September 11, are not as trivial or fleeting. They impact us significantly — morally, spiritual-ly, politically, and in many other ways. The events of that day sure-

1

ly changed our entire world. However, trying to understand what is different is much harder to quantify since the escalation of terror simultaneously effected us as individuals and as a society. Besides, we are not far enough from that day and its aftermath to place any change in perspective.

But change is nothing new. In our lifetimes, let's include in that approximately the last half-century, there has been only one true constant — rapid change (I deliberately do not term this progress since some of this change has been for the worse and some advances and breakthroughs have bred new and even greater problems).

In a song titled "We Didn't Start the Fire" singer-songwriter Billy Joel captured the major images, events, and personalities of this half-century in a three minute song. (A group called Shlock Rock actually did him one better describing 4,000 years of Jewish history in a parody of the same tune!) For a relatively monotonous song, it was clever. It was a song tailor-made for Music Television; just add the appropriate video clips from the film archives and put it on the air every hour. It was pure information overload, a song that assumed we knew exactly what he was singing about. Music, movies, science, revolutions, and wars. Liberation, equalization, assassination, and plenty of sensation. Equal rights, civil rights, gay rights, and whale's rights. Rock stars, movie stars, sports stars, and media stars. What was truly alarming was the realization that for the most part we, the listeners, understood the references.

It makes little difference how isolated one chooses to be or where one lives. Change and all of its baggage, blessings and curses, has altered who we are, how we experience and feel, and how we perceive the world around us and the spiritual world within us. Pen and paper, electric typewriters, word processors, personal computers and PDAs. Radio, television, cable, satellites, wireless, and fiberoptics. Soncino, Artscroll, Dial-A-Daf, CD Daf, and Torah on line. How much change have we witnessed? How much has this change affected us and the choices we make?

One of God's greatest gifts to man is free will. Man can choose. In our day and age, the array of choices, both good and bad, is almost limitless. In *Devarim* (30:19), Moshe describes the two paths that lay open before the Jewish Nation, the Chosen People, after forty years of rigorous preparation in the dessert. He places good and evil before them, life and death. He advises them to choose life, the way of God's Torah and commandments.

Life was simple then, perhaps as simple as it can possibly get, sand, water, and sunshine all while being surrounded by 600,000 of your closest friends and relatives. Even so, it was doubtful whether our ancestors truly knew what was good and what was evil. Just move a holy book or two farther (e.g., *Shoftim, Shmuel*) and you watch them sin and then get trounced by the Philistines, and sin and get trounced by the Amalekites, and sin and get trounced by the Midianites etc., etc., etc.... If they had a clear notion of good and evil, they certainly gave that free choice of theirs a Body by Jake workout.

The reality was that they faced extensive and constant change and were challenged to deal with it. One day they were slaves — tortured and abused. The next they were liberated. Although free, they lived for a complete generation in a protective cocoon, a womb for their nascent development. They did not have to farm or cook or launder their clothes. But they likewise did not have the freedom to choose where to go each day or what to do. They were children in an Eden-like existence. They lived in a wondrous, miraculous, nurturing environment, but they were children nonetheless. Any individuals or group that rebelled or tried to travel along another path — in any way questioning or challenging the established directive — were not simply placed in "time out" like a rambunctious toddler. No, they were either burned alive, swallowed by the ground, stoned, or attacked and killed by one marauding tribe or another. Even Moshe himself was ultimately punished for raising his hand instead of talking in class.

As the forty year timer went off, they were pointed in the direction of the Holy Land and told, "go and fight,"— conquer, rule and govern. By the way, they also had to build homes, plant fields, establish courts, transact business, and interact with foreign nations. To top it all off, they were also expected to maintain a steadfast course of religious observance in the face of intense temptation from those immoral and decadent Canaanites, while being truly free from hand-holding teachers, protective leaders, and whip-snapping overseers for the first time in their or their parent's lifetimes. They faced extreme change in virtually every facet of their lives and true freedom of choice for the first time.

Did you find the first moon landing amazing or miraculous? Think about witnessing the splitting of the sea or the sun standing still on command. We have super computers, but they saw the *Urim V'tumim,* precious stones set in gold that functioned as an interface between the High Priest and God, in action. The Chicago police at the 1968 Democratic Convention or the National Guard at Kent State would not have handled the Korach rebellion with any more violence. The smart bombs that hit Iraqi targets with such precision in the Gulf Wars were not nearly as effective as, or more devastating than, the shofar blasts at Jericho.

The Torah is a book about rapid change — cultural change, societal change, economic change, and scientific/technological change — that occurred and affected real people with faults, vices and temptations during times that mirror ours in more ways than one would think possible. The Torah is also the ultimate "Never Ending Story," a work "written" by God a thousand years before the creation of the world that contains the script for all that was or will be until the end of days.

We read the cycle of Torah portions each year. For some, it is a mere recitation; ancient words in an unfamiliar language and the difference between a two hour and a three hour service each *Shabbat*. For others it a review of the familiar — favorite stories and fables that remain static. For many, especially for many rabbis, it is the ultimate well-stocked private fishing lake. If one simply baits the hook with a relevant theme or a current event and casts his line into the multitude of commentaries, *Midrash,* or Hasidic parable, the line will be taut in no time.

But the key to understanding the Torah, as intended by the very sages that instituted the system of reading the weekly portions, and, dare I say, as intended by God, is for it to be the guidebook of and for our lives. The Torah is described as white fire on black fire — flickering and moving, consuming and energizing. Every Jew is a letter in the Torah and a Torah with even one missing letter is incomplete and invalid. I sit to write this as a way of discovering my letter, my personal key to not merely studying the Torah but to entering it and being a part of it 24/7.

In order to do this I am undertaking an experiment (if you are reading this, it means that the experiment worked!). My hypothesis is that everything that will happen in my life this year can be filtered through the Torah. More specifically, I intend to produce a diary of sorts, in real time, where I relate whatever is important in my life week by week. Since the Torah is the blueprint for all of existence, one would expect to be able to interpret the events from somewhere in the universe of Torah and its commentaries — that would be almost too easy, not a challenge at all! What I will attempt is to see whether my life is connected to a major theme of the Torah portion to be read during that very week. Is the Torah so eternal, so in tune with each individual Jewish soul, that it can guide a modern 21st century man as he is living his life, no matter what the issue? Is the Torah so "user friendly" that one can find such guidance and inspiration with as little effort as fulfilling the requirement to review the weekly portion?

This work is intended as a tool for me and my personal spiritual growth. But my hope is that it can also be a guide or example for others, to focus their own thoughts and experiences week by week through the source of all life and all thought, our Torah.

With that in mind, I am setting another control on this experiment. I have been blessed during my life to learn from renown Torah scholars, to set aside time each day for in depth study, and, as a Rabbi and teacher, to have been stimulated to greater insight by students and congregants. I also have an extensive library of Torah commentary and Jewish law. These weekly diary entries cannot be research projects or treasure hunts for some obscure or esoteric source. The connections and messages that I expect to find must be contained in the Torah text itself or in an examination of the plain meaning of the text that is accessible to everyone — regardless of their level of scholarship. In shul each week the entire congregation, from young children (if they can sit still) to the wisest scholars, listen attentively to the reading of the Torah. They all hear the same words, read the same way. Yet they understand the reading differently, based on their experiences, base of knowledge, background, and perspective. To be effective, and to encourage you, the reader, to personalize the process by trying it yourself, I have chosen to work from the common denominator.

This undertaking, of course, raises one of the most difficult theological questions. If every choice, decision, and event in my life is already written in the Torah and is preordained by God, how much am I choosing and how much has been chosen for me? For now, I am content to establish my link to the Torah and perhaps better understand how to best benefit from its guidance. If I ever master these basics, perhaps then I will feel bold enough to tackle philosophy.

One final warning. I carry the baggage of my past experiences and reflect the society and times in which I live. Accordingly, much of what I may find as I gaze at the Torah to try and understand my letter may only be a distorted reflection of the truth — not necessarily what God intended to teach. Well Alice, let's plunge through the looking glass!

BEREISHIT
Beginning With Two

Another round of holidays have come and gone. Eat, sleep, go to shul (synagogue), eat, sleep, go to shul, eat, sleep, go to shul. This has been a month-long endurance test. We have faced judgement, confessed and repented, received atonement (hopefully!), braved the elements, helped out the Israeli agricultural industry as well as the network of booksellers who collect hundreds of dollars from us for a piece of fruit and some drying leaves, and "rocked" around the shul fourteen times. We have done this together as families, friends, and communities. We sang familiar tunes and learned a few new ones. We reached out to God in prayer — asking our Father to forgive and to care for us — asking our King to commute the sentences of loved ones for whom every day brings poignant questions about their own continued mortality.

We also shared experiences with our own selves (memories, not reincarnation or channeling) as these holidays converged with and overlaid those of the past. Our memories work in strange ways — we usually cannot remember what we did two weeks ago last

Thursday or what we wore last Monday; but we can picture many of our prior holiday observances like they just happened: the "ritual" of lifting our children on our shoulders while dancing on *Simchat Torah* merges with the sensation of being lifted on our own fathers' shoulders; it is cold in the *succah,* but still not as bad as the time it snowed in 1984; and remember 1978, when our thoughts on Rosh Hashana, in *yeshivah* no less, were sidetracked by the Yankees/Red Sox do-or-die playoff (thanks again Bucky Dent!!!).

Perhaps the most important and effective part of this past holy month was the fact that we shared this experience with others who observed as we did. I deliberately chose the word observe because I do not know if there are two individuals on the planet who think alike, worship alike, or believe alike. Yet, without those others who are like us, who take up little pieces of our attentions and concerns, we would be alone.

What is so bad about being alone? When I arrive home after a long stressful day in the office, a bit tired and ready to eat dinner and one child wants my help on a school project and another is crying because her brother teased her and another has just scattered a pile of important papers and my wife, who has been dealing with this chaos for the past two hours while trying to prepare dinner and helping the children with their schoolwork and keeping a lid on any one of a number of domestic crises, gives me one of those looks that simultaneously says *boruch Hashem* (thank God) relief is here, where the heck has he been, and he thinks his day was tough — I'll show him tough, a bit of aloneness seems like *Gan Eden* (Garden of Eden). But, of course, were I to seek that solitude, I would be depriving my loved ones of their needs. I would also be someone far less than the person I strive to be.

The Torah conveys this idea with its very first letter, the *Beit.*

The *Midrash* recounts an fanciful dialogue, one that has been the source for a number of charming children's books, between God and the letters of the *Aleph-Beit.* God is preparing to translate

His Torah into a written form. Like politicians in New Hampshire early in an election year, the letters of the *Aleph-Beit* are vying for the top spot; desiring to be the first letter. Beginning with the last letter *Tav* and moving forward in reverse order toward the first letter *Aleph,* each one states its case. Now, mind you, every letter is a power in its own right. Each letter represents an aspect of God. Each letter contains forces that were used to create the universe. Nevertheless, one by one they get gonged — until the *Beit* comes forward. God embraces the *Beit* and proclaims that it will be the first letter because it represents *berachah,* blessing.

This is all well and good, except one letter has been deprived of its right to a fair trial. The *Aleph* did not present its credentials. Not wishing to appear unfair, God unilaterally proclaims that the *Aleph's* suitability for the pole position has been ruled out insofar as *Aleph* is the first letter in the Hebrew word for curse, *arur.* God, thus, expressly desires to begin His Torah with blessing rather than with a curse.

This legend is a nice story with a nice message, but something is missing. The explanation that God provides to the *Aleph* seems too shallow. There are many words and concepts in Hebrew that begin with an *Aleph* — love begins with this letter (*ahava*), as does belief (*emunah*), and the name of God denoting mastery over the world (*Adon Olam*). *Aleph* is even the first letter of the Ten Commandments, not exactly an insignificant part of Jewish heritage. Likewise, *Beit* certainly has its dark side — full of idols (*Baal Peor*), evil prophets (*Bilaam*), and assorted other abominations (*bizayon*). Why then is the *Beit* preferred over the *Aleph*?

The answer may have nothing to do with these letters as parts of words. It instead may involve their other aspect — the letters as numerical representations. Hebrew letters are also numbers; *Aleph* is one, *Beit* two, *Gimel* three, etc. God is alone, God is one. Man by nature and by creation is two. Man was never alone — there was always God. Man was never intended to be a solitary creature.

In fact, after creating man God immediately proclaims: "it is not good that man exist alone." (Bereishit 2:18).

For Man, in this world, being *one* is a curse. One is the loneliest number!! Without others he will not receive or appreciate God's blessings. A solitary man can not do kindness or acts of charity. A single person cannot spread the beauty of belief in God or even deepen his own understanding of Torah by sharpening it on the reasoning of others. *Beit,* two, is the blessing of Torah when viewed this way.

God, thus, wanted the Torah for mankind to begin with the *Beit*.

If the holidays and their focus on family and community were part of my two, these days of reentry in their aftermath return me to a one of reality. We live in a wonderful society where we have unparalleled freedom to live and worship according to our beliefs. My colleagues and co-workers respect my lifestyle, even if they sometimes can not fully comprehend it. But part of what they do not understand is that observing as a Jew is not limited to a few days a year or one day a week or even to fourteen or sixteen of the twenty-four hours each day. It encompasses every second and every minute of our lives. It is what we wear, how we eat, when we arrive and depart, and how we interact with the world.

After nearly a month of the two of family, community, and ritual, the everyday one is lonely indeed. One plus one equals two. If I confidently feel and experience the "One" of God wherever I go (or at least when I feel the isolation of differentness), the *Beit* of the beginning will have proven its point.

We recite *"Shema Yisrael"* (the "Hear O Israel" prayer) and proclaim that God is one at the beginning and end of each day. By doing so we remind ourselves that we are part of a greater whole, the nation of Israel, while simultaneously reinforcing that we are never alone because our own personal one is accompanied by His. *Shema* is not only for little children and martyrs. As a Jew you can choose "Two be, or not two be." Only this is not the question, this is fact, the truth as laid out from the Torah's very first letter.

NOACH
Cyber-Babel

The portion of *Noach* has seemingly little to do with the dominant event in our home this week. About a month and a half ago, our new computer system arrived and everyone's focus (except for my two-year-old's) became centered on the white machine on my office desktop. The computer reads animated interactive stories to the younger children, presents the older ones with new educational opportunities and some kosher fun (a la Mitzva Mania — a Jewish-themed computer game), helps my wife more efficiently prepare and organize her teaching regimen, and provides me with the motivation to jot down or tap-tap these musings.

Armed with some basic familiarity with the system and what it can do, we were finally ready for the next step. As of this week, our home is part of the world wide web — the Internet. That sounds pretty impressive and imposing — and it is. This information superhighway provides a link to virtually everything (including "Virtual Jerusalem") and everyone. This vast net is limited only by the technology of delivery and our available time. It is an ocean of information containing the pure waters of Torah thought, as well as vile (and often illegal) polluting hate and pornography.

This week's portion of *Noach* contains a description of two different versions of society. Both were flawed, both were doomed, and both were ultimately dealt with by God. He destroyed one physically and the other ideologically.

The society Noach lived in was so corrupt that God literally had to flush it away and begin again. What were the crimes of that generation? Did they seek to ethnically cleanse their neighbors; did they pollute their environment with poisonous waste; did they develop weapons of mass destruction; did they fail to comprehend that objects in the mirror are closer than they appear? Their sinfulness is described as a state where they were full of *"hamas."* Hamas, today, has a particular meaning as a destabilizing fundamentalist group in the Middle East that is dedicated to destroying westernized society, in general and more specifically, Israel and the Jewish people. *"Hamas"* in Noach's time, however, did not **merely** represent chaos, corruption, hatred, insanity in the name of religion, or homocidal/suicidal acts. The *"hamas"* detailed in the Torah was something worse, something that resulted in the destruction of nearly the entire world. The biblical term has been loosely translated as robbery.

This robbery was not of the gun-toting, switchblade-flashing, or even the confidence-gaming variety. It was much more sly. Stealing a little here and a little there. Amounts too small to be noticed, too small to even be actionable in court.

A useful analogy is that incident a few years back where an accounting/computer drone in the employ of a public utility company somehow diverted a fraction of a cent from each customer's payment into a dummy account that only he could access. As time rolled by, based on the millions of payments and hundreds of millions of dollars in billings, he accumulated a small fortune — until he was caught. The robbery in Noach's time was pervasive. Everyone did it, as everyone figured they were going to get away with it. This, in turn, became "everyone is doing it so it must be o.k.!"

The cumulative effect of this robbery added up to a huge defect in mankind's character. Soon there were no barriers, at all. This was not some early form of collectivism or communism, it was an outright free for all. As this corruption progressed like a disease, man was not content to take from his fellow man. His now covetous and lustful eye (do you ever find the words "covetous" and "lustful" anywhere other than in a biblical diatribe? ...discuss!) was turned towards the animal kingdom. Man, thus, plunged to the lowest depths of moral depravity (even worse than Snidely Whiplash and Darth Vader). The intensity of this corruption became so great that God purged the land-based animal kingdom. Except, of course, for Noach, his family, and the animals on the ark.

Through that small band, mankind was reborn. It flourished with a new creative focus and with renewed purpose until the generation of the "Towering Inferno," a.k.a. the Tower of Babel. The organizer of the Tower project is not identified directly in the text. The *Midrash* and other commentaries, however, are nearly unanimous in depicting King Nimrod as the protagonist. (The same Nimrod who threw the young, innocent, and soon to be monotheistic, Avraham into the fiery furnace.) In a history replete with villains, Nimrod seems to be a mere footnote. Yet, in many ways he was the prototype or archetype for all evil megalomaniacs to follow.

What exactly was Nimrod trying to accomplish? The narrative implies that he was coordinating construction of a structure that would reach the heavens. Ostensibly, Nimrod the mighty warrior would use it as a platform to wage war against God for dominion over all existence. Such a notion is patently absurd. As I am sure some famous general once said, "you can't fight what you can't see." Man can barely comprehend God, let alone try to challenge Him directly and physically.

Moreover, how high do you think that the Tower realistically

could have reached? Nimrod's engineers likely could not have cal-
culated the correlation between the foundation needed and the
weight of the structure — a structure of solid stone. His crews did
not have massive cranes and other machines. The architects did not
design with structural steel. Could it have risen even as high as our
modern skyscrapers; the Empire State Building or the Sears Tower?

As the Tower rose higher, all of mankind, with its one language,
became subsumed by the project. Nimrod, thus, took man's unity,
creativity, and energy and twisted and corrupted it into a tool for
his own nefarious purposes. God charged man with the task of
subjugating the world with God-like creativity. Nimrod converted
mankind's energy, as manifest by God's directive, into the tool for
its own subjugation. In the end, bricks were more valuable than
bodies; perspiration meant more than inspiration; and the Tower
became both the beginning and end of man's earthly experience.
Nimrod was the first to try to dehumanize man. Dehumanized
mankind is juxtaposed and linked in the same Torah portion with
corrupted mankind.

There is one part of the story of the Tower that I find particularly difficult to understand. At first, God stands passively by and
allows the project to progress. Then, the Torah relates that God
finally "descended to see the city and tower which the sons of man
built." (Bereishit 11:5). When He descends, He observes that the
project is corrupt. Accordingly, He reacts by taking away mankind's
ability to communicate effectively by "confusing their language."

Certainly God knew where the project was headed from its
inception. Moreover, He knew that He was ultimately going to intervene and halt it. Why then did He wait?

I believe the answer to be that the project actually served a useful purpose, to a point. Reflect over history. Many of mankind's
greatest accomplishments have been founded on near lunacy and
folly. Advances in modern chemistry and physics can be traced to
the works of the medieval alchemists who searched for the secret

of making gold from the four elements. Man has been to the moon, but likely would never have left the launching pad without the curiosity of generations of ancient astrologers. Building a tower to reach the heavens was a farce, but it encouraged man to develop engineering skills, to invent the simple machines, to move from cave, tent, and tree dwellings into constructed structures.

God was patient because He knew that man needed a project like the Tower to advance. However, when the project outlived its usefulness, when Nimrod replaced progress and innovation with endless goal-oriented repetition and inhumane efficiency, then it was time for a new direction.

Is the Internet a modern day Tower of Babel? Will it reunite mankind with a single language for a glorious and creative purpose or will it create a generation of plugged in automatons? Could a modern day Nimrod, a Bin Laden type, emerge to seize this power to influence through mass communication and technology? Perhaps I will post these questions on a chat board and see what responses I receive.

LECH LECHA
A Mint on Your Pillow

In today's world, a man's home is not merely his castle, it is an almost impenetrable fortress. If not for minor annoyances, such as going to work or purchasing food, a person could stay shut in with most everything literally within fingertip control. Automatic deposit and ATMs have rendered trips to the bank unnecessary. Pay-per-view brings a vast assortment of live entertainment events and second run movies into the house through a satellite or cable hookups. After flipping through a catalogue, with a credit card and telephone or web connection, you can order anything that can be delivered by common carrier. If you want to buy it and you can pay/borrow for it, someone will find a way to get it to you with as little trouble and effort on your part as possible.

Most religious needs can be serviced at home as easily as the personal ones: Torah study by phone, tape, or computer; weekly Torah portion updates by fax; Jewish music by 800 number; and someone in Israel will place a note for you in the Western Wall if you press on a button. What about the synagogue? In our neighborhood, and in others around the country, people who do not feel like walking the few extra blocks on the *Shabbat* (Sabbath) have actually set up mini-synagogues in their homes. Most neighborhoods where Orthodox Jews reside are densely populated with others of like persuasion (everyone needs to be within a reasonable walking distance of the synagogues because of the requirements of Sabbath observance) — so a *minyan* (quorum of a minimum of ten adult males required for communal prayer) can generally be rounded up from people living on the block. Even such revered institutions as the *yeshivah* and *kollel* (institutions of intensive religious study) are facing competition from an increase in private in-home study groups.

It is quite understandable, therefore, that the first words that God speaks to the first Jew are *"Lech Lecha"* — leave home without it — hit the road Jack! Avram had a good life, had a nice wife, a good family business to go into, an open relationship with his family — in short, everything a person could ask for. He was also a local celebrity, having defied King Nimrod, emerging from the fiery furnace unscathed. Why was it necessary for him to leave home? What traps lay in wait for us in our homes (even with smoke detectors, radon gas detectors, carbon monoxide detectors, burglar alarms, and baby monitors)?

One insight can be gleaned by understanding the *"Cheers* Principle." Cheers, for the culturally disadvantaged, was a popular television situation comedy set in a Boston bar. The regular characters were the denizens of this bar: the bartenders, the waitresses, the bar owner, and assorted patrons. The show seemed premised on the notion that these people had no independent existence, no *raison d'etre,* outside of the bar. It was the place "where everybody knows your name." Cheers was a place with its own rituals and where the patrons and employees were surrogate family for one another.

Two of the supporting characters in the ensemble cast were a postman named Cliff and an accountant name Norm. Both men had dysfunctional family lives. Neither accomplished much in their careers or for their community. While likeable, these men were simply lonesome losers. (How motivated and accomplished could they be if they spent nearly every waking non-working hour on a barstool sipping beer and eating nuts?)

Yet in the bar they were somebodies. They walked through the doors to calls and chants of "Norm!!!" and "Cliff!!!" When they offered advice or opinions, their words mattered. If a stranger challenged them, the other regulars in the bar came to their defense. Inside Cheers, they had names, and everybody knew them.

At home, everybody knew Avram. But that name had to change; he had to change and grow. He had to become Avraham, the father of Yitzchak, the "father of the multitude of nations." The cocoon of his father's house in Aram would not suffice as a catalyst for his new persona as Avraham. Ironically, when asking Avram to leave, God promises that ultimately, everybody will know his name — and will be blessed by and through it.

We also left home this week. I was invited to lecture as a scholar-in-residence at a weekend Torah retreat. So, we packed, loaded up the car, and "moved" into the Doubletree Suites hotel (non-kosher chocolate chip cookies at check in, not mints on the pillow!). Leaving home for *Shabbat,* even under nearly ideal circumstances, provides a fresh perspective on the usual.

A usual *Shabbat* has its own rhythm and pace. We take the usual route to and from shul. We sit in our usual seats. The same people cluster together and talk during the service until the rabbi makes his usual announcement for them to cease and desist. Upon our return home, we sit at the same set table, start with the same warm up songs (*"Shalom Aleichem"* and "Woman of Valor"), and perform the same rituals (make *kiddush* over the wine, wash our hands and eat *challah* bread). Then comes the obligation of listening to the children read their nearly endless list of meaningful insights into

the Torah portion of the week during the meal. (PLEASE NOTE —
this is the meal that my wife painstakingly prepares, with much
effort and sacrifice. It most certainly is not included in this recounting of the sameness of the usual *Shabbat.* Each meal, with its
unique its texture, taste, composition, and balance is a culinary
delight... Except for the potato *kugel,* which she can not consistently prepare to save her life.) As we fast forward through sleep,
go to shul, eat, sleep, go to shul, eat, with some Torah and social-
izing mixed in, you have the picture of a usual *Shabbat.*

Going away mixes things up a bit. Being in new surroundings
is interesting, though it can be somewhat disorienting at first. The
time schedule is not within our control. There is no way to skip the
fish or to serve the soup more rapidly. Some of the tunes for the
Shabbat songs are unfamiliar. I am tired, but I can not dive under
the covers since I have to deliver a lecture in an hour. One of our
boys has just spilled grape juice on the second of the two white
shirts we brought for him — he will not be able simply to go to his
room and get another one out of the closet. And yes — WHO ARE
ALL OF THESE OTHER PEOPLE?

Here at our table is the person who is experiencing *Shabbat* for
the first time. There, one table over, is the person who never read
the words of a weekly Torah portion before. Everywhere I look I
see people who are curious, who want to learn, to experience, and
to understand. The room is filled with the spirit of *Shabbat,* a holy
separation from the rhythm of the workweek.

This particular *Shabbat* is separated from the cookie-cutter
sameness of the ordinary at-home version. This *Shabbat* is a paradigm for how all the others should be celebrated. One day away
from our home provides a new perspective on the Day of Eternity.

Avram perceived the world differently from his fellow man. He
could sense the presence of God everywhere and in everything.
This set him apart and dictated that God choose him as the prog-
enitor of our monotheistic nation. However, had Avram remained

in Aram, his grasp would have been limited to those who knew his name. He would have achieved nothing more than spiritual influence over Aram (Avram = *Av Aram,* father or master only of Aram).

When he left at God's request, his horizons broadened. He was made aware of the entire world's greater diversity, beauty, majesty, and holiness. He understood that there was a wide range of other peoples and false deities. He was destined to bring belief in God to the world. For him to live up to the responsibility of being Avraham (Avraham = *Av Hamon Goyim,* father of the multitude of nations), however, was not a simple task. In fact, it was one that would take his entire lifetime, and the lifetimes of many succeeding generations.

Avram's move provided more than a mere change in focus or a refreshed perspective. It also provided a model for the many moves that would be forced on his children in the centuries to come. We, his children, have endured many harsh exiles. We have witnessed how easy it is to be uprooted from even the most secure homes and communities — both voluntarily and forcibly. Yet, we have survived and prospered precisely because of Avraham's example and his blessing.

Next week, we will be home again (unless *Moshiach* comes). Hopefully, our *Shabbat* will be a little different, a bit less routine, and a touch more appreciated because of our experiences this past weekend. (Come to think of it, this has not been significantly different from the experiences we shared on *Succot* — when we left our permanent homes for the temporary *succah* dwelling. Think about it!) As nice as it was to be away, I missed my own *Shabbat* table and bed — too bad they do not likewise come with maid and waitress service. Oh well, at least at home, the cookies are kosher.

VAYEIRA
Baby with the Bath Water

Like the weekly Torah portions, our lives cycle around and around again. Each experience returns at a new angle. The first day of elementary school brought anxiety, excitement, fear, and eagerness — as did the first days of high school, college, graduate school, and the start of various new jobs. Each of them were filled with a similar mixture of emotions. Yet, in each of these different times and places, I was also different.

Think back to your first summer at sleep-away camp. Through eight-year-old eyes the grounds are vast. The distance from cabin to dining hall to baseball field to camp office is imposing. Through twelve-year-old eyes, this same campus is stale; been there, done that. Twenty or so years later, returning for a reunion, you find facilities that seem both full of magic — with the ability to trigger long forgotten memories, and melancholy — so small and worn out, so unlike the retouched and polished memories.

How about that first Disney World vacation. You arrive, for three or four days of escape, armed, at considerable expense, with the passport that will grant access the various fantasy areas. You pull out your annotated guidebook and work with the maps and schedules to plan out maximum park coverage. We **will** experience all of the major rides and attractions, we **will** see the spectacular shows, we **will** avoid the long lines, we **will not** dally and waste time and considerable amounts of cash browsing through every gift shop.

After about a day and a half, reality sets in. This is a vacation. This is about relaxing. We'll ride Space Mountain next time... who needs to see Michael Jackson as Captain Eo in three dimensions. By the third day, you begin to appreciate the sights and sounds — the detailed and clever robotics, the humor and artistic flourishes in the various international exhibits and the neat t-shirts in the gift shops. You are in the same location as you were on Day One, but your ongoing experience has altered the perspective.

No force is more perspective altering and experience bending than our own children. Whatever it is that they are doing now, good or bad, we likely did once upon a time, as well. In this regard, we are somewhat different from our own parents who grew up as bridges between two worlds. All four of my grandparents were European immigrants with little formal education. They simply did not have the same cultural reference points as their American-born and college-educated children. Through the two world wars and the Depression, they had to work almost endless hours to make a life for themselves and their families. There was no time for Little League or Boy Scouts! Additionally, their world was technologically different from ours and changing rapidly. They had few electrical appliances and no televisions. Even the automobile was more a luxury or novelty than a necessity for everyday transportation.

This is not to say that our grandparents were in any way deficient as parents. On the contrary, they raised, fed, clothed, nurtured, and educated their children; equipping them to achieve and accomplish in life, both as secular Americans and as religious Jews.

They were also more than capable of instilling within them solid moral and family values. Yet, their baseline experiences were vastly different, so foreign.

We "the Baby Boomers," and "Generation Xers" on the other hand, have benefitted from parents who wanted us to have it all; to have and to do all that they pictured as the American-Jewish dream. They also, in most cases, have had the resources and freedom to, at least, point us in the direction of attaining these goals. From the first days of grammar school through the receipt of a law degree, my education, secular and religious (Torah U'Mada), was integrated in one system. I participated in the full range of sports leagues, youth groups, and cultural activities. I played with GI Joe, creepy crawlers, a frisbee, and a whiffle ball. We watched television (probably too much), read comic books and listened to popular music, both Jewish (Rabbi's Sons, Mordechai ben David, Carlebach, Ruach Revival) and other. We played video games (Intellivision and Odyssey), and were sports fanatics.

How significantly different will the experiences of my children be? If you walk into Toys R Us and manage to get past the video games, what is it that you find being marketed to today's children? Barbie dolls, Mr. Potato Head, Etch-a-Sketch, Spyrograph, Kerplunk, Yahtzee, and on and on and on — our toys!

Which brings us back, full hula hoop, to returning experiences. I certainly do not want to be the kind of parent who lives vicariously through his children — correcting past mistakes and achieving through their achievements. As my children progress to ages within my own clear and present memory (about age seven or eight), however, I find it more and more common to observe them and to picture the little me. I also preferred to do my homework at the kitchen table rather than at the desk in my room. I often came home requesting the "must have" fad of the week (then — a Footsie, today — devil sticks). When would I ever want to come in for supper when it was nice out and we had a good street hockey game going? Peter Frampton once sang "I'm in you, you're in me" — this is full scale harmonic convergence.

This perspective can certainly wreak havoc on parenting. How can you discipline your children for disturbing your *Shabbat* nap by playing too loudly with their friends when, week in and week out as a child, you did the same thing? How can you advise your son not to socialize so much with the young ladies in synagogue, when you ignored similar admonitions? How can you insist that your daughter write her school report all by herself, as requested by the teacher, when your parents sat with you and guided you through a nearly identical project? These are the easy questions for which there is an easy answer — you simply live the fiction, act ignorant and old fashioned, and play the parent game.

But what happens when the issues become more serious? What do you do when your child who has been cruising along as a responsible student, begins to be disruptive or starts to associate with and emulate behaviors of others that YOU would prefer he avoid? When do you counsel and guide? When do you intervene? When do you allow a mistake so that a lesson can be learned? These are issues that my wife and I were called upon to face this week.

(AUTHOR'S NOTE: The family and friends that surround me, and their experiences, are central to my life, affecting me, directly and indirectly, in different ways. As you will see, more often than not, entries in this work will be triggered by these very interactions. I can and do choose to lift the "cone of silence" or raise the "deflector shield" protecting aspects of my privacy. But I do not have the right to violate theirs. Therefore, this is as good a place as any to say that while the situations I write about, and will write about, resemble the actual events that are taking place in my life and motivating these musings, they have been altered, exaggerated, combined, sliced, diced, "ginsued", "vegematiced", and generally scrambled to suit the needs of the message and to protect the privacy of those I can not otherwise avoid describing.)

Harsh choices and unpopular decisions are often necessary for effective parenting. But how far should we go? What right do we have to meddle in the lives of our children? Can we dictate who their friends should be? Should we control their environments?

I am not a parenting expert (though as the father of six I am not exactly inexperienced in such matters). However, as I wrestle with just such an issue, I realize that in this week's portion of *Vayeira* the first Jewish parents, Avraham and Sarah, are forced to deal with several of these same difficult issues.

After enduring years without the presence of the vitality and youthfulness of children, yet without questioning the Divine promise of multitudinous offspring, Avraham and Sarah recognize that they are getting on in years and need to take a more proactive approach to procreation. Sarah suggests that Avraham utilize her maidservant Hagar (according to the *Midrash,* an Egyptian princess) to build a future. Avraham is successful in this undertaking and a son, Yishmael, is born.

Yishmael is a vigorous, active, and likeable child. Avraham enjoys having a son and Hagar enjoys the fact that she, rather than her mistress, is the one that bore him. To make the first part of a long story short, after Hagar flees harsh treatment from Sarah, she encounters an angel in the desert who instructs her to return and to endure. In exchange, Hagar and the child receive a quite elaborate blessing (which may have something to do with the vastness, influence, and wealth of the modern day Arab world). So Hagar returns. Yishmael is raised by Avraham and participates in the first circumcision ceremony at age thirteen.

One year later, Sarah finally gives birth to our forefather Yitzchak. He is the long awaited son of destiny. One would think that Yishmael, who has grown and developed under his father's tutelage, would be extremely resentful and jealous of the new little prince. Yet we find just the opposite reaction. Yishmael plays the role of a true big brother (Wally to Yitchak's Beaver). He plays with

Yitzchak, he spends time with him, and he entertains him. A real bond begins to form between the boys. (It is a bond that is so strong that later in life, after Avraham's death, they become neighbors. In fact, Yitzchak's son, Eisav, attempts to curry favor with his father by marrying Yishmael's daughter.)

Sarah observes the strengthening bonds between the boys and the influence that Yishmael is exerting on Yitzchak. She is aware of the Divine intervention that kept Hagar and her son in the household, yet she is even more attuned to the needs of her son's spiritual growth. The presence of Yishmael is simply not compatible with the perfection that will be required from Yitchak. Sarah finally reacts by demanding that Avraham send Yishmael away.

Avraham had been through this before. He knows that Yishmael has a historic destiny and he has invested much of himself into his son's upbringing. Needless to say, Avraham is quite reluctant to comply. After appealing to a Higher Authority, Avraham realizes, however, that Sarah's judgement and decision is correct. Avraham must sacrifice a son in order to develop the son that he will later be asked to sacrifice. The history of our nation rests on this difficult choice and decision.

I hope that as a parent I will never be called upon to make a choice as difficult as Avraham's. I could not imagine being forced to choose one child at the expense of another. But there will be critical moments in the lives of each of my children when my wife and I will be required to intervene, to discipline, to shelter, to teach, or merely to stand back and watch in ways that will seem counter-intuitive, inappropriate, maybe even cruel.

What ultimately allowed Avraham to accept Sarah's assessment was the reassurance from God who seconds Sarah's radical notion. Avraham truly understood, as he would show so much more directly during the *Akeidah* (the binding of Yitzchak), that children are created through the three-way partnership between God, a man and his wife. When the concerns of all three partners are addressed, the decision will most assuredly be correct.

Unfortunately, we do not have the same kind of direct hotline to the Almighty that Avraham and Sarah had. But we have other resources; rabbis and teachers in our schools and community that can help provide the perspective or reality check that is needed when we are emotionally too close to a situation to act with clarity. Generally, father, and mother do know best. However, they are not always honest enough with themselves. We must emulate Avraham and Sarah and their handling of a delicate child-rearing issue as a reminder of how we are supposed to manage the process.

CHAYEI SARAH
Youth in Age — Huh?

My youngest daughter, Yo-Yo (short for Yocheved), turned two this week. For some reason we usually make a big deal over the first birthday: grandparents, video cameras, hats, party favors, a cake... as if the kid knows what is happening! For a "terrible two," however, celebration is more muted, more private. Rather than planning and producing a major social event, we simply bought her a few presents and took the kids out for pizza.

I know that my other five children were sweet at this age, but Yo-Yo definitely has my number. One of her favorite games is "Again." When I arrive home, she runs up to me yelling "Daddy," with her arms out to signal that I am to lift her. As I do, she turns her cheek toward my lips for a kiss. I accommodate, after which she says "again." This sequence is repeated quite a number of times — she does not seem to tire of the game, and I certainly do not tire of hugging and kissing her.

These are not mere "Kodak" moments. The emotions and feelings, the love and joy, bond the two of us together and shape us.

My daughter, young as she is, learns that she is loved, that she is important, and that she is safe. I get the chance to readjust priorities after a long day in the outside world and to soften some rough edges.

When we returned from our "dinner party," it was time to hit the phones. Yo-Yo is not communicating yet in full original sentences (she is a great parrot, though), but her grandparents would never forgive me if I deprived them of the opportunity to *kibbitz* and offer birthday wishes. Soon it was time to place that special call to my grandmother, Bubbie Annie.

May she live and be well, Bubbie is in her mid-nineties. Until about a year ago, she lived and cared for herself in her own apartment in Far Rockaway, New York. She currently resides in an assisted living complex in Brooklyn.

My relationship with Bubbie is and has almost always been nearly as close as that with my parents. During my *yeshivah* and college years, with Mom and Dad a thousand miles away in the deep South, I spent nearly every *Shabbat* at her apartment. I actually lived there for a few months between the beginning of year two of law school and my wedding. Bubbie Annie is a deeply religious woman, who puts family and feeding them above everything else. Hopefully, as these weeks roll by, I will have other opportunities to share more about this remarkable woman.

Bubbie is in as good health as one can be in their mid-nineties. Unfortunately, some things are starting to wear down, like her memory. When I visited her for the last time in her Far Rockaway apartment, with the kids in tow, she did not want to let us in — she did not recognize us or comprehend our attempts to explain who we were (please realize, I spoke with her earlier that morning to confirm our visit and to inform her of our approximate arrival time). She would not even open the door (I mean how threatening could I have looked holding a then one-year-old baby while surrounded by five other children?) until her neighbor and good friend assured her that everything was fine. She then greeted us and played along, never quite sure who we were.

That day hurt because I simply wanted her to be who she always was. That hurt was a bit selfish because, thank God, she was alive and healthy and we could hug her and plant kisses on her cheeks.

During my last in-person visit a few months ago, the experience was quite different. Rather than displaying a lack of recognition or a blank reception, Bubbie's memory was in overdrive — with a few twists. First, she thought I was my father. (Note: I do not look or sound anything like him. I take after my mother's side of the family.) She did not perceive me as my father, a great-grandfather himself, but my father the fourteen- or fifteen-year-old in school. She asked about classmates and teachers, she discussed financial arrangements for tuition payments, and she gave me a mother's blessing to succeed and accomplish. At first, I tried to explain who I was, to bring her back to the present. Eventually, I relented and played my assigned role. I was simply content to know that she was happy reliving milestones in her life, that she was alive and healthy, and that I could hug her and kiss her, again.

If you have not figured it out yet, the phone call with my daughter on one side and her uncomprehending great-grandmother (who is also hard of hearing) on the other was short. Neither knew who they were talking to or what was being communicated. But at the end of the call, at our prompting, my little sweetheart blew a kiss into the phone that I know was more than a bunch of electrical impulses — a kiss I hope was full of all of my "agains."

Current pop psychology, of the radio talk show variety, extolls the need for the male to get in touch with and to become comfortable with his feminine side. (Being ignorant, I thought that the feminine side was excised when God split Eve off from Adam.) The rap is that the typical aggressive male is wary about revealing emotions ("big boys don't cry") and has difficulty dealing with interpersonal conflict through communication rather than action or inaction ("Men are from Mars, Women are from Venus"). By opening up and embracing his feminine side, a man can grow as a complete person.

I do not know if I or any other man, has a quantifiable internal feminine side. What I have, and have had throughout my life, are a number of important feminine influences — namely, my mother, grandmothers, sister, wife, mother-in-law, and daughters.

Traditional Judaism deals with the differences between sexes in a variety of ways. There are laws and observances that are uniquely male (e.g., circumcision). There are laws and observances that are uniquely female (e.g., family purity and laws of childbirth). There are even *mitzvot* (commandments) that are mandatory for men and optional for women (positive time-bound commandments). Finally, there are certain areas where the responsibility is divided between the two with one having a more primary role — the home v. the synagogue, Torah study v. child-rearing are examples. Torah Judaism, thus, is a religion for both sexes. But it generally does not encourage them, outside of the family unit, to participate, worship, or study together.

At synagogue services, men and women sit separately. Likewise, many carry this over to communal and social events. While there are some national coed Jewish youth groups (NCSY and B'nai Akiva) there are others that are not (Pirchei and B'nos). In Orthodox day schools today, the question is not whether to separate the girls from the boys, but at how early an age.

In *Ethics of the Fathers* (1:5) , Rabbi Yose ben Yochanan warned against casual conversation with a woman (even one's own wife!) as such conduct would lead to *Gehenom* (essentially, Hell). This had nothing to do with intelligence, religiosity, superiority, or inferiority. The statement conveys an attitude — study Torah, improve your spiritual self, and focus on your own obligations. Nevertheless, this attitude fosters a separation, an invisible barrier, that results in a Jewish male having reduced contact with his companion sex. Thus, in situations where the barriers are officially absent, the role and influence of an "approved" contact is thus magnified.

My wife, my main conduit to understanding the feminine side and the true other half of my soul, will likely get plenty of ink as the weeks roll by. I would therefore rather examine the female of youth and the female of age with whom I shared experiences this week.

This week's Torah portion, *Chayei Sarah,* opens with a one line summation of the first Jewish woman. She was also the first Jewish mother, daughter, sister, mother-in-law, etc. No less important, she was the feminine (not feminist) influence on Avraham, the first Jewish man. The opening verse states, "And these were the days of Sarah, one hundred years, and twenty years, and seven years, the years of Sarah's life" (*Bereishit* 23:1). If you've been reading this diary from the beginning, you know that I am certainly not a expert grammarian. However, even I would not compose a verse with that much redundancy. The Torah, which does not contain superfluous verbiage, should have simply stated, "One hundred and twenty seven years," not "One hundred years and twenty years and seven years."

Rashi, the classic commentator (Rabbi Shlomo Yitzchaki, born Troyes, France, 1040, died 1105), explains that the words are not extra — each phrase reveals something about Sarah. At age twenty, she was as free of sin as a small child of seven. At one hundred, she was far from being old and shriveled, she was instead as comely as a twenty-year-old.

Each of these characteristics is quite remarkable. A seven year old is full of life and vitality; curiosity knows no bounds; the world is full of black and white, no shades of grey; and so many thing are learned and experienced for the first time. That same young child, in theory, is also watched, protected, supported, and dependent.

Obedience and conformity flow from love, fear of consequence, desire for praise and acceptance, and most likely, ignorance and naivete (not too different from the adult relationship with God!). Innocence is the norm — a magical innocence that sees the rose of the world. This child is Adam and Eve before the apple, too young to appreciate subtle, sophisticated temptation and too inexperienced to weigh consequences.

Fast forward to age twenty. This is the age of physical maturity — prime appearance and strength (just look at those Olympic athletes). For the first time there is true freedom of choice; parents have little true control (what do they know anyway!). Financial constraints and personal needs are relatively few. What responsibilities are there — certainly not jobs, children, or ex-wives (o.k., there might be military service). The only things lacking (although none would admit it at the time) are wisdom, knowledge, and experience. While the world is full of opportunities and options, it is likewise full of pitfalls, traps, and temptations.

We all fall prey to temptation. For some, these are mistakes to learn from, bruises that soon heal. For others, especially those who forayed into experimentation with sex and drugs, the consequences may be longer lasting, even permanent. But for Sarah — beautiful, vigorous, vivacious, Sarah — there was control and purity. She was tempted but not tainted by possibility.

Old age arrives and again reduces choice. Some potential sins become physically impossible. Others are not worth the price of reputation or notoriety. As the time remaining shortens, the *carpe diem* attitude of youth gives way to nostalgic reflection, preparation for the approaching end, and a desire to be rather than to do. Sarah, however, still had all of her cylinders running. She had beauty, she even had a child to rear. She was an object desired by kings, a true princess. Yet her purity held; her consistent and internal unity of being never wavered.

Rashi seems to leave one question both unasked and unanswered. What was Sarah like at age one hundred and twenty seven? The answer can only be, the SAME as she was at one hundred and at twenty and at seven. Sure she grew and experienced. She loved and was loved. She endured emotional pain, witnessed wars, survived famine, and watched her husband leave on a mission to sacrifice the son that was her ultimate purpose in life. Everything around and about her changed. But, the more things changed, the more they stayed the same.

A kiss on my daughter's cheek and on my Bubbie Annie's cheek — the same. The love they inspire — the same. The thanks I express to God for making them a part of my life — the same. The appreciation of feminine virtue they paint on my inner soul — the same.

The youth of the two-year-old is still in my bubbie — she experienced the nurturing of that age so long ago. The age of my bubbie is in my daughter, her great granddaughter, the same genetic way it is in me. They are both assimilated in me and continue to shape who I am presently and who I am yet to become in the future.

TOLDOT
The More Things Change...

The Presidential elections have come and gone. America voted and the exit pollsters told us who we had chosen. This is all yesterday's (or in this case, last week's) news, except in my house — and in the home of any other parent who has a child wrapping up a report or project on "Decision 'xx."

This was the first election in which I cast a vote for President as one Constitutionally qualified to hold office. As a native born United States citizen over age thirty-five, with no felony convictions (at least none that have not been expunged or placed under seal), I could have run for and been elected President. In this great country, many a speaker has gazed out over a group of bright eyed and talented youth and proclaimed "you can, one day, grow up to be President." However, reality has finally set in. I am never going to be President. I am also never going to be a Major League shortstop, or a NASA astronaut, or a neurosurgeon, or host of "Late Night," or a best-selling author.

There is an obvious reason why I will never be President —

America is simply not ready for an Orthodox Jew as Commander-in-Chief (Joe Lieberman may get close). America is similarly not yet ready for a female President or an African-American President — though the pendulum of possibility is at least moving in those directions. Without stirring up kettles of racism, sexism, bigotry, and all the other wonderful varieties of ignorance and hatred, the reason, presently, is rather clear. For now, the politics of the Presidency is not about ability, fitness for leadership, merit, morals and character, or personal philosophy and vision. Winning a presidential election is about positioning the image of the candidates to appeal to the lowest common denominator of the electorate. Today, that means the Christian white male who voters can identify with in a personal way. The candidate with the greatest appeal to the key demographic groups, as determined by an army of pollsters and consultants, is the winner.

Former President Clinton's handlers were geniuses at applying this formula. They took a lifelong liberal Democrat, whose party was rocked in the midterm Congressional elections, and were able to envelop him in conservative Republican values — even while the example of his own life ran counter to those same values. I am not judging the man or this strategy. After all it was this very strategy that served our people so well in the first, and in some ways most important, election ever held.

In the Torah portion of *Toldot,* Rivkah is informed that she will be giving birth to twins. They will not be ordinary children, mind you, but the progenitors of two great nations. We are told little of these nations or their destiny. The most pertinent distinction is that the *Rav* (older, greater, stronger) will serve the *Tzair* (younger, smaller, weaker).

The identities of the *Rav* and the *Tzair* are somewhat obscured. Eisav is the first birthed. He is physical and powerful, and more outgoing and vigorous. Yaacov emerges second. He is cerebral and studious. He also seems to be less worldly. This would imply that

Eisav is *Rav* and Yaacov is *Tzair*. Later, however, Yaacov purchases the birthright making him legally, perhaps, the *Rav* and Eisav the *Tzair*.

The determining event would be the election, an election with one voter, the twins' father Yitzchak. His vote, to be cast in the form of a blessing, would settle the issue of who would continue as successor in the family business of heralding God's ideals and values.

We all know the literal story, one that would make Chicago Democrats proud, of how Yaacov and his mother deceived Yitzchak and rigged the election. As believers in God, who is Truth and whose Torah is truth, it is quite unsettling to think, however, that the very foundation of our status is a cloak (or sheepskin rug) of lies.

There are nearly as many explanations of this incident as there are commentators. Some focus on the technical legality of the claim (the earlier sale of the birthright for the lentil soup), while others seek to prove that Yitzchak was indeed aware of what was transpiring. I tend to favor the latter approach, as I find it far too difficult to accept that Yitzchak 1) was oblivious to the differences between his sons, 2) did not communicate with his wife, and 3) would transmit blessings of cosmic and historic significance without care, planning, and foresight.

Yitzchak had to choose between two very different candidates for the office of "Forefather Number Three" for the Jewish People. He was faced with a real "chicken or the egg" dilemma. On the one hand, he wanted to assure that his children would be worldly enough and strong enough to withstand the burdens of chosenness — exile, pogroms, inquisitions, holocausts, etc... — and to adhere to God's ways. On the other hand, his children needed the intellectual discipline and mental acuity to study and teach the Torah and thereby to cleave closer to God. Which would be easier — for the 98 lb. egghead to muscle up or for the thoroughbred to ask the wizard for a brain? Since Yitzchak knew that at the end of time they would work together, the *Rav* serving the *Tzair,* he wrestled with who should be chosen as the dominant first.

This is where the campaign handler came in, our mother Rivkah. She was certainly no silent partner. We saw her gregarious nature last week during her initial encounter with Eliezer, as well as through the active role she took to seek out advice during her unusual pregnancy. As the election neared, she, no doubt, voiced her opinion and eloquently stated Yaacov's case. But Yitzchak was not convinced by her words, nor by Yaacov's actions and demeanor. If only the vigor of Eisav could be tempered with the faith of Avraham, he would be the dream candidate.

Rivkah intuits the ageless winning strategy — the candidate who most reflects what the voter wants to see and hear, will win. If the voter wants a hairy man of the field — put on the costume, and smear on a little dirt. If the voter wants a chicken (or venison) in his pot — serve it to him. If the voter wants the aura and persona of Eisav — adopt it. Rivkah and Yaacov were not deceiving or fooling Yitzchak, they were proving a point. If Yitzchak chose Yaacov, he could rest easily knowing that he chose the candidate that embodied the quiet spirituality of generations of rabbinic scholars, as well as the candidate that would slay the Goliaths, Antiochus', and Nassers of history.

When Yitzchak chose Yaacov, he finally recognized that only this son could actualize his vision and bear the responsibility. He was a successor with both the voice of Yaacov and the hands of Eisav. This is how the choice was made. All that remained were the ethics investigations of history. The more things change...

VAYEITZEI
"None of Your Business"

This is a diary and not a mere pretense to moralize or preach using the weekly Torah portion. The one problem that I knew I would face sooner or later with this format is how to discuss important events without betraying personal or professional confidences. This issue becomes particularly acute when I want to focus on something that occurred "on the job."

When I am not busy being a parent, teacher, husband, and observant Jew, I am a tax lawyer for a large manufacturing corporation. Lawyers are ethically and legally (not contradictory terms) bound to maintain client confidences. Tax lawyers, with their access to detailed financial and other proprietary information, must be particularly careful about safeguarding the privacy of what they know and have been told. Since I intend to keep my job and to preserve my professional reputation (such as it is), I am thus limited in what, when, and how I can disclose or discuss something — no matter how interesting it may be.

There are exceptions that would allow me to relate otherwise restricted information. One such exception pertains to information in the public record and another to information that the client has consciously chosen to disclose. As of this writing, a project I worked on, albeit in the deep background (revising and generally wordsmithing the operative agreements) is a matter of public record. My employer has pledged $30 million to establish a business school at the Technion, in Haifa, Israel. That many shekels will ensure a fully equipped school building, communications center, faculty, library, and provide some incentive to lure a quality student body. The vision is that a combination of Technion's technological expertise and the resources of the world class business school will produce men and women who are equipped to advance Israel's economy in the technology based world of the 21st century.

I feel pride and admiration for my company's role in this endeavor and marvel at the foresight of those who "made it happen." I also find it interesting that my most significant involvement in this project and its ultimate approval by our Board of Directors are taking place during the week we read about the first Jewish business school student.

Yaacov has left home, or is on the run, depending on how one looks at it. He has no real assets (he sleeps with a rock for a pillow) and his main concerns are merely "food to eat and clothing to wear." (*Bereishit* 28:20). He eventually arrives at his Uncle Lavan's house (his mother Rivkah's brother). Lavan is portrayed by the commentaries as a personification of evil. At the Passover *seder* we recount how he wanted to destroy Yaacov and nip our nascent nation in the bud.

In the Torah itself, however, Lavan is not portrayed quite as malevolently. Yes, he tricks Yaacov again and again, switching wives, underpaying and overworking him — but he always seems to do it with a smile and a wink, always with a rationale or an explanation, always within the rules. Lavan is an experienced business man, the ultimate used car salesman. Yaacov arrives as a naive

ivory-tower intellectual. However, even worse for Yaacov, he likely fancies himself a capable player — after all he outwitted his
brother in the birthright deal and pulled off the blessing sting.

A better analogy for the early stages of their relationship might
be pool hustler and mark. A hustler never challenges an inexperienced player or one with little confidence. The hustler wants the
guy who is the king of his pool hall, the big fish in the little pond.
Such a player is confident, cocky. He thinks he is better than he
truly is, especially when his cronies encourage him. The pool shark
can smell the blood — he observes and spots the weaknesses in
the mark's game, even while boosting his ego with some early, low
stakes losses. Eventually, the stakes are raised, the pump is primed,
and the hustle is completed.

When Yaacov first encounters Lavan, he was ripe for the taking.
Lavan, the master manipulator, simply took the candy.

Yaacov could have run. After all, fleeing was a relatively effective solution to his prior difficulties. Sure, he was in love with
Rachel, but was she worth another seven years, for a total of fourteen? However, he was smarter than that. His desire to stay was not
hormonal, it was intellectual. He had to learn Lavan's lessons, he
had to complete the program and to pass the final exam. The proof
of this is in the extra six years he worked to complete his doctoral
thesis on the workings of the commodities market. In the end,
Yaacov's ability to combine science and technology (genetics) with
finance and marketing allowed him to meet his objectives, and to
gain his independence from Lavan.

Without a doubt, Yaacov learned much about business and business practices from his uncle. Much as we believe that the actions
of the fathers are a sign for the children — that the lives of our
fathers foreshadow later events and imprint national characteristics
— this, in no small measure, contributed to the famed business
acumen of our people (of course, it was also helped along by hundreds, if not thousands of years when Jews could not own land,

were barred from participation in certain trades, and were so scattered as to become natural conduits for what passed as foreign commerce in the pre-industrial world). However, we must at least consider the impact of this experience on the murky side of business — business ethics. There is a very fine line between disclosure and *caveat emptor* (often the line between a great deal and break even). Truth comes in many flavors; whole truth, half truth, white lies, omissions, and unclarified misconceptions. It is so easy to rationalize that the ends justify the means, when we end with profit and success. Was Yaacov's business school curriculum deficient? Was he faced with a paucity of ethical teaching, or even worse, was he taught to go over the line?

The answer comes in next week's portion as Yaacov prepares to encounter his older brother Eisav for the first time since he fled his wrath nearly twenty years earlier. He sends messengers (perhaps actual angels according to the *Midrash*) to deliver greetings. The very first words they are to relate are, "I lived with Lavan and I safeguarded God's 613 Commandments" (see, Rashi, *Bereishit* 32:5). He did not rely on trickery nor did he try to buy his way out of trouble, as Lavan might have. Yaacov proudly and directly answered our question about the impact of his "graduate" education on his personal ethical values, while at the same time responding to the threat posed by Eisav. Yes, he earned his Ph.D.while he absorbed all of Lavan's lessons. But they were a mere overlay for the ethical, moral, and truthful foundations of his fathers Avraham and Yitzchak and their God. This combination of wits and morality was the same formula that allowed him to prevail in the previous contests with his brother. If anything, Yaacov is even more prepared now.

Yaacov did not sacrifice ethics, he in fact lived them. This grounding did not hinder his success, it explained it. The voice of Yaacov can subjugate the hands of Eisav.

The world has changed. Economic might and technological knowhow can be more crucial to national survival than planes,

tanks, and missiles. Israel grows stronger with start-ups and strategic business alliances while her enemies wrestle with their own
ignorance and resist change. I am proud that my employer has the
foresight to provide Yaacov's children with the means to integrate
the business and engineering skills necessary to compete on a
global scale in the 21st century and to build and safeguard a lasting peace without further bloodshed. I am equally glad that this is
being done within the walls of an institution like the Technion that
understands and can instill its students with the critical ethical
direction.

VAYISHLACH
"I Wish to Thank"

When I set out to write this diary, I knew that I would only be able to complete it if I could discipline myself to produce a meaningful entry each week. Of course, this presupposed several things: First, that there would be something interesting to write about; second, that I would not be at a loss for the proper words to describe that "something;" and finally, that between family, community, and professional responsibilities I would actually find the time to write contemporaneously.

During these first seven weeks, I learned that I can really do this. This week, however, has given me a better sense of the challenges that I face.

Twelve years minus one week ago, my sister-in-law gave birth to a beautiful little girl. She was particularly special to my wife and me because we all lived in the same apartment building in Bayonne, New Jersey and we had just brought our first-born son home mere weeks earlier. For most of our waking hours, especially on the weekends when I was home from work, it was like having twins. The kids ate together, played together, and (major embarrassment here kids) bathed together. Of course there was no end to the diapers, real cloth ones with pins. Whichever father was nearest to the crying baby got the assignment (my memory is quite clear on this, the fathers usually changed the diapers). In the course of this first year of her life, a strong bond formed between niece and uncle. This bond, in turn, lead to that fateful phone call earlier this week.

"Uncle Steven?"

"Yes, Annie."

"I need some help with my Bat Mitzvah speech."

"Here's my fax number. Just send it and I'll try to beef it up."

"I was hoping that you could help me write it."

"O.K., what do you want to speak about?"

"I'm not sure."

"Annie, your Bat Mitzvah is this weekend. Surely you must have... no, don't worry about it. I'll throw something together and fax it to you in a couple of days."

"Thank you Uncle Steven."

Needless to say, this was not going to leave me with any spare time to write and I really would have liked to write about the upcoming Bat Mitzvah. Then inspiration struck! Why not kill two birds with one stone — write a killer speech and include it, in toto, as this week's entry? So beloved grandparents, parents, family, and friends, picture nicely decorated tables, a festive celebration, and a special Bat Mitzvah girl standing in front of a microphone nervously speaking the following:

At the beginning of this week's portion of *Vayishlach* we find our father Yaacov faced with a very complicated situation. After twenty years of being away from his family, from those he loved most — his mother, father, and brother — he is finally returning home. I am sure that he was full of excitement, What would his mother Rivkah think of his children? Would his father approve of his choice of wives?

At the same time he had to deal with another emotion, fear. He was afraid that his brother Eisav was still angry at him. He was afraid that Eisav would come to fight, that Eisav might kill him and his family or that he, Yaacov, might be forced to kill Eisav.

In order to face this, Yaacov knew that he had to prepare. Rashi says that he prepared in three important ways: with a gift, with prayer, and with a military or security plan.

Today we are gathered to celebrate my Bat Mitzvah. While I certainly am not dealing with a moment as critical as Yaacov's in our *parsha* (weekly Torah portion), this is a time of conflicting emotions for me — it is exciting to think that I am an adult Jewish woman, that I can fulfill *mitzvot* and look forward to a life as a contributing member of our religion. Yet, it is also scary — so much responsibility and accountability, so much to learn.

What we learn from Yaacov is that we have to prepare for such times — to prepare using different tools. Perhaps if I examine Yaacov's method, I might have a better game plan for dealing with today's emotions.

Let's start with the most important part (pause) PRESENTS! Now of course, Yaacov gave them and I am getting them. However, they are certainly helping me through this crisis. So you should all feel really good about how you are contributing to my emotional well being today.

All kidding aside, I would like to briefly look at the other two parts of Yaacov's plan — his *tefilla* (prayer) and his security plan. His *tefilla* begins:

"Then Yaacov said, 'God of my father Avraham and God of my father Yitzchak; God who said to me return to your land and to your birthplace and I will do good with you' (*Bereishit* 32:10).

He prays to *Hashem,* the God of his father Avraham and the God of his father Yitzchak to save him from Eisav.

I have one simple question — isn't Avraham also the grandfather of Eisav? Isn't Yitzchak likewise Eisav's father? How can Yaacov ask for God to respond to his prayers instead of Eisav's in his father's *zechut* (merit) — when he and Eisav share it equally?

The answer that we can derive from this verse is that only one who follows in the footsteps of his parents may invoke their merit. Yaacov followed their path, maintained their ideals, and internalized their approach to life. Eisav, of course, did not. Yaacov could, thus, seek their assistance.

I am blessed with two wonderful parents. My Dad is a true *av*, a father who brings the *Aleph* of the *echad* (one) who is God into our *Beit*, our *bayit* (home). He has always made sure that the values of Torah and being Jewish are of primary importance and he gives us the most valuable thing that he owns — his time and attention. My mom is the classic *aim* — a mother who gives us life and cares for us, a mother who sacrifices for us, a mother who teaches us, and a mother who serves as an example of what we must strive to be as Jewish women.

My *tefilla*, on this day, is simple. Not to invoke the merit of my parents — but to merit to be like my parents — to follow in their footsteps and to cherish their values.

Yaacov employed a direct and simple strategy for confronting his brother physically. He split his camp into two parts:

"And he said: 'If Eisav comes to the first camp and destroys it, then the other camp, which is left, shall escape' (*Bereishit* 32:9).

I have two family camps that have brought me to this day - the Shulman camp and the Jacobs camp. But I would never think of splitting these camps. They are too important to me and too much a part of who I am. However, in one respect, they have been split already —— not along family lines but in a bitter-sweet way, between those that are here and those who are here in memory and emotion. There is the Bubbie and Zaiyde that are here with me — my Bubbie Leonore Shulman and my Zaiyde Jack Jacobs loving me and giving me so much, and my Bubbie Gertrude Jacobs and Zaiyde Herbie Shulman who love me and are protecting me in ways I can't ever know.

There is a story told of the Rebbe, Reb Dov Ber of Radeshitz who once arrived in a village near sundown and looked to rent a room for the night. The innkeeper didn't have any rooms left, but out of respect for the Rebbe gave him his own room and volunteered to sleep in his office, next to the bedroom. The innkeeper did some work at his desk and finally lay down to sleep. But he could not — there was too much noise coming from the bedroom — the Rebbe was joyously singing and dancing — hour after hour. The innkeeper fell asleep but the Rebbe kept going. When he awoke he wondered why his visitor was so happy.

When he saw the Rebbe the next morning, before the innkeeper could even ask a question, the Rebbe approached him and asked, "Can you tell me where that remarkable clock in my room is from?" The innkeeper answered that a few years earlier a guest came and rented a room because the weather was too bad to travel in. He expected to stay only a day or two. But the weather didn't clear for almost two weeks. When it finally cleared, the guest said "I'm sorry, I have no money to pay you with, but would you take my belongings instead. I have just inherited them from my father." The innkeeper looked through the man's things — he had inherited his father's silk robe, a hat, and a clock. He had no use for the robe or hat, so he took only the clock and hung it in his room.

The Rebbe asked — Was that man, by any chance, Reb Yosef of Tulchin, the son of the Chozeh of Lublin?

"Why, it was!" exclaimed the innkeeper. "How did you know?"

"Because I know that the clock must have belonged to the Chozeh. The Chozeh used it to tell when it was time to pray and study."

"But how could you know that?" the innkeeper asked amazed.

"Because it is different from other clocks. Usually when a clock chimes you feel sad because it means you are an hour closer to the end of your life. But this clock makes you feel happy because every time it chimes you know you are one hour closer to Mashiach (Messiah).

When you celebrate a particular time in your life, like a Bat Mitzvah, you can be sad — sad about having responsibilities rather than being a care-free child, sad about loved ones who are not here to share in your *simcha* (joyous occasion), sad that we live in different places and live different lives and cannot always be together feeling as good as we do today. Or you can feel the joy of knowing that each moment together, each *simcha* celebrated, each hug, each lesson learned and each person we love is a *berachah* (blessing) from God to cherish for now and forever — a *berachah* we should appreciate to grow closer to Him.

Today, I feel this joy. May I merit to always feel it — as I see my parents and grandparents do.

I wish to thank...

No thanks are necessary, Annie. Just continue to grow into the fine young woman you are becoming.

VAYEISHEV
Lots of Little Pieces

Chanukah is coming at the end of this week. That means it is time for all of us parents to do our patriotic duty and to help out the economy. I have reviewed the laws and the various sources about this holiday many times and have never discovered a reference to obligations regarding video games, dolls, sports equipment, board games (except *draidle,* of course), home electronics, or action figures. Yet there is a driving force, a compulsion to seek and to acquire these items that is nearly as strong as the urge to purchase Israel Bonds on *Kol Nidre* night or to create hundreds of feet of paper chains on *Succot,* or to stockpile macaroons before Passover.

About two to three weeks before Chanukah, my wife and I survey the playroom and take a mental inventory of games with missing pieces, dolls as multiple amputees, and the assorted twisted and cracked pieces of plastic that were more fun to break than to play with. At this point we vow not to repeat past mistakes. We will not purchase any new toys this year: clothing — yes, books — yes, toys, especially toys with lots of little pieces — most definitely and positively NO!

As the *chag* (holiday) approaches, our resolve begins to falter. We cannot be such fuddy duddies. How will the children feel when they go to school and listen to their friends bragging about the gifts they received? Just picture the scene:

Little Moshe to my son Avi: "Hey Avi, last night my parents gave me battle-armor Batman with a rocket launcher and a Batcave play-set with remote control door opener — what did you get?"

Avi: "I got a new pair of Land's End pajamas."

If our county prosecutor frees up some time by giving up on Dr. Kevorkian, he might go after this high profile and inexcusable instance of child endangerment. Hence, we had a focus shift.

If our initial strategy avoided toys, the modified game plan involves developmental appropriateness, educational value, and a total absence of lots of small pieces. The hunt begins with the circulars from the Sunday morning papers. The huge toy stores have their glitzy catalogues filled with discount coupons. Of course, you will spend five times as much as you ever considered if you do nothing more than step in their front door. The department stores offer a few nice items, but the prices do not seem to be as good. Then there are the discount stores, K Mart, Target, Walmart, Meijer, etc. — those of us blessed with large families know them well. Their advertisements are jam packed with the trendiest, faddiest toys — those reflecting the warped imaginations of Hollywood's premier promotional tie-in marketers — and deeply discounted Lego.

For a relatively modest price our children can have an assortment of Lego kits; the 90 piece pre-school bucket, the 270 piece starter kit; the 1900 piece pirate adventure set, and the 2500 playland construction set. These toys are educational. These toys can be given in an age appropriate manner. THESE TOYS HAVE LOTS AND LOTS AND LOTS OF LITTLE PIECES! Needless to say, we bought about a quarter of a million Lego pieces (at least it seems that many).

What amazes me most about this toy is the gap between packaging and product. Let's look at the pirate adventure set. On the box we have the obligatory two smiling kids holding a completed pirate ship (booms, masts, sails, cannons, etc.) surrounded by a number of pirate figurines, a fort, a small island, and a treasure chest. Open the box and you find plastic bags filled with (repeat after me) lots and lots and lots of little pieces. Those pieces come in all different sizes, colors, and shapes. How are my little *kinderlach* (rocket scientists in training) going to progress from point A, lots and lots and lots of little pieces, to point B, a completed pirate action adventure?

The answer is that the toy designer had a plan. The plan may not be readily apparent, but all the pieces are there in the box. Everything that is necessary to achieve the end result is prepackaged and awaiting interaction and involvement with creative and energetic little minds. After hours of experimentation, trial and error, fun, and a little frustration, recognizable objects begin to take shape. With effort, the pile of loose parts starts to look less imposing. In the end, all of our concerns are put to rest as smiling children play with their pirate ship... for about 10 minutes, after which it gets left on the floor to be put away and slowly decay back into lots and lots and lots of little pieces.

The Torah portion of *Vayeishev* is a lot like that Lego set. It has lots of pieces — many actors (and actresses), many scene changes, and a range of emotions. We know what is "on the box" because we know how the stories end. The Yoseph arc builds a royal viceroy from a favored and perhaps spoiled adolescent. The Yehudah arc, which starts with a desperate, but righteous woman, will culminate in the Davidic line of kings and ultimately the Moshiach.

At first I found it quite odd that the Torah chose to relate these two stories in the same section. The story of Yoseph's descent into slavery and subsequent ascent to near royalty seems so different from the nearly tragic episode involving Yehudah and Tamar. Yoseph was the victim of circumstance — because his father favored him and because he had the dreams, his brothers hated him. In fact, they hated him enough to consider killing him, but a caravan **just happens** to come by, which allowed the brothers to sell him and profit instead. It then **just happens** that he is acquired by an important government official and as things start to look good — he's placed in charge of the household — the master's wife **just happens** to cast her eyes on him, ultimately landing him in jail after he rebuffs her advances. While he is rotting in jail, who **just happens** to show up to keep him company? Pharaoh's wine butler and baker! You all know the rest of the story, coincidence, after happenstance, after fortuitous occurrence, and in the end, Yoseph, as viceroy of Egypt helps to move his father and family to the Land of Goshen to begin their exile.

Yehudah's story is less grandiose, with far fewer twists and turns. Nevertheless, it does contain a classic moment of high drama. Yehudah marries and has three sons. The oldest marries a woman named Tamar and is killed by God because of sinful conduct. The next son, under the laws of laverite marriage, also takes Tamar as a wife and he soon shares his brother's fate. When Tamar approaches Yehudah expecting son number three, who is still a young lad, she is told to return to her father's house to allow the boy to mature.

Time passes and Tamar realizes that while she is not getting any younger, her in-laws are not exactly beating a path to her door. So she takes the initiative when she hears that Yehudah is visiting her neighborhood. She dresses up as a prostitute and seduces Yehudah, all while concealing her true identity. A few months later her indiscretion is revealed by her bulging waistline (they had not yet heard of the immaculate conception defense), which due to the fact that she is reserved for Yehudah's son, constitutes adultery and is punishable by death.

In the end, she is saved at the very last moment from the burning stake when Yehudah takes responsibility and admits his role, a role that Tamar herself stoically refused to directly reveal (although she gave Yehudah some good hints). A nice drama, a classic morality play, but it does not seem to be a story with the lasting historical significance and surrounding prophetic aura of the Jews' initial descent to Egypt through Yoseph.

The real connection between these two stories is not fully clarified for hundreds of years, in the Book of Ruth, and will not be fully realized until the fabled "end of days" as related in prophecies and in the legends of the *Aggadah*.

At the end of the Book of Ruth, itself a book of emotions, personalities, and coincidences, we learn that Peretz, one of the twins resulting from the Yehudah/Tamar incident, was the direct lineal forefather of the future King David — whose dynasty will produce the Moshiach of our hope and belief. (Equally interesting, but not worth a diversion now for the full analysis, is the fact that Ruth, another important part of David's ancestry, was a direct descendant of Moav, one of the sons born of the fateful coupling between Lot and his daughter in the aftermath of the apocalyptic destruction of Sodom.) David was able to rule and assert dominion over the land that Joshua, a descendent of Yoseph, was commanded to conquer initially.

At the "end of time," *Moshiach ben Yoseph* (the Messiah descended from Yoseph) will lead the war against and consume the forces of Eisav. Unfortunately, he will also lose his life. This will pave the way for *Moshiach ben David* (the Messiah descended from David) to lead us into an era of redemption and a new world order — a world where "God is one and His name is one." This will be the final repetition of our pattern — first Yoseph, then Yehudah.

Many little pieces, like family squabbles, human passion, characters and personalities and big pieces like kings and nations, wars, exile, and redemption are put together and taken apart over and over again to form the tapestry that is both our history and our destiny.

God's plans stretch over millennia, from the beginning of history to its end. They include every person, every living thing, and every inanimate object. Each component of the plan has layers and layers of complexity. The designer of the Lego kits knows that all those little pieces can be properly connected to create pirate ships, space stations, and medieval castles. God likewise knows that when His pieces are all finally put together, they will create and embody the Torah that was their schematic.

MIKEITZ
The Show

Human power comes in many flavors. There is the near absolute power of the dictator or ruler; the positional power of the boss, professor, or clergy; the situational power of the bank teller, government clerk, or customer service representative; the emotional power of a parent, spouse, or child; the inner power of the accomplished self-confident person; and, finally, the power of celebrity. Because of the power presently enjoyed by the various forms of modern media, this latter power is the one that seems most prevalent. Yet it is, perhaps, the hardest to really understand.

The twelfth man on the bench of a professional basketball team, a man who may average a minute of playing time and less than a point per game, can field non-stop requests for autographs for two hours at a local sporting goods store from fawning and adoring fans. A television talk show host can mention a book and it zooms to the top of the best sellers list with millions of copies sold. At an auction, costume jewelry from a former First Lady, purchased for practically nothing, can fetch prices as high as several hundred thousand dollars.

If you have ever been in a restaurant or a store when any kind of celebrity walks in (sports, entertainment, media, politics), no matter how immune to it all you may otherwise be, you notice — and you will probably relate the experience to countless others.

To his day I remember the evening when my wife and I entered revolving doors at Lincoln Center just as Bob Hope was exiting from the other direction. I felt a link to history when I rode up an elevator one morning with Richard Nixon and his two Secret Service agents (his office was one floor above mine in the Jacob Javitz Federal Building in Manhattan). My stroll into the Federal courthouse was just a little more special the morning I passed Robert Redford and Debra Winger filming "Legal Eagles" in the lobby. I could go on and on detailing my encounters and near encounters with the rich and famous (including my stint as an extra in the blockbuster film "Turk 182" starring Timothy Hutton). However, I would like to turn this around and look at it from the other side. What is it like to be the recipient of such adoration and to have the power and responsibility such fame bestows? How can celebrity be handled responsibly?

What triggered this discussion is an event I participated in this week. As I might, or might not, have mentioned before, I enjoy studying Torah with others. Since we moved to Detroit, I have become involved with Machon L'Torah, a local Jewish outreach organization. In the past year, I have given a series of classes on *Ethics of the Fathers* and lectures on a broad range of topics for Machon, in Detroit and at their center in Ann Arbor.

This week, Machon sponsored its annual Chanukah concert. The concert serves both as a fund-raiser for the organization and as a treat for the community, since Machon tries to book the most popular traditional Jewish musical performers on tour.

One day before the concert, the person who had agreed to M.C. the concert had to leave town on urgent business. At approximately 10:30 P.M. that evening, Machon's Director, who we lovingly call Rabbi J, called to ask if I could fill in (from the lateness of the hour I surmised that I must have been number 27 or 28 on his list). I declined, he kept asking, not taking no for an answer, and ultimately I relented and consented.

As hesitant as I was to serve, I am nevertheless glad that I did. In my role as M.C., I had a chance to interact with the performers and gain some small insights into the personality of celebrity (if you define celebrity as making one or two records of highly religious music, performing at maybe ten or fifteen concerts a year, and selling fewer than 10,000 copies of each album). I am not talking about on stage repartee, but backstage schmoozing (light-hearted small talk). I was not a fan or a groupie. I was part of the show, a colleague.

About a half-hour before the show, I went backstage and introduced myself to the three acts. Interestingly, they each responded with the same request — to hear my introduction. They were first and foremost concerned about their image. I enjoy Jewish music and have a large collection of records, tapes, and CD's. I own nearly every recording any of these performers had been associated with and had written introductions covering the spans of their respective careers, noting appropriate highlights, and praising them as stars, trendsetters, classics, or whatever other spin was appropriate. These mini-masterpieces were carefully crafted and designed to inform, to entertain, and to whip the crowd into a frenzy of adulation for these musical heros. In short, the proffered introductions were perfect. How dare these minstrels presume that I should change a word or two here and there — to shift an emphasis, to delete an anecdote. I would soon radiate out of the same microphones and speakers. I would soon command the same stage. I would also garner laughter and applause. With due respect to Sinatra, I would do things my way (see, I learned how to be an egotistical, temperamental, prima donna — all in under half an hour).

All kidding aside, I had written serviceable introductions. The performers offered a few suggestions and requested additional plugs for the albums on sale in the lobby. I truly had a nice time getting to know people whose music I have enjoyed over the years. I filled my role passably, they played wonderfully, and a good time was had by all.

One perk that evening was being able to view the concert and the performers backstage. Since there were three separate performers or groups playing sets, there was quite a bit of time to talk and to observe. These performers, though talented and popular, have a very limited audience. They are professional, but by no means are they full-time, big-time musicians. There is simply not a large enough demand for this product. In "real life" these guys are lawyers, dentists, teachers, doctors, and businessmen. Nevertheless, tonight they are "the show" they are "sensations," "stars," and "internationally acclaimed recording artists." As the evening goes on, it is interesting to watch them slip into these roles. One minute we are a group of regular people talking about some mutual friends, then, as some young fans slip back for autographs, they transform into celebrities. On stage, of course, they are the center of all attention.

Most of the evening's performers were experienced veterans of the Jewish music scene. They have been around — seen it all. They are married, family men who know how to relate positively to the young fans pressing close for a chance to approach an icon.

One of the acts, however, was a rookie. He is a talented young man promoting his first album, and hoping to launch a successful sidelight as a premier Jewish music performer. The concerts this Chanukah, in Detroit and a few other cities, were his first professional road trips. As the veterans joked and talked, he paced; mouthing lyrics and visualizing the performance. While some of the veterans were sipping soft drinks, he opened a briefcase; first taking out some concoction to gargle with, and then drinking the fabled raw egg. Next out of the case came a hairbrush — used both to smooth down his hair and then to meticulously groom his beard. He performed first, for about fifteen minutes, and then, except for a grand finale at the end of the concert, was basically free for the rest of the show. Once his bottled-up performance was loosed, quite successfully I might add, he relaxed. We talked a bit, and I learned a few things about him — where he lives, which *yeshivah* he (still) attends, what he plans to do in the future, etc.

After the next act finished playing, it was time to "go on out to the lobby and have a 7-up" — intermission. As a wise move to promote album sales, the performers went out to greet and meet the fans. A large group surrounded the rookie, thrusting pens, programs, and album covers in his general direction. There were also a number of young ladies who, in groups of two and three for courage, came forward to chat. At first, he greeted everyone with a demeanor resembling shyness. This soon grew into a smiling friendliness. This, in turn begat puffy chested, peacock plumed "I am the man"-ness. Finally, near the end of the session, I observed a faint touch of arrogance.

Essentially, what we have here is a nice *yeshivah* boy with talent and a dream. The question that lingers is, in the long run, what effect will the dream have on the boy?

In this week's portion of *Mikeitz,* we follow the further adventures of the first *yeshivah* boy who faced the challenge of actualizing his dreams. Yoseph dreamed of dominion over his family and this week he becomes viceroy to Pharaoh. He started out preoccupied with grooming his hair, but in the end, he is the true *baal hachalomot* — the master of the dreams. This name, initially hurled in ridicule, is quite fitting because he mastered his dreams rather than letting the dreams master him. Whenever he attained a position of responsibility, he never took advantage and he never acted "too big for his britches."

In contrast even with his forefathers, Avraham, Yitzchak, and Yaacov, Yoseph is identified as the *tzaddik* — the righteous man.

Some identify this with his self control in refusing the advances of his master's wife, Mrs. Photiphar. Others link it to his treatment of his brothers — he not only refrained from extracting a full measure of revenge, but he sustained them and provided for them during the famine and through their transition onto Egyptian soil.

I prefer to view his righteousness in light of his dream consciousness. Boys have dreams and men have dreams. Servants have dreams and Pharaohs have dreams. When dreams come true, when goals are achieved, when greatness and celebrity is attained, it is so easy to take prideful credit — I worked hard, I sacrificed, I suffered, I met the challenge, I saved the day, I made this happen. But Yoseph never lost his perspective. He knew that the dreams came from God. He therefore accepted the twists and turns of his life as part of God's plan, and when faced with ultimate power and the opportunity to crush any and all that had troubled him throughout life, he merely acknowledges, as related in next week's portion *Vayigash,* "But for your sustenance God has sent me here" (*Bereishit* 45:5). Yoseph thus views his own celebrity merely as a component of God's will, an instrument in His symphony.

If I did a good job as M.C. and everyone had a good time — maybe more people will attend the concert next year and Machon will raise even more money to spread the teaching of Torah. But that is as close as I will ever get to celebrity. Our rookie may well develop into a premier performer — popularizing songs that bring joy to people, enhance their weddings and other occasions, and livening up their *Shabbat* tables. But the dream will be truly real only if he never loses the *yeshivah* boy inside, the true essence of what makes him God's instrument.

VAYIGASH
Lawyers and Light Bulbs

There, up in the sky, it's a bird, it's a plane, it's... super lawyer. Although being a lawyer is, theoretically, about truth, justice and the American way, most people (non-lawyers and lawyers) generally do not have warm and fuzzy feelings about these purveyors of the legal trade. I have a number of friends who take sadistic pleasure in sharing the latest "lawyer joke" with me. (You know the kind — Q: What do you call 500 lawyers on the ocean floor? A: A good start!) Dealing with lawyers can be gut wrenching, exasperating, and frustrating (just ask my wife). Lawyers can complicate the easy deal, find the cloud on the silver lining, and confound plain language and common sense with artifice and rhetoric. But this week I must admit — I love what I do.

I am writing this in the gate area at La Guardia Airport in New York. I am returning home after a frantic day that was part of a crazy week that will culminate in the closing of a mega-deal. What made this process so much fun was that I got to play with the big boys in the "Legal Major Leagues." This was a time filled with corporate officers, big-time New York law firms, and lots of heated negotiation. I actually enjoyed these past several weeks full of drafts and revisions, deeds and assignments, and indemnifications and guarantees.

To the naked eye, the transaction was relatively simple — my company wanted to sell some shares of stock it owns in another company. The deal should not have been significantly different than you buying a loaf of bread at the bakery (o.k., maybe more like you buying a new car). This was strictly a corporate deal. As a tax guy, even as tax counsel, I was not even initially informed of the transaction (I was only remotely aware that we even owned the shares being sold).

Then, as the closing approached, some of the lawyers finally began to "what-if." Are there domestic or foreign tax consequences? Can we meet other objectives with this deal? Should this trigger other corporate activity? Enter the tax guy! Finally.

At one point, this simple little sale was going to trigger two corporate restructurings, the sale of one subsidiary, a distribution of shares in another, and the purchase or sale of major operations in four foreign countries. By the time reality set in, as well as the awareness that whatever we did, it had to be signed, sealed and delivered in a total of fourteen days, we had it pared down to a more modest scenario involving us, the buyer and four other parties. Our tools included telephones, fax machines, personal computers, copy machines, pens, paper, and the all important post-its. The path we chose to the objective of a completed transaction involved a 65 page initial agreement (with about 400 pages of supporting opinions, exhibits, and other good stuff), several side agreements, as well as a number of authorizing corporate resolutions, transfer deeds, bank instructions, and escrow agreements.

This was a formidable undertaking in its own right, even if the project would have been kept fully in-house. However, because of the multiple parties involved, each document had to be reviewed, discussed, debated, and modified several times over (oh yes — add red marker to the list of tools).

On Day Five a complication arose involving an agency of a foreign government. After more phone calls, more documents, and some help from the son-in-law of a major political figure in the country in question, we dodged the bullet. No, there was no *payola* — actual or implied, involved in this episode — just good old fashioned advocacy.

On Day Seven all *Gehenom* (the place some believe all lawyers belong) broke loose. Management decided to take a slightly different approach to the deal. The easy part was negotiating the change with the buyer. Likewise manageable was the process of editing, revising, and conforming the paperwork. Somewhat more daunting was the need to sell the changes to two of the parties in New York and their big-time Manhattan law firms. We spent several days preparing the documents. By then it was Day Twelve. Day Thirteen was key; things had to get done, decisions had to be made and documents had to be executed and finalized for the closing. Hence, it was a most frantic day.

The day started with a 7:00 A.M. flight, scheduled to arrive at 8:45 A.M. The inevitable and predictable mechanical problem delayed takeoff until 8:30 A.M. with deplaning a little after 10:00 A.M. (already 1 and 1/2 hours lost). The cab ride into Manhattan brought me to destination #1 at 11:00 A.M.

The meeting with the corporate Senior Vice-President for Finance went fine. He truly understood the changes (and the additional benefit for his company). He was willing to sign, but wanted his attorney (who had received copies, via fax, the day before) to take a last quick look. This attorney voiced a few new misgivings and felt compelled to involve his partner, the one with more of a feel for securities law issues. I left them to mull the issues while I trucked to destination #2 to get that ball rolling.

I will not bore you further with the ping-pong nature of the rest of this day. Questions and answers, revisions, and modifications, conditions and contingencies, lawyers and more lawyers, meetings and conference calls — all under the gun of the closing deadline. But I loved every minute of it — especially since, at the end of the day, despite all the posturing and preening, we had what we wanted and needed. Game, set, and match.

What I have described is just a superficial overview of the undertaking. Think of the countless man hours, late nights, the applied expertise, and the focused concentration of the many professionals involved. All of this effort was employed just to sell a few shares of stock. If you multiply this by a factor of 1,000, (conservatively) you have the O.J. Simpson murder trial.

His trial involved serious issues dealing with the capital crime of murder. However, it was only a trial of one insignificant, albeit famous, man. This man has not contributed to humanity in any significant way or lasting way ("Naked Gun" and "Capricorn One" do not count as significant contributions, the Bills never won a Super Bowl, and Eric Dickerson and others later broke his single season rushing record), other than changing our strategy on how not to miss a flight when arriving at the airport too close to take off time. In the end, his trial did not seem to be about innocence or guilt — it was about lawyers, lawyers, lawyers.

Upon reviewing this week's portion of *Vayigash,* one is drawn to the reunion of Yoseph with his brothers and later with his father. My attention, however, is drawn to an earlier section, right at its very beginning. The portion opens with a court case of immense religious and historical significance.

At the end of *Mikeitz,* the eleven brothers, including Binyamin were returning home with the bags of food they purchased in Egypt. Yoseph had instructed his servant to hide his "magical" silver chalice in Binyamin's sack. Yoseph sends out a posse to recover the "stolen" chalice. When accused, the brothers are astounded. They firmly believed that they were not responsible for the theft.

To make a long story short, the portion ends with Binyamin being hauled back to face the consequences of this action — he is now destined to serve as a slave to the Egyptian viceroy (Yoseph), never to return to his father. The brothers, especially Yehudah, recognize the severity of the situation, and return to Egypt to win his release.

Yehudah emerges as the family lawyer. He pleads and threatens. He argues, reasons, and appeals to the emotion. He presents and eventually wins the case.

Think what was on the line — his brother's life, and likely his father's as well (the souls of Binyamin and Yaacov were bound together), the legacy of a "Tribe," and an opportunity for personal redemption from the millstone that was his leadership role in the sale of Yoseph and the subsequent cover-up. What prepared Yehudah for this task? Why was he an effective advocate? Which characteristics allowed him to meet his burden of persuasion?

First was commitment. Yehudah had a personal stake in the outcome of this case. That stake was not in the form of a book deal or a syndicated talk show. Rather, it was personal, as personal and as permanent as it gets. Yehudah had pledged the fate of his everlasting soul to Yaacov as a guarantee that he would return from Egypt with Binyamin (an offer Yaacov accepted, in contrast with Reuven's foolish pledge of the lives of his own sons as collateral). With so much on the line, he had to do his best since only this would be what was best for his client. Unfortunately, many lawyers today are not committed to their client's best interests or even to their own moral convictions. Billable hours and dollars are the engine that drive the system.

Second was responsibility. Yehudah, except in the aftermath of the sale of Yoseph, was a person who uniquely understood what it meant to accept responsibility. The denouement of the Tamar episode (described in *Vayeishev*) is cogent proof of this.

Interestingly, this characteristic is encoded in Yehudah's very name. Leah named her son Yehudah to express praise to God for giving her four sons while her sister Rachel, more favored by Yaacov, remained childless. The name Yehudah derives from the same root as the Hebrew word for praise. Casting that same root into a reflexive construction, the result is the term that connotes confession. Praising God and confessing to Him are two sides of the same coin. On one side, when a person praises God, he or she implicitly acknowledges that He is responsible for the action that was the catalyst motivating the praise. On the other side, through confession a person accepts and verbalizes responsibility for actions that were inconsistent with God's credo. Yehudah intimately understood all aspects of the responsibility he bore.

Ironically, the laws governing attorney conduct in most states are called the Rules or Code of Professional Responsibility. Effective and ethical legal practice rests upon notions of responsibility. The fact that my profession has such an image problem (only slightly better than car salesmen) may well be linked to the fact that for many attorneys CYB (cover your behind) is far more important than PYC (protect your client). The term plausible deniability had to be coined by a lawyer!

Finally, there is integrity. Yehudah spoke as if he was answering Detective Friday's questions, "just the facts." Everything he said was straightforward, direct, and honest. He did not shade or hedge his words like his zaiyde (grandfather) Lavan would have. He did not exaggerate or use hyperbole or unduly flatter. Neither did he cower or speak too brazenly. In fact, the sages of Talmudic times suggested that Jewish leadership review Yehudah's words and his style whenever forced to confront hostile gentile authorities. Yehudah's words persuaded effectively because they were reinforced by his integrity.

Today, a lawyer would likely be exposing himself to a malpractice claim if he took an adversary's written or spoken statement at face value, without considering other possible shades of meaning that could affect his client's circumstance. In recent months, in dealings with a number of adversaries, I have been lied to outright on several occasions (with others witnessing both the original statement and the prevarication). After calling the party to task, rather than being offered an apology or an explanation, I have been accused of making too big a deal out of things. This is a sorry state of affairs that can spoil many other productive and professional interactions.

Yehudah had what it takes; commitment, responsibility, and integrity. This is why he prevailed (though not quite in the way he expected) and why his descendants were and are destined to provide majestic leadership for our people. In a society where many of today's young lawyers will inevitably become tomorrow's political leaders, it would be refreshing if the values embodied by Yehudah would be cherished and emulated. Perhaps then lawyers would not be viewed as such a fertile source of humor.

VAYECHI
Fathers and Sons

It is hard to ignore the impact of popular music on American society. Music, at times, has been a mirror of the social and philosophical changes that we, as a country, were experiencing. At other times, it has been a catalyst for change.

In the flapper/Charleston era of the Roaring '20's, the music reflected both the atmosphere of the Prohibition-era speak easy, as well as the carefree innocence of a country basking in its role as a victorious world power, unaware of the depressing darkness about to crash down on it. The music of the '40's was big-big band and big guns, tanks, and planes. The beat masked anxiety, stirred patriotism, and ultimately celebrated victory. In the '60's, however, music emerged as an agent of change; civil rights marching, anti-war protesting, a changing role for human sexuality, freedom from the boundaries of polite conformity.

The mood of that music was mind altering and consciousness raising. It was not simply to be labeled and placed on a shelf — folk, acid rock, psychedelic rock. It was experienced — Woodstock, the

Bay Area, the Village. Musicians experimented with new sounds and new technologies. But perhaps the greatest experimentation was with lyric.

Popular performers still sang about love, longing, and sentimentality. Love did, does, and always will sell lots of records. However, they also wrote songs about prejudice, the assassination of important leaders, the senseless sacrifice of innocent youths on foreign soil, and revolutionary change. The songwriters fused their lyrics together with the music to deliver messages that suggested new perspectives, different ways to react or to behave, and that allowed the artists a means of free self-expression.

In light of the charisma of the performers and the impact of the songs, popular music, as a force, could not be ignored — not even within the walls of a traditional *yeshivah*. Recall, if you can, the attitudes and reactions of secular American parents to the emerging of the "Rock and Roll" genre in the late 1950s. Rock was the music of the Devil, a corrupting influence on our youth. Christian clergy hurled fire and brimstone at it from their pulpits. Records were gathered, broken, and burned. Now try and picture how the head of a rabbinic academy, an institution labeled a "Talmudic Institute," would likely react in the early '70's.

Indeed, in other schools rather harsh measures stood in defense against this incursion of foreign values and ideals. At the *yeshivah* my cousin attended, the rabbis confiscated transistor radios and expelled and suspended boys for listening to and singing "unclean" songs — they took a hard line. Our faculty took a more tolerant approach. It was not quite "if you can't beat 'em join 'em," but it avoided creating a new forbidden fruit, a tantalizing temptation to which many would otherwise have inevitably fallen prey.

Part of their benign, yet rather insidious strategy, involved incorporating the lyrics of a number of popular songs into our 10th grade English curriculum on use of language (creative writing) and poetry. I do not remember all of the songs that we analyzed as a part of this unit, but two stick out in my mind. One was "All the Lonely People" (Eleanore Rigby) by the Beatles. I still chuckle at our classroom discussion of her keeping "her face in a jar by the door." The other song was the late Harry Chapin's "Cat's in the Cradle."

If you haven't heard it you should seek it out (download it legally!). The song will touch you. In its three plus minutes, Chapin captures the lifelong relationship between a father and son in a series of lyrical snapshots. The journey through the life of this father and son starts with a father's hope that his newborn will be like him, and envisioning the good times they will share together. It moves to the scene of a small child eager to be with and to be like his father — even though the father is too busy with his life and career to spend any quality time with him. The father, however, promises to play with him later; they will "have a good time then."

Soon, the child is grown, home from school on a break. Dad wants to chat and catch up, but Junior just wants to borrow the car keys and be busy with his friends. This time, it is the son who holds out the promise of later good times.

By the end of this parable, the father makes a late night phone call to his son, to whom he has not spoken in a while, and who is married, living far away, and raising a son of his own. The son is in a rush, has no time to make small talk. After exchanging a few pleasantries, the son ends the conversation with talk of the elusive "then" when they will get together and have a good time. As the father hangs up, he realizes that his long ago hope and prayer has been answered — his son is just like him — although not quite in the manner he had hoped. Nevertheless, he cannot complain since he got out of the relationship what he put in. In phrasing tinged with regret, the father, in the end, recognizes that the responsibility was his. It is a powerful song, with a powerful message.

I am thinking of this song and its message because of the convergence of this week's portion of *Vayechi* and this week's central event, a too brief visit from my father (and mother). *Vayechi* is primarily about the final days of Yaacov's life. He has moved with his family to Egypt, is reunited with his beloved, favorite son Yoseph, and is living out his final seventeen years in near tranquility (especially when contrasted with the rest of his life). As he senses the end approaching, he gathers his sons to impart blessings, to convey words of guidance and to share prophecy with them. (He also wishes to reveal the time for the coming of Moshiach, but is prevented from doing so by God).

I look at *Vayechi* as an opportunity to evaluate the Yaacov-Yoseph relationship as a paradigm for future similar relationships, including my own with my father.

It is no coincidence that both Yaacov and Yoseph endured twenty-year separations from their own fathers. Yaacov, forced to flee from the wrath of Eisav, spent twenty years with his Uncle Lavan. Yoseph, sold by his brothers into slavery, endured twenty years until he was finally reunited with Yaacov. Some of the sages view the Yoseph separation as a punishment for the twenty years Yaacov spent away from Yitzchak — a "measure for measure" equation.

However, that would not explain why Yoseph had to suffer similarly. I believe there was something else at play — some lesson or trait that had to be engineered into our national make-up.

Let us fast forward a few thousand years to the present, and then rewind a little. As a sixteen-year-old, I was privileged to attend a fine *yeshivah* high school. However, in order to attend this school, I effectively had to leave my parents' household and move to another city. One year later, the distance became much greater and the opportunity for in-person contact much rarer, as I departed to study for a year in Israel. Thus by age seventeen, the same age Yoseph was when his adventure began, I was displaced from my family, living in a foreign country, destined never to return home for any period longer than a short vacation or school break.

Through the approximately twenty years to follow, years spent at *yeshivah,* at college, graduate school, with my wife and later with our children, in our first apartment, second apartment, first, second, and third homes — life never moved me closer than a thousand miles from Mom and Dad. Yes, we have the telephone today, and jet airplanes, and e-mail — but I have never permanently come home again, despite having established my own. My father and I have endured our own twenty-plus year separation, that will likely last until Moshiach comes. We are destined to spend no more than a handful of days in each other's company in any given year.

Let us turn back to Yoseph, to seventeen-year-old Yoseph. We view him as a lad, a naive and vain boy. Yet, he was so much more than that, he was a son of Yaacov. He was raised with the values and lessons of our religion, internalized and manifest as the likeness of his father. This likeness, which stood out before his eyes for twenty years, gave him the fortitude to endure slavery, the balance to handle responsibility, the steel to withstand temptation, and the courage to step forward responsibly and to lead. This is not dissimilar to Yaacov's own experience — living with Lavan for 20 years, yet safeguarding the 613 commandments.

In *Bereishit* 49:33, the Torah describes the end of Yaacov's physical existence. The phrase used is "he drew his feet back into the bed, expired, and was gathered to his people." There is no reference to the death of Yaacov. The usual Hebrew word expressing death (*mita*) is absent from the verse. Rashi comments, quoting the Talmud, that this teaches us that Yaacov, indeed, did not die (*"Yaacov lo met"*). This is quite a strange comment considering that succeeding verses describe the past-mortem embalming procedures, the mourning period, the funeral procession, the exit visa for the trip to Israel and the burial in the sacred family burial plot in Hebron. How can anyone claim that Yaacov did not die?

The answer is that Yaacov lived on in Yoseph, and in Yoseph's children after him. The Torah does not really even have to tell us this fact — since we knew it already. Yoseph lived apart from

Yaacov for twenty years, as we noted, all the while keeping his father's likeness foremost in his mind's eye. What impact! What influence! What parenting! What immortality!

My father and I have similarly lived apart for over twenty years. I have studied in many fine institutions, emulated the life-style and example of a number of renown rabbis and teachers. I have worked and studied in environments not even remotely similar to that of my childhood home. Yet after Dad visits, my wife will inevitably point out what she perceives as the numerous likenesses in our mannerisms and personality.

Like most any son, for years I protested, distinguished our personalities, and distanced myself from the comparison. The bird just learning to spread its wings wants to preserve the illusion of independence. He wishes to fly high and accomplish without having to give credit or to acknowledge a debt to his ancestors. It is so easy for a child in early adulthood to look back critically — to see bad decisions, poor choices, and lost opportunities without understanding the responsibility, the need to balance, the restrictions, and the sacrifice. If that child reaches higher and has more opportunity, it is only because of the push, the support, the foundation provided by the parent. Being "like him" is more than a matter of pride, or even of time and effort — it is, or should be, a spiritual legacy; a legacy that the passage of years and the imposition of separation cannot diminish. However, sometimes it takes that same time and distance to allow the lessons to seep, to allow the son to appreciate.

Yaacov signals this in an interesting way. He blesses all of his sons, yet he directly blesses only two of his grandsons — Ephraim and Menashe — the sons of Yoseph. This is no longer a simple matter of favoritism. The time for games and misdirection has long since passed. Yaacov singles them out to amplify the message of likeness — to provide additional momentum for the lessons Yoseph learned so well — to assure that each succeeding generation will receive this legacy. His words rang out, as they do in many Jewish homes every Friday night at the *Shabbat* table, when fathers place their hands lovingly on their sons' heads (and as Yaacov himself dictated when he stated "Through you Israel shall be blessed."), proclaiming: "God shall make you like Ephraim and like Menashe" (*Bereishit* 48:20).

Just as they had a father to guide them, and a grandfather to guide him — no matter where they were, no matter what the separation — so too every father must instill these values into his own children. Each child will develop their own unique persona, but they will only succeed as Jews if, on some level, they are like their parents.

Thanks for the visit Mom and Dad, even if it has been, as it usually is, far too short. Even as you leave to return home, you are still here, in me and in my children — your Ephraim and Menashe's, Sarah, Rivkah, Rochel, and Leah's. We may be departing the Book of *Bereishit,* but we certainly never leave our forefathers and mothers behind. Their likenesses inspire us daily.

SHEMOT
Commander-in-Chief

One of the most fundamental rules of military service is "don't volunteer." You may ask, what do I know about military service — I have not served in either the American or Israeli Defense Forces, I did not attend a military academy (although a few of my *rabbeim* (teachers) in high school may have wished that I did), and I have never even been a card carrying member of *Tzivos Hashem* (literal translation: "God's Army" the name popularized by the Chabad, Lubavitch youth corps). To answer this we must travel back in time to the summer of my 19th birthday.

Had I been born in the 1950s instead of the 1960s, my 18th and 19th years could have been spent in a rice paddy in Southeast Asia. Yes, while famous former Presidents and Vice-Presidents had the influence, wherewithal, or lack of moral character and scruples to proudly serve this country, many thousands of the youth of America were shipped from the world of "Gilligan's Island" and "Andy in Mayberry" to the "Twilight Zone." Would I have spent the war years on some form of deferment or evasion or would I have seen action? Who knows! Thank God, I never had to face such issues. By the time I hit high school the war in Vietnam was over, and abolition of the draft soon followed as a consequence of harsh anti-war sentiments.

However, at some point in the late '70s reality set in — American military success in this century — through the World Wars and the conflict in Korea — was predicated on its industrial base and on its ability to raise a standing army. Future defensive capability could require either and likely both. Accordingly, Congress instituted a Selective Service registration requirement. This is not a draft and no numbers are assigned. Our country, nevertheless, feels that it is necessary to maintain a database of available fodder in case the need arises to restart the war machine.

Upon completing my first full year at Yeshiva University, I spent the summer as a counselor at an Orthodox sleep-away camp in the Poconos (in the heart of Pennsylvania). It was truly an ideal summer. The camp had a beautiful lake for swimming and waterskiing, tennis courts, an indoor gym, nice bunks, good food, and, of course, a great staff. All I (and a group of other school friends) had to do was supervise a dozen or so kids from families who were wealthy enough to afford this Rolls Royce of child care facilities... and we got paid for it.

As the summer wore on, we faced two major challenges. First, we had to be nice enough to the spoiled brats, oops, I mean "little darlings" in our charge, so that they would encourage their parents to lavishly tip us (who but those parents could truly appreciate and value what it meant to cater to those little monsters without either strangling them, tying them to their beds, or leaving them in the woods on an overnight). The second was to put a little life into the precision scheduled, education valued, and otherwise quite bland camp programming. Don't get me wrong — the camp and its experienced head counselor Larry were professional in every respect. They had all aspects of camp life from morning assembly at the flag pole, through prayer services, Torah classes, sports events, meals, special activities and trips, and showers and letters home down to a science. But too much of it seemed prepackaged — "have fun because this is supposed to be fun." We felt this recipe needed a little spice... but not so much as to ruin the casserole.

We started with a few small pranks to get things stirred up — removing the wheels from Larry's golf cart, hiding the flag pole, and substituting the usual wake-up in the morning tape with one of a recitation of "One Hundred and One Pickle Jokes." We graduated to a surprise cameo performance as very large Oompa Loompas in the camp production of "Willie Wonka and the Chocolate Factory." (The camp drama coach, an imposing 300 pounder, nearly stormed the stage to flatten us — until he saw that we actually bothered to correctly learn the Oompa Loompa dance.) With my Selective Service Registration date, a.k.a. my birthday, approaching, we had to plan the ultimate operation.

With some help from the drama coach (my new best friend), the arts and craft staff, and the camp mailman, we planned our campaign against the service, the United States Postal Service — my designated registration site (this was in those innocent carefree days before disgruntled postal employees asserted their right to bear arms to an illegal, and sometimes bloody, extreme). I outfitted myself in green army fatigues (Israeli Army Surplus, that I had purchased while studying there) and two squirt guns. The "boys" dressed in commando black with camouflage paint on their faces. They loaded onto the camp bus clutching the wooden Uzis they had fashioned as a crafts project. At zero hour, we burst through the front door of the small rural Pennsylvania post office. After securing the premises with true military precision, and giving the postmaster a knowing wink, we marched to the counter where I received the registration forms. I filled out the forms, submitted them for filing, led the group in a crisp salute and kazoo rendition of "Taps" and led a charge to the candy store down the block.

I can, thus, puff my chest out and proudly proclaim "I am a patriot." When I was called upon to serve my country, I stepped forward and met all required obligations — and I did it with style.

Now that you have all the facts pertaining to my spotless and honorable military record, we can get back to this week's event, the whole point of this rambling preamble. If the military is an institution governed by chain of command, discipline, teamwork, and the need to sometimes blindly follow orders from a superior without question, any (and probably every) Jewish organization (excluding the IDF) is the polar opposite.

Few of our co-religionists can accept any order or even a polite request, without questioning it, the person giving it, as well as the time of day, the overall reason for existence and the meaning of life. If you want a good lesson on what discipline isn't, monitor the decibel levels in synagogue during services. Teamwork is fine, until someone in the group receives some *"Kovod"* (honor or acknowledgment) that someone else just realized should have been theirs. Chain of command only rests with the rabbi if his contract is not subject to periodic review.

Don't get me wrong, there are many fine Jewish organizations that accomplish great things for our people and for all of humanity. However, the same traits — drive, will, persistence, creativity, and goal orientation that foster success, also lead to bruised egos, one-upmanship, and sometimes even violent conflict.

Over the years I have participated in a variety of such organizations — youth organizations, student government, day school board, Israel Bond and Jewish Federation — the whole gamut. In fact, one of the nicest things initially about moving from Cleveland to Detroit was that I could extricate myself from all the meetings, time demands, and personalities that I (and especially my family) was suffering due to my basic inability to say no to worthwhile projects. In fact, I have relished this time as just a parent, just a shul goer, just a person who spends a little time each week learning

Torah with others. This low profile is liberating. But, it was far too good to last.

Earlier this week the Director of Machon L'Torah, Rabbi J, called (yes, the same man who put me onstage in that Chanukah debacle). He informed me that the same person who was supposed to M.C. the concert, the current president of the organization, felt that he had too many other commitments to continue to lead Machon effectively. As the saying goes *"mitzvah goreret mitzvah"* (one good deed leads to another) (*Ethics of the Fathers* 4:2). According to the good Rabbi, my M.C. stint turned into an audition for the job. Would I please agree to a leadership role at Machon?

I declined the offer and protested — I valued my newfound liberation; I disliked community politics; I enjoyed the extra quality time I had with my family; I am too new to the community and have not networked sufficiently to be of value to the organization; I want to have time to work on my book; and I prefer teaching classes to helping support the framework that attracts students and allows others to teach.

But, But, But, But... The Rabbi was persistent, and likely knew he had a real live one (after all, I never hung up on him or insulted him). In the end I agreed to a "limited" leadership role as part of a Presidium with two others — either a good way to reasonably divide responsibility, or a formula for disaster. I did not fully ignore my military heritage. After all this was not the same as volunteering. However, I now found myself in a position I did not want to fully occupy, at least until I started reviewing this week's Torah portion of *Shemot* — with an extra boost from a passage of Talmud I studied with my regular *chavruta* (study partner) Dr. S. (who, by the way, actually served in the Israeli military!).

Shemot opens with a description of the worsening conditions for the Jews in Egypt. This is immediately followed by the story of the birth of Moshe. Considering that every weekly portion except one (*Tetzaveh*) from *Shemot* until the end of the Torah mentions Moshe, it is remarkable how little we are told of his birth and development.

An anonymous Levite and his wife, a daughter of Levi, have a baby. Due to Pharaoh's decree to kill all male children, they hide him. Soon, even this becomes dangerous. So he goes white water rafting, where he is found by Pharaoh's daughter and raised in the royal household. Fast forward about eighty years (we know nothing, except from the *Midrash,* of his childhood, his education and identification as a Jew, or his role in the royal family), and we meet an individual who has deeply held attitudes about man's injustice toward man, a man who is unafraid to speak up ("Wicked one, why do you hit your friend?" *Shemot* 2:13), and a man who gets his first glimpse at what it's like to try and lead other Jews ("Who made you our boss?" *Shemot* 2:14).

In quick succession, he then flees Egypt and the consequences of his actions, arrives in Midian to assist some damsels in distress, meets his soon-to-be father-in-law, gets married, has a child, and settles into life as a shepherd. One fine day he follows a lost sheep in the desert, encounters the burning bush and voila! — Moshe the Redeemer, Moshe the Miracle Worker, Moshe the Law Giver, Moshe the Leader, Moshe the King, Moshe our teacher!

Maybe I went through this a little too quickly. Let us back up to the famous scene by the burning bush. In a nutshell, God introduces Himself to Moshe and offers him the rewards and responsibilities of leadership. We do not know much about Moshe at this point, but we can tell that he is very intelligent, because he turns the offer down. God can be very persistent and persuasive, so as Moshe gives his excuses, He gets back the "But... But... But." Eventually, Moshe relents and accepts (and I can now well sympathize with him). Before we go on with Moshe, and what *Shemot* teaches me as I face a new leadership position, we must detour to that Talmud passage I mentioned earlier and that I, not coincidentally, reviewed just this week. The passage in the tractate of *Sanhedrin* (14a) is discussing the requirements for rabbinic ordination. In those times, it was not a mere degree or certificate of completion. Ordination was the cloak of authority. A true rabbi was more than a scholar, he was a leader.

The Talmud relates that R' Zeira would hide to avoid being ordained, for he used to say, "One should always be in the dark (out of the spotlight) and if he stays there, he will live." (Sure, no stress, no aggravation, no death threats!) But then he heard the following statement from R' Elazar and strove to have himself ordained: "No person rises to a position of greatness unless heaven forgives all of his sins." (Sure, what greater punishments could *Gehenom* hold!). As the old commercial tag line went — "You can pay me now, or pay me later" — it looks like I'm back to paying.

Shemot, however, holds two more important lessons about leadership, perhaps the two **most** important lessons, hidden in a very strange incident.

Moshe is on board, signed up, with the program. He packs up his wife, Tzipporah, and newborn son, Gershon, puts the carrier on the caravan, and heads to Egypt with a large "M" emblazoned on his chest and red cape all aflutter. Just think, one minute he is an exiled shepherd and the next he is second in this universe only to God Himself.

They stop for the night at the Holyday Inn (I couldn't resist) and they encounter a lot more than bad room service. A fiery, avenging, big bad angel is about to kill Moshe. Yes, that's right, God just spent an afternoon and a few good miracles on Moshe to recruit him for the most important series of events in the history of the world, and now, practically as he pulls out of the driveway, God dispatches a heavenly hit man? Could you imagine Dean Smith benching Michael Jordan in the NCAA Final? Would you pull John Elway with the ball on your own twenty, two minutes to go, down two? This simply does not make sense.

Before we try to understand this, we should let the scene play out. The angel appears and is threatening to kill Moshe. Tzipporah leaps into action to save Moshe. She circumcises their son and flings his foreskin at the angel's feet.

We now know what the problem was. Moshe was eager to assume his new job — so eager that he did not want to delay the journey long enough to circumcise his newborn son. In essence, he allowed the most holy of ends to justify cutting a few corners on the means. Tzipporah, his wife, immediately and innately understood that this was wrong and acted quickly and decisively to save him.

I've gone on too long this week as is (the BENEFIT of having a few days off for the secular New Year), so I'll jump right to the punchline. Every Jewish leader must keep two things rooted firmly in mind:

One — by definition, what you are doing is *l'shem shamayim* (for the sake of heaven). The work you are seeking to do is in furtherance of God's will. Nevertheless, no matter what the goal, no matter what the greater good, you may not ignore any other aspect of God's Torah in achieving the objective. Redemption from Egypt and the giving of the Torah do not outweigh the timely circumcision of one small (and historically, rather insignificant) child.

Two — a Jewish leader cannot succeed without the guidance and support of his or her spouse. Without Tzipporah, Moshe is a footnote. With her, he makes history and changes the world.

I will not embarrass my wife, because she is likely going to read this quite a number of times. However, any success that I will have in this or any other holy undertaking will only be achieved together with her. How fitting that *Shemot* is the only portion where her Hebrew name, *Shifrah,* appears. A righteous woman who helped ensure Jewish physical survival in Egypt has a namesake who is devoted to supporting Jewish spiritual survival today.

VA'EIRA
Twinkies and Ring Dings

As a veteran corporate employee, I've seen restructuring, re-engineering, downsizing, decentralizing, re-centralizing and virtually every other initiative that the management gurus have implemented in an attempt to justify their own excessively high levels of compensation. Most of these programs boil down to a simple formula — cut costs (usually reducing the work force) and the bottom line will look better, at least for a short while. If business begins to slow, do it again — call it something else — but do it again anyway.

This is something of an exaggeration. Businesses, especially successful ones, do need to step back once in a while and to evaluate process. What strengths are not being maximized? How can things be done more efficiently? Are there needless redundancies? Is the organization encouraging its employees to "work smart?" Groups of employees are sometimes sent off site for team-building workshops and focus groups to ponder these issues. In these sessions the emphasis is not on "why," but on "what if." The operative term is

"Brainstorming." I read an item in the newspaper today that caused me to reevaluate the process revealed in this week's Torah portion of *Va'eira*. The profundity of this article merited status as a discrete and discussible event.

Last week, God instructed Moshe to go down to Egypt and to request that Pharaoh release the Jewish People from servitude. Other than arming Moshe with a couple of parlor tricks (like the staff turns into snake routine), God did not lay out the full game plan. This week, we are shown most of this plan — the first seven plagues, signs, wonders, heart hardening, psychological warfare, diplomacy, and negotiation. As we know from our *seder* table experiences, by the time it is all over, there will be a total of ten plagues in Egypt (sidestepping the *Haggadah*'s discussion of whether there were forty or fifty, in total).

Our sages have asked the obvious "why" question: Why did God smite (that great Biblical word) the Egyptians with ten plagues? Certainly, God could have skipped plagues one through nine, gone right to number ten, and swiftly redeemed His people. Likewise, He could have devised some awesome "super plague" that would have forced Pharaoh into whimpering submission.

They provide a sagelike (meaning, mystical and somewhat cryptic) answer. God, as we all know, created the world with ten utterances or sayings (*Ethics of the Fathers,* 5:1). Early man, Adam, could almost directly see and experience God. In a sense he could still likely hear the echo of the creation utterances. However, in order to allow man and mankind to exercise free will, God had to mute those sounds. When the barriers imposed by man's own evil actions in succeeding generations were added to this diminution, the world fell to a state so far removed from God, that it could no longer serve as a receptacle for His Torah. Through the ten plagues, God, figuratively, broke through these barriers to allow the essence of the original ten utterances to resonate throughout the world. God's greatness and power, the same power used by God during creation, was, once again on full display This also explains why in the *kiddush* on Friday night (the blessing said over wine to sanctify the day), the *Shabbat* is identified both as "a memorial of the Exodus from Egypt" and "a remembrance of creation." The same characteristics of God utilized and revealed in one (creation), were re-utilized and re-revealed in the other (the Exodus).

However, our sages never asked the what if — what if God had tried a different approach, used different plagues or sent Moshe armed with a different sign? To be honest, until I read the following article, I never though much about how things could have gone differently — how God, through Moshe, could have convinced Pharaoh to raise his hands and cry "Uncle" with any greater effect. But this week, I saw this in the news:

> NASHVILLE, TENN. — Hundreds of people are flocking to a small Nashville coffee shop to see a likeness of Mother Teresa — on a cinnamon bun.
>
> Visitors lined up at the Bonga Java coffee shop Saturday and Sunday to stare at the bun, which looks like the nun's face, complete with her head covering.

If hundreds flock to a coffee shop for a cinnamon bun, just think of the reaction Moshe could have stirred with a lemon meringue pie or a seven (or TEN) layer cake. More incredibly, if people can acknowledge the miraculous nature of a piece of pastry, why do they ignore blatant evidence of God's handiwork in this world? Why do people no longer hear the sounds of creation?

BO

The Three Bad Wolves

There is an old expression that bad things come in threes. I do not know whether this is pure superstition (a.k.a. nonsense) or whether there is some mystical source (a secret of *kaballah*). However, there would seem to be a hint for it in the very name of the Torah portion *"Bo."*

Numbers in the Torah have great symmetry. Man's awareness of the seven days of creation (six plus *Shabbat*) is complemented by seven specific laws or commands from God, the "Seven Noachide Laws." (As an interesting aside — the sages of the Talmud derive all seven rules from the wording of the single command not to eat from the fruit of the tree of knowledge). As we discussed in the essay for *Va'eira,* the ten utterances of creation were amplified by the ten plagues. Even the famous "Ten Commandments" have a certain balance with five on one tablet and five on the other.

Why then does the Torah split the ten plagues in such an uneven way? There are seven in last week's portion of *Va'eira* and three this week, in *Bo.* We can not claim that this is mere happenstance, because the number of plagues to be found in each portion is intertwined with the portion's very name.

The first two Hebrew letters of the word *"va'eira"* are *Vav* and *Aleph*. The numeric equivalent of these two letters (each Hebrew letter has a corresponding numeric representation, termed *gematriah*) is six and one, a total of seven. The portion *Bo*, is spelled with only two Hebrew letters, a *Beit* and an *Aleph*, or two and one, a total of three. Remarkably, we find, as stated above, seven plagues in *Va'eira*, and three in *Bo*.

I believe the ten plagues were split up in this uneven manner to teach us a lesson. The three intense plagues in *Bo* have an impact equal to, or even greater than the seven lesser ones in *Va'eira*. The Torah does not place six balanced against four or eight versus two — specifically seven and three. Why? Because God knows the balance and because His Torah says this is so.

That is not a particularly satisfying answer. It is even less satisfying when we recognize that the plagues involved varying levels of real human pain and suffering. But then again, this past week has not been particularly satisfying either — as it has been full of the suffering of family and friends.

In this week of the "big bad three" of *Bo*, I encountered three troubling incidents. First, my mother-in-law, who has been courageously battling the rigors of a difficult illness, was hospitalized with an assortment of complications. Second, Harvey, one of our close friends, lost his father to the long, slow decline of Alzheimers. Third, one of my childhood teachers, a man who was truly one of the great influences on my life, lost his sister, which necessitated his coming to Detroit for the funeral and the Shiva observance.

Such a convergence of suffering. What a range of circumstances and emotions!

Mom has been battling various cancers for a few years now. Rather than "Blood, Frogs, Lice...," she has faced plagues of radiation, chemotherapy, surgery, rehabilitation, more treatments and medications, etc. Harvey, and his mother who valiantly stood by her husband through it all, watched almost helplessly, as the functions of the mind and body — memory, reasoning, speech, mobility — slipped away one by one, leaving the shell of a loved one to succumb finally to the ravages of infection — a drawn out succession of plagues. Rebbe's sister passed swiftly as her heart simply gave out.

These people, these loved ones, and their travails, raise many tough ethical and philosophical questions. Why do good people suffer? Is there any benefit to a long painful death over a quick and relatively painless one? Is there a point where death, rather than continued life, is a relief? Is it better to be aware or unaware of the suffering? How do people find the fortitude and courage to battle for life day after day without giving up?

As a child, I enjoyed reading comic books. I particularly liked the super-heroes: Superman, Batman, the Fantastic Four, Captain America and many others. Although the books were in full color, the stories were so black and white — the heroes were clearly good and the villains, Lex Luthor, Joker, Dr. Doom and the Red Skull, were clearly evil. In the end, the heroes would prevail and the villains would be thwarted. No matter how bleak things sometimes looked for a hero, there was always a solution. Sometimes, through some quirk of science, time travel, or an alternate dimension, a character would even be revived after certain death.

Life is not so black and white, and every difficulty does not have its sure solution. If the portion of *Bo* shows us the ultimate troubles and plagues, it also shows us this ambiguity of life, as well.

As explained above, *Bo* contains the last three of the ten plagues, "locusts, darkness, and the plague of the first born." These are the ones that force Pharaoh to capitulate. In a sense, each plague in this group was an ultimate.

The plague of "locusts" was the finishing touch in the assault against the land and property of Egypt. Anything that had withstood contamination, pestilence, and the destructive bombardment of the fire and ice mixture of hail was simply and effectively consumed.

God intended the plague of "darkness" was to be the ultimate assault against a living person. As described in the *Midrash,* this plague was not a mere absence of light, it was tangible darkness. Every Egyptian experienced total sensory deprivation. They could not move since their limbs were weighed down. They could not speak, see or hear since everything was filled with and muffled by the deep darkness. Each person was completely alone, isolated from all other contact. It was as if they existed as pure thought; conscious minds aware only of the seemingly endless and panic-filled night.

With the "plague of the first born," Pharaoh and Egypt faced the final assault — death. Those who died suffered and those who remained alive suffered as much, perhaps more. The bad guys faced off against the biggest, baddest guy, the "Angel of Death." (In the text, God states that He would personally deal with the Egyptian first borns. Nevertheless, the Angel of Death was also unleashed to wreak havoc with a license to kill. The Jews needed to smear the blood of the Pascal lamb on their doorposts to ward him off). Talk about ambiguity; our great moment of national triumph comes, in part, through the ministrations of the one entity, other than God Himself, we perhaps fear most. Likewise, reading the biblical description of the plague in each Egyptian household, a plague that took the first born of every family, from Pharaoh to lowly maid servant, fills us, as compassionate people, with a sense of their sorrow and with a measure of pity.

Is the Angel of Death a hero? Is Pharaoh a villain? Are their roles black and white or are there shadings of meaning with lessons for us to discover?

Death is too difficult a topic to comprehend fully. It is both an angel or messenger of God and a personification or aspect of evil.

(Of course, God is everything, good and bad. We are commanded to bless the bad as we would the good. Trying to understand or to explain why God looses such forces on the world are beyond my limited narrative abilities). While the Angel of Death was a beneficial part of God's gameplan for the Exodus, we can only hope that he will face his own destiny at the time of the final redemption, as described in the *Chad Gadya* ("One Kid Goat") parable at the conclusion of the Passover *seder* ("and God will come and slaughter the Angel of Death").

I would like, instead, to center on Pharaoh and an important lesson we should learn from him. We often look at characters like Pharaoh through children's eyes — the way we first viewed him. With these eyes we see an evil man, a baby killer, a despot, and a man who enslaved our people and approved of their cruel oppression (or we see Yul Brenner). This could very well be who he was.

But it would seem that he was much more complex than this. As with the "Angel of Death," ambiguities surround him, ambiguities that are amplified in the rabbinic sources.

According to some, the Pharaoh of Moshe was the same individual as the Pharaoh of Yoseph. That Pharaoh harbored no particular ill will against the "Sons of Yisroel;" he even promoted one of them to viceroy, the number two position in his palace. He also gave them choice Egyptian real estate, in Goshen, and treated them as honored guests. Moreover, as a personality, he represented a balance between imperial strictness (killing the royal baker) and fairness (sparing the wine butler, allowing Yaacov to be buried back in Hebron). Finally, he cared enough for his people and his land to implement the measures necessary to survive the years of famine.

Others identify the Pharaoh of Exodus with the King of Ninveh in the book of Jonah. Without getting lost in the details of that story and explaining the significant passage of time (several centuries) between events, the central theme of such identification is the fact that Pharaoh repented. Yes, in the end, "Mr. Hard Heart" himself, repents.

In a way, I have placed the answer before the question — kind of like the gameshow "Jeopardy." The category, "the Book of *Shemot* for $100." DAILY DOUBLE! The answer is "because Pharaoh repented." The question is, "if Pharaoh is so malevolent, why does the Torah not explicitly record and celebrate his death?"

Many of the evil men of the Bible come to inglorious ends: Korach was swallowed up by the earth; Avshalom was hung by his hair; Haman was hung from a high tree; Sisra was impaled with a tent stake driven through his head; etc... Yet Pharaoh merely fades into obscurity as the waves come crashing on his army. Why was he spared? Why did he deserve to be spared? Some say he repented as he witnessed the events at the Red Sea. Yet, if his repentance was so crucial, why did God not publicize it in the Torah?

I would like to suggest a somewhat radical answer. Pharaoh was spared because he taught the Jewish people an important lesson; a lesson critical for their personal and national survival. It is a lesson so important, that he could be viewed as a step-father of our people (do not laugh at this notion — Moshe was, in fact, raised in his royal palace!). He taught us how to be stubborn.

I am not referring to your five year old's "I won't eat this and you can't make me" stubbornness. I am talking about a cosmic stubbornness — the stubbornness to withstand the ten plagues without buckling and the stubbornness to face exiles, inquisitions, pogroms, and holocausts and still believe in and worship God; the fabled Jewish "stiff-necked" stubbornness. This is, of course, the same stubbornness that allows an individual who suffers through illness, deterioration, and pain, to live through today and to look forward to and hope for tomorrow.

Like Pharaoh, we all must face plagues. We all, at one time or another, face devastating plagues. Like Pharaoh, we are ambiguous mixtures of good and bad. If we ultimately do not outlast the Angel of Death, may we, like Pharaoh, be able to overcome our own natures, stubbornness, and spiritual blindness, and turn the pain into something positive; emerging repentant rather than victimized or punished.

BESHALACH
"Listen to the Music"

The *Shabbat* on which we read the Torah portion of *Beshalach* has a special name. It is called *Shabbat Shira,* "The Sabbath of Song." This name is not a call or an invitation to celebrate music and song — a Jewish Music Week to complement Jewish Book Month. Nor is it reflective of our desire to hear the song of the birds of spring as we lift our heads from the depths of a slumbering winter and realize that it is already *Tu B'shevat,* the 15th day of the Jewish month of *Shevat,* the New Year's day for trees and the signal that nature is preparing to revitalize and to renew. Instead, the name comes from a key portion of the week's text, the *Shirat Hayam,* "The Song of the Sea," that Moshe and the Children of Israel sang as God crushed Pharaoh's army under the force of the Red Sea while simultaneously delivering His people to redemptive safety.

The song reflects their joy at that moment, as well as the promise of future redemption. It contains a graphic description of the devastation inflicted on the Egyptians. The lyrics also bespeak pride, the national pride of a fledgling nation of formerly weak and powerless slaves that attains a realization that it is destined for greatness because God is so powerful and so great.

What joy! What a high! Yet, if it were not for the actions of one man — not a Moshe, or an Aharon, or a Yehoshua, not the leader, high priest, or army commander, but one ordinary man who made a difference by acting — the liberation of our people likely would have been permanently derailed.

Before we discover the identity of that person and what he did, I should backtrack and identify why I am so fixated this week on what a single person can do or can prevent. Last week as I wrote about the plagues that many people are forced to endure, I mentioned that my mother-in-law is battling cancer and had been hospitalized due to some side complications. Her initial expected stay of a few days turned into a several weeks of confinement to bed while hooked up to a variety of machines, monitors, and medicines. This forced inactivity, unfortunately, reversed some of the wonderful progress she made following orthopedic surgery last spring. As a consequence, her doctor informed us that when the primary medical problems were sufficiently under control, she would have to return for a few weeks to the rehabilitation facility she visited during her prior recovery.

This is not exactly wonderful news. We want her back home where she is most comfortable, as soon as possible. However, the therapy she received there before was professional and the care was more than adequate. Therefore we simply look at this as a necessary evil, a small bump on her road to recovery. The fact that she has experienced this all before, with success no less, means that while her stay would still be unpleasant, it would at least not fill us with the added anxiety of the unknown.

My wife has been shuttling back and forth to New Jersey to spend time with her mother, and she was there most of this week. Based on the early reports, Mom looks and feels better than she has for several weeks and the immediate problems seem to be under control. It is just up to her doctor to authorize her release from the hospital. Thursday morning, after a brief examination, the doctor said that Mom could be discharged on Friday and he requested that the floor nurse prepare the necessary paperwork for Mom's transfer to the rehabilitation center.

About an hour later, the assigned social worker, who has maybe spent a few minutes with Mom during her stay, walked in with a stack of papers for Mom to sign and inquired about the transfer. One of the assembled family crew identified the name of the rehabilitation center. The social worker immediately responded that Mom could not go there and that they should locate another suitable facility. When challenged about this last minute change of plan (the question asked with the panic of realization that things are about to be turned inside out), the social worker declared, "after observing your mother and monitoring her condition and needs, I classified her as **subacute.** The facility that serviced her last time will only admit patients classified as **acute.**"

Mom's doctor did not make this determination and was not consulted. Mom's primary care nurse did not make this decision and was not consulted. The system had delegated responsibility to a social worker with no real interest in, or connection to the patient. This petty, bureaucratic, stubborn, woman (I am sure the peanut gallery used descriptions that were far more abrasive) threw the family into a "two minute drill." They had less than a day to find a suitable facility, with the necessary therapy available, within a reasonable proximity to family members, with bed space, and with the willingness to admit a new patient on Friday afternoon, with an early *Shabbat* looming.

To make a long story short, and to the great credit of my brother-in-law and sister-in-law, they found a convalescent facility nearby that would meet Mom's needs and would admit her immediately. But let us return to the social worker. She is stereotypical of all the court clerks, airline gate attendants, title company assistants, bank tellers, and other "little people" who have the ability at critical moments in our lives to muck up the works and aggravate us. They can delay your move into a new house, cause you to miss an important meeting, or prevent you from capitalizing on an investment opportunity simply because they have the power to — and they know that for a brief time you are completely at their mercy. If we are lucky they only cause inconvenience. Sometimes, however, they can cause real lasting harm. (I do not mean to slander everyone employed in these positions — only those who have a real talent for making others miserable for no good reason. Such people are clearly not performing their jobs with the requisite professionalism a service provider should display)

This week also marked the celebration of Martin Luther King Jr.'s birthday. Dr. King is the symbol of a single person who made a difference and was able to promote change in our society. Dr. King was also a unique person — a born leader, and powerful speaker, with courage, passion, talent, vision, and energy. (The other day on the radio I was listening to a tribute to Dr. King by Andrew Young, former U.S. Ambassador to the United Nations and Mayor of Atlanta. Mr. Young spent a few moments reflecting on his private personality. He described Dr. King as a playful humorous person and stated that the contemporary person who reminds him most of this side of Dr. King is [and I am not making this up] Eddie Murphy. Go Figure!)

Very few of us have been blessed with the package of abilities possessed by Martin Luther King Jr. However, his success, and the success of the entire civil rights movement, was built on the actions of ordinary individuals who acted appropriately when called upon. People like Rosa Parks or the African-American students who defied then Gov. George Wallace to attend classes at the University of Alabama helped deliver the change.

The Children of Israel literally had their backs up against the wall. In front of them was the Red Sea, with no "Bridge to the Future" in sight. Pursuing from behind was the still mighty Egyptian Army. They looked to Moshe for guidance and he told them simply to enter the sea. But they just could not do it. Despite witnessing the hand of God at work through the plagues in Egypt and despite the fact that Moshe had been consistently true to his word, they could not, would not, make that leap of faith into the sea.

Sure, Moshe could have gone first. The sea would certainly have split for him and our nation would have responded to the miracle by moving forward on the now dry path. But the fledgling nation had to learn that a society, a nation, does not function and thrive that way. Leaders can and do accomplish great things (and sometimes, unfortunately, they do evil and wicked things). But true progress and lasting accomplishment is the result of cooperation and timely, responsible behavior by regular people.

Fortunately, a man named Nachshon the son of Aminadav pushed forward and leapt into the sea. When this "everyman" acted, the sea split. Everyone and anyone can make a difference. No, we do not all get the chance to change history or to save thousands or millions of lives. However, we all are occasionally given opportunities to improve the lives of others, to help, to comfort, to support, or simply to do the right thing.

When a musical piece is being performed, if even one singer or one musician is off key or misses the beat, then the entire song can be ruined. Every participant makes a difference — a noticeable difference. In the portion of the "Song of the Sea," read on the "Sabbath of Song," we are reminded, as the Doobie Brothers so eloquently stated, to "listen to the music all the time." We have to pay attention to the music of the lives of those around us. We must stay in synch and play our personal notes in harmony with our fellow man. Ms. Social Worker — pump up the volume and get in step with the beat!

YITRO
Little Miss Sunshine

There she is, our little "Miss America." She is resplendent in her crown. Colorful streamers flow from her wrist. Her long wavy hair is bouncing around her head and her smile is beaming.

There is electricity in the air. Everyone in the room reflects the excitement. We are all anticipating that magical moment. Parents, grandparents, and younger and older siblings are assembled for a symbolically important event.

Our little "Queen Esther" (the full Hebrew name of our daughter Esti is Esther Malka, literally Queen Esther, after her great-grandmother) moves forward toward the stage. The regal nature of her bearing has nothing to do with the pageantry of Purim, that holiday is months away. Nevertheless, this day resonates with history. Esti, adorned with a cardboard crown, is about to join generations of ancestors in receiving a precious spiritual crown — the very crown received in this week's portion of *Yitro* — the crown of the Torah.

The spectacle of *Matan Torah,* God's giving the Torah to our people at Mount Sinai, is detailed in *Yitro*. The event was a special effects spectacular — laser lights and stereo surround sound. The experience was so intense and stimulating that the people actually "saw the thunder." Even the nation that witnessed God's power and creativity during the Exodus from Egypt and the crossing of the Red Sea was not adequately prepared for the spectacle and grandeur at Sinai. In fact, the *Midrash* relates that as they experienced the moment of Divine revelation, their souls left their bodies because the essence of their beings was simply overwhelmed. They survived solely because God drew their souls back and revived them.

Today's sounds are not quite as imposing. Our daughter and her classmates are singing sweetly as they take their places. However, this does not mean that the sounds are any less significant. They likewise echo in lofty spiritual realms and may well impact future generations.

The girls then focus their attention on their principal, who steps up to the microphone at the podium to welcome the assembled guests and to praise and encourage her students. She notes that just four months ago these girls were kindergarten graduates — masters of coloring, scissors, glue, finger paints, and the letters of the *Aleph-Beit*. Today, she proclaims that they are princesses, pupils who can blend those letters into words — words of *tefillah* (prayer), words of *shira* (song), and in a few minutes, words of Torah.

The principal turns the microphone over to Esti's teacher, who calls her and the other students up by name, one by one, to receive their first Torah texts — the Book of *Bereishit*. Each girl, smiling ear to ear, returns to her place, after a short pause at the podium for her parents to take a picture and/or to get appropriate video footage. The teacher then instructs her class to open their new books to the first page and to place their fingers on the first verse. The girls, shyly and carefully, lovingly and tenderly, open to *"Bereishit bara Elokim..."* ("In the beginning God created the heaven and the earth..."). The smoothness and harmony of their reading bespeaks some advance rehearsal. Nevertheless, we take this moment for what it is, symbolically, if not actually, the moment that our Esti begins to receive and study the Torah.

When our sages discuss the events at Mount Sinai, they refer to *"Matan Torah,"* (the "Giving of the Torah"). In fact, the festival of *Shavuot,* when we celebrate and commemorate the actual calendar day of the experience, is also referred to as *"Zeman Matan Torateinu,"* (the "Time, or Season of the Giving of our Torah"). The emphasis seems to be on God's giving of the Torah, not on the Jews receiving it. Why is the one aspect given more emphasis than the other?

I pondered this question as I watched Esti and her classmates. My mind wandered to a recollection that my childhood Rebbe shared with me when I sat with him during that *"shiva"* (seven day mourning period) visit two weeks ago (see, *Bo:* The Three Bad Wolves). He reminisced about a child, the Torah, and how we receive it.

In the fourth, fifth, and sixth grades, I was Rebbe's student at the Arie Crown Hebrew Day School in Chicago. Arie Crown was (and still is) a full service school with Judaic subjects taught in the morning and secular or general studies in the afternoon. The alternative for Jewish education to such a school, and one that unfortunately has been less than successful at motivating and inspiring religious feeling among our children, is the afternoon Hebrew school. I do not mean to demean or belittle these programs. There is simply too much competition for a child's attention — especially after a full school day, especially when other friends and classmates do not have such "burdens," and especially when parents do not reflect or reinforce the lessons taught in their homes or in the priority schemes of their lives.

Nevertheless, there are exceptions. A few precious students do accept the challenge of caring, dedicated teachers and demand and seek more. Rebbe's day at Arie Crown ended early in the afternoon. He, with his teacher's soul, ran an afternoon Hebrew school program where he could make a difference to those precious ones.

One year, with one particular class of eleven- or twelve-year-olds, he spent a few weeks teaching the children about *"Matan Torah."* Knowing Rebbe, he likely brought the Biblical narrative alive with the colorful embellishments of the *Midrash*. Equally likely, he must have brought in his guitar to sing some of the songs associated with the event — perhaps the very songs my Esti and her friends sang this week. After a few class sessions, however, it was time to move on to the next topic, for the boys and girls to learn other important material.

During the following week, one of the students, a little boy, approached Rebbe at the end of class. He was holding a blank piece of paper and his pencil. He asked Rebbe to write down the Hebrew words of the Ten Commandments for him.

Rebbe began to write the words across the paper.

"No, No, No," exclaimed the boy. "Please write them like they are on the tablets — five going down one half and five going down the other."

Rebbe was somewhat puzzled by this request, but he nevertheless complied. After all, how often did one of his students show such great interest in "old" material, in last week's lessons?

One evening, several weeks later, there was a knock on Rebbe's door. He opened it to find his student, the little boy with the expressed interest in the Ten Commandments, standing there holding a piece of plywood almost as big as he was. Rebbe looked more closely and realized that at the top of the board were two curved mounds. The boy had apparently fashioned a replica of the two tablets.

The boy was grinning from ear to ear and stated that he wanted to give Rebbe a present. Rebbe invited the boy in. When presented with the gift, Rebbe noticed that his student did not simply prepare a symbolic representation of the commandments (either letters of the *Aleph-Beit,* Roman numerals, or the familiar two word shorthand for each of the ten commandments) but had actually copied every word as Rebbe, himself had written down on the paper.

In those days, B.V.G. (Before Video Games), kids actually engaged in many hobbies and outlets. Some built model planes and cars. Others would play stickball or football in the school yard. Still others were collectors — stamps, coins, bugs, rocks, comic books, baseball cards, etc. One such hobby, not particularly common or popular today, was wood burning. No, not arson. This involved purchasing an electric wood burning tool (a pen-like device with a red hot tip, somewhat like a soldering iron) and writing or drawing with it on a wood surface. Essentially, the tool allowed the "artist" to burn the text or design into the wood. The tint of the burns and the depth and thickness of the lines was a function of the intensity of the heat and pressure applied to the wood.

What was remarkable about the boy's work was that he did not merely write or paint the words on. It appeared as if he had meticulously burned each letter in a skilled, almost artful, manner. Realizing this, Rebbe praised him for his wonderful talent at wood burning.

"But Rebbe," he explained, "I did not make this with a wood burning kit."

"Then how did you make it," asked Rebbe.

"The letters and words came from God!"

"But I taught you in class that the first tablets were fashioned by God, and the second by Moshe thousands of years ago. God did not fashion the letters on your tablets — you did!"

"No Rebbe, I mean it," he insisted — "The letters came from God!"

Rebbe did not want to get upset with a student who exerted the effort to make him such a meaningful gift. However, he felt himself get frustrated at the boy's insistence that God somehow directly assisted in the project and carved the letters. After a brief pause to inspect the "Tablets" and again to decide on the right approach to take, he looked the boy in the eyes and simply asked, "Why do you insist that this came from God?"

The boy smiled sheepishly and slowly reached his hand into his pocket. He pulled out a magnifying glass and while pointing with it to the sun emphatically repeated, "I did not etch or draw these letters, they came from God!"

Three thousand years ago our ancestors received the Torah, from God. This week, my Esti received the Torah, not merely from her teacher's hand, but from God. Our sages, thus, emphasize the fact of the giving rather than the receiving of the Torah because any act of God, like God Himself, is outside of the boundaries of time. God was, is, and will be. God gave, gives, and will give. All as one act, all at one time.

We, on the other hand, each receive Torah differently. At Sinai, Torah was received amidst miraculous revelation and special effects. In the era of the *Mishnah,* when the Romans ruled the world, Torah was received by dim candlelight in caves and attics. Today, Torah is received in our beautiful Day Schools and *Yeshivot* — as well as on audio tape, the internet, via satellite, and on cable television. Sometimes, as my Rebbe witnessed, Torah even comes through solar power. It is important for each generation to receive the Torah its way, as long as the method and medium are in accord with the long chain of transmission (*"mesorah"*) tracing back to Sinai (see, *Ethics of the Fathers,* 1:1).

The Torah describes the fact that Moshe's face shone when he returned from Sinai. In fact, it shone so brightly he had to wear a veil in order to shield the others around him. Esti's face, and the faces of her friends were shining in a different way when they "received the Torah" this week. Maybe Rebbe's wonderful and motivated student perceived something very deep when he chose to shine and to channel the light of the sun into his Torah project. Perhaps he was in tune with the timeless energy of God giving us the Torah every day and charging and energizing us with its study and observance.

MISHPATIM
Live Long and Prosper

Only eight feet away. Standing on stage a mere eight feet from where I sit is Mr. Spock. No, not someone dressed as a pointy eared alien in a colorful uniform with green tinted skin. It is really him, Leonard Nimoy.

Like many others of my generation, I am a huge "Star Trek" fan. I have seen nearly every episode of the original show and the various sequels. I have gone to see each of the motion pictures, on opening day. As a pre-teen I read James Blish's novelizations of the classic episodes. Over the years I have accumulated and read the nearly one hundred and fifty books, by a variety of authors, that contain new adventures of these space faring crews of familiar characters with their imaginative plots, far off worlds and alien species. No, I have never quite been a card carrying fanatic, a "Trekkie" — rushing off to conventions, redecorating my room or home with "Trek" memorabilia, or naming my children Kirk, Scottie, or Bones. However, I am admittedly more than just a casual fan. A few examples:

On occasion, I have been known, even from the rabbinic pulpit, to use a reference from the Star Trek Universe — terms like "warp speed" or "holodeck" — or to allude to a particular episode or plotline;

I did, in fact, show up to a synagogue Purim party one year dressed in a Stafleet uniform shirt with rubber pointed alien ears; and

Several years ago, at Universal Studios in Florida, I made a short video film using technology that allowed me to participate in a Star Trek adventure with the actual cast members, including William Shatner and Mr. Nimoy. (To this day, my wife enjoys playing it for friends and family and watching my face turn as red as the uniform shirt.)

Thus, it is a real thrill to be sitting in an auditorium eight feet from Mr. Nimoy (great seats, third row center), listening to him lecture about his life, career, and experiences. But it gets even better. The lecture topic is "Spock in the Diaspora" (it is, after all, being sponsored by Hillel, the largest Jewish organization on America's college campuses). As advertised, Mr. Nimoy speaks about his experiences growing up with Jewish immigrant parents in Boston [he speaks Yiddish fluently (he even acted in the Yiddish theater)], various film projects that allowed him to tap into his Jewishness, and finally, how his religion influenced his most famous character.

At one point in the lecture he describes his influence on a particular episode involving Spock's return to his homeland, the Planet of Vulcan. This was the first time on the show that we, the audience, would view Vulcan civilization and observe Spock interact with others of his species. Recognizing that until this show the only Vulcan depicted was Spock, a uniformed Starfleet officer, the writers and producers virtually had a clean slate on which to create

Vulcan costume, ritual, and social interaction.

One of the key moments in the show was to be an exchange between Spock and the Vulcan matriarchal leader. As they rehearsed the scene, Nimoy felt that something was missing; a simple bow, nod, or salute would not sufficiently convey the uniqueness of Vulcan, in contrast with human, behavior in this situation. He strained his mind and memory for the right gesture; something simple, yet ritualistic.

As he describes this dilemma, Mr. Nimoy reaches into the podium and takes out a black velvet bag. He unzips the bag and removes a folded blanket-like piece of fabric. As he continues to speak, he unfolds the fabric, which turns out to be a large wool *talit* (prayer shawl) complete with decorative black stripes and the requisite fringes. This is not, mind you, one of those silky little blue and white "drape it over your shoulder" *talitot* (plural of talit). The *talit* in Spock's bag is the real deal.

Mr. Nimoy drapes the *talit* over his shoulders and stops his narrative for a moment to describe what it is. He explains, quite accurately, that the important or symbolic part of the garment is the knotted strings or fringes (*"Tzitzit"*) and not the fabric (in fact, he references his current studies with a rabbi to learn more of its significance). After a cute joke involving a *talit* and a dry cleaner, he proceeds to lift the top of the *talit* over his head. He pulls it out approximately half an arms-length in front of his face and places his two hands together while dividing the digits of each hand between the middle and ring fingers. He then loudly chants *"Yivorechecha Hashem V'yishmerecha,"* ("May God Bless you and Watch you") the Hebrew words of the priestly benediction.

It seems that as a child, Mr. Nimoy's parents attended an Orthodox synagogue. He recalled that on the holidays, the *kohanim* (priests, descended from Aharon the Priest) would bless the congregation with the biblical priestly benediction. During the ceremony they covered themselves with their *talitot* and positioned their hands in the manner described above. He explains that tradition has it that we are not supposed to look at their hands during this ritual since the *"Shechinah,"* an aspect of the presence of God, is flowing through them to deliver the blessing.

Little Leonard was instructed by his father not to look. But being a curious child, he nevertheless did. He was so impressed with the hand gesture, that he actually practiced it, to the point of becoming proficient in forming the "V" with either hand. When his role as Spock required a significantly appropriate gesture, he simply raised his hand, as he had seen the *kohanim* do so many years earlier. Since then, it has been an important part of Spock's character and of Star Trek lore.

What a thrill, I actually watched Mr. Spock *"duchen"* (perform the ritual of the priestly blessings). My holiday services will never quite be the same! But even such a memorable display did not prepare me for the one line spoken by Nimoy/Spock that profoundly explains this week's Torah portion of *Mishpatim*. That's right, his one line does not merely explain one incident or one law, but virtually the entire portion.

Last week, in *Yitro,* the Torah described the events at Sinai. God presented the Jewish People with His treasure amidst a spectacle of sights and sounds. Prior to Sinai, these people had witnessed an impressive array of miracles and plagues — so you can imagine just how awesome the revelation had to be to waylay a "been there/done that" attitude. (If you think that I am exaggerating about how small an impression some of these events seem to have made on the people, realize that they began complaining about the lack of water just three days after crossing the Red Sea and that they worshiped the "Golden Calf" a mere 39 days after they heard the Ten Commandments.)

After describing the experience at Sinai, one would therefore think that God would want to declare those laws that outwardly appear special, unique, symbolic, or even mystical. God's intricate plan of redemption and revelation involved so many elements that capture the imagination. The story of the Exodus is wondrous even in today's world of enhanced special effects. Thus, one would have expected that the first laws presented would have been designed to emphasize the fervor and passion of Judaism — to build on the intensity of "and they believed in God, and Moshe, His servant" (*Shemot* 14:31).

Instead, we have *Mishpatim* — literally, laws. In this portion we find laws about slaves (which you would not think a nation of recently freed slaves would be particularly eager to hear about), laws of torts (e.g., goring oxen, personal injury, fire damage, safety hazards, public nuisance), court procedures, and criminal law issues. This is supposed to be a new religion, not the Code of Hammurabi. One could liken this to filling a theater with a group of patrons eagerly awaiting the re-release of the digitally enhanced, souped up, special edition of "Star Wars" (with its 4-1/2 minutes of new footage) and screening for them reruns of "The People's Court," instead. Why were these laws presented first? Why the mundane rather than the metaphysical?

In the question and answer session following Mr. Nimoy's talk, someone asked him what he found so interesting about Star Trek. The series was full of imagination. It provided a glimpse of a possible future, explored new worlds and people, and functioned as a forum to metaphorically examine issues that effected 20th century man (such as the Cold War and civil rights). There were also the neat gimmicks; starships, transporters, tricorders, and computers (in 1966, the PC was just about to be invented!). Mr. Nimoy's response to the question, thus, was unexpected and quite enlightening.

He said that it was not, so much, the wonder of the show that intrigued him, as it was the ethic.

To elaborate: yes the show was dressed in special effects and makeup. But at its core the stories were about people — good, moral, caring, loyal, and brave people. Gene Roddenberry, the creator of Star Trek, was adamant about portraying the future of humanity as a rosy one. The crew members of the Enterprise were not prejudiced, they did not take advantage of technologically inferior races, they avoided war, they battled disease, etc. Collectively they were not religious, but they upheld an ethic. They represented an ideal humanity.

What if... three thousand years ago a powerful starship, piloted by a technologically advanced race, discovered the earth. After its occupants observed a while, let's say they found the oppression of the Jewish People at the hands of the Egyptians to be morally repugnant and decided to intervene. If we can assume, for argument's sake, that most of the ten plagues can even be imitated today with our more limited technology — putting a chemical in the Nile to turn it red, rapidly cloning a horde of frogs, seeding the land with lice larvae, making the animals go mad using a virus or perhaps high frequency sound waves, etc. Then these advanced aliens more than likely could have pulled off the Exodus (heck, they could have split the Red Sea with a laser and a tractor beam!).

Having interfered with the lives of these former slaves, it would not have been fair for the aliens merely to turn them loose to fend for themselves. The only responsible thing would be to give them guidance on self-governance and national survival. Thus, the aliens, not willing to reveal themselves personally, could have hooked up a computer interface to the top of a mountain like Sinai and programmed/created/bestowed a rulebook on the people. Presto!

Do not fit me for a strait-jacket. I do not, by the wildest stretch of any imagination, even one as warped as mine, question the Divine origin of the Torah or the veracity of the events recorded within it. Yet fifty, or perhaps one hundred and fifty years ago (I want to steer clear of the imagination of Jules Verne) nobody could have even postulated such a preposterous scenario. Today, it can not only be articulated, but it can probably be filmed with live actors in a very convincing manner (if you disagree, check out the movie "Stargate"). Fifty or so years from now, it is possible that the actual miracles of the Torah will seem like child's play in comparison to what technology will be capable of accomplishing.

The wonder God generated had a purpose. It captured the Jews' attention. But it was not the wonder that would keep their attention — it was the ethic.

We conclude the *Shema* prayer by proclaiming that *"Hashem, your God, is truth."* Just as God is truth, so too is His law. Through the spectacle, the Jews discovered and learned that God was truth. He delivered on every promise. Once this was established, God immediately presented them with His law — the nuts and bolts of functioning as a society and living according to His ideals. The law was ethical, the law was true, the law was from God.

These facts and the laws themselves became imprinted on the Jewish psyche, not the special effects. If the foundation of Judaism was the supernatural, how would the religion have survived these past few thousands of years without recorded prophetic revelation or overt miracles?

We have been able to "live long and prosper" as a people precisely because of the *Mishpatim*.

TERUMAH
Built to Last

Like snowflakes, no two people are alike. However, also like snowflakes, most lives follow a pattern of formation and development, leading to self-actualization, and finally terminating in descent and assimilation. In plain English, we are born and raised, we fulfill a destiny, and then we perish and return to the earth. With few exceptions, this is the normal flow of a human life.

Some of us share other details and particulars of life; a mold or pattern that is repeated, with little variation, in what is still the mainstream fabric of our American society. We are born and raised by two loving parents. We go to school to receive an education that will give us the tools to survive and, hopefully, to succeed in life. We marry, start a family, and try to provide our children with a supportive atmosphere and appropriate developmental experiences. We try to contribute to society in a meaningful way and then we pass away.

But people are not snowflakes, and lives can not be diagrammed with the precision of a simple flowchart. Extraordinary events, both joyous and tragic, disrupt the orderly journey. In the daily paper we read of lottery winners, high tech entrepreneurs, and miracle cures. On those pages we also encounter random terrorist acts, evil and sick murderers, and unexpected disasters of an almost infinite variety. Yet even that which is random, unexpected, or unknown is part of a pattern and a plan. It is all part of God's plan for each person and for the entire universe.

In past weeks we have seen this illustrated with clarity. In the narratives involving Yoseph and Moshe we saw how seemingly random events, some as minor as the birth of a baby or an inter-family squabble, others as major as famines and plagues, formed the pattern of the descent to Egypt and the redemption from it. As we have followed the text of the Torah, from creation through the giving of the Ten Commandments and the other laws at Sinai, we have studied a linear progression — A leading to B leading to C — actions and reactions, decisions and consequences, generations and succeeding generation. (Another great example of this is the "Book of Esther.")

Although until now some incidents may have been reported out of their correct chronological order (i.e., there is a debate among our sages whether Yitro advised Moshe before or after *"Matan Torah"*), no portion or section has been noticeably out of order. That is, until this week's portion of *Terumah*. What does the building of the *Mishkan* ("Tabernacle") and the fashioning of its vessels have to do with the experience of *"Matan Torah"* detailed in the portion of Yitro and embellished at the end of *Mishpatim?* The building campaign for the *Mishkan* did not get underway until after God forgave the Jewish People for the sin of the Golden Calf — which will be described two weeks from now in the portion of *Ki Tisa.* Moreover, since the entire book of *Vayikra,* book three of the five, is devoted to the duties and responsibilities of the *kohanim* — it perhaps would have been editorially more sound to juxtapose the construction of the objects with the description of their use and function.

Perhaps the Torah is not always bound by decipherable, comprehensible order because we, who use it as a guide, can not expect our lives to run their courses with connect-the-dots predictability. If we ever forget this, there are plenty of reminders around, reminders much closer to home than the daily newspaper.

As an "old married couple", it has been quite a long time since my wife and I have veered anywhere near the dating scene. Most of our friends have been married as long as we have (give or take five years) and, thank God, our children have a ways to go before it is their time. When we do get together with friends for an evening out, all of the couples collectively have the mutual casual comfort of a well broken-in pair of slippers — the husbands know what type of quip will provoke a good natured glare from their wives, the wives know the punchlines and details of whatever story their husbands are recounting, and any given spouse can generally finish a sentence for the other. These are evenings of friendly social interaction. They have not had the pacing and energy of a date for a long time.

So in a way it was refreshing to actually go out on a "double date" one evening this week with a dear friend and a woman who hopefully will become one, if it is God's will and their relationship continues to flourish. (In describing this "event," I once again am treading dangerously in that area called privacy. Therefore, the names and personal details of our friends are, by necessity, being fictionalized.)

While refreshing, the evening should be more accurately characterized as bitter-sweet. Our friends Dan and Ora, are two people who started with flowchart lives, but for whom God has since prepared a new design.

Dan was married to a special woman and together they began a family that outdid the "Brady Bunch." Everything was just right: the kids, thank God, were healthy and bright, their home was warm and loving, and their lives were suffused with Torah learning and values. Then one day, with no warning, tragedy struck and the family lost its "Woman of Valor."

Ora's experience was not dissimilar, the only real difference being that the number of children who were left without a father was fewer.

I have truly understated the magnitude of these tragedies and the seeming senselessness of these losses. Similarly, I will not describe the incredible strength and fortitude of these two people. I merely marvel at their ability to hold together, avoid the paralysis of depression, and get on with their lives. Our evening, however, was not about the pain of the past. It was an evening of cautious discovery, of reawakening emotion, and of the hint of spring after a harsh winter.

We met at a small New York-area kosher restaurant. After a slightly forced, somewhat awkward introduction, we sat to eat, talk, and get acquainted. Now realize, Dan and his wife were relatives, best friends, and classmates of ours — we have know them practically forever and shared many memorable and pivotal moments in our lives, both good and bad, together. Thus, while we wanted, and certainly want, more than anything, for Dan to find someone to complete himself and to resume a more typical life, we could not help but hold Ora to an incredibly high standard. One can only imagine then the close examination that Dan and Ora were giving to each other.

I expected that the conversation would be stimulating, mainly because of the challenge presented and the finesse required. We wanted to acquaint without prying or interrogating. We also wanted to steer clear of potential landmines, like past times spent together with Dan or the challenges of a large family (combined, they would reach double digits which puts our mere six into a different perspective). Yet, we did not want to be casual and shallow.

I would like to think that we were all so sharp and quick witted that all these objectives were met. The truth is, after a few minutes, we all just acted and spoke as ourselves — no calculations, no weighing of words — and a pleasant time was had by all. I must admit, the ease with which Ora entered our world told us the most about her — followed, as a close second, by some of the non-verbal signals we observed — the way Dan and Ora glanced at each other, the way each could cause the other to smile, and the way they paid attention to each other as if no one else mattered. (Watching these two novices reminded me of a cartoon I once saw. Man #1: "I've been married so long I think I have exhausted all the ways to express my love. I've said it in words, letters, cards, flowers, gifts — you name it! What else can I do to express my love for her?" Man #2: "Start expressing it all over again." — A useful thought!)

As the evening ended, we drove away feeling hopeful for both Dan and Ora. Had they found the right person to fill the voids in their lives? Only time will tell. But, possibly for the first time since their losses, they both now know that there are good people out there — people who can make them happy, people with whom they can rebuild lives, and people with whom they can build homes.

Interestingly, this same portion of *Terumah* that shows us that life is not necessarily lived in a straight line also shows us what it takes to build a lasting home — a home that can withstand change and tragedy. The Torah uncharacteristically, spends a lot of words discussing the *Mishkan* and its vessels. Now understand, we have a complete description of this in the portions of *Terumah* and *Tetzaveh* and then a detailed repetition in the portions of *Vayakhel* and *Pekudei*. Certainly the *Mishkan* was holy and important. But it was also quite temporary, lasting only until King Solomon built the *Beit Hamikdash,* the Temple in Jerusalem. Even the *Beit Hamikdash* itself and its successor functioned for only a small fraction of our history, fewer than 850 years. Why all this emphasis and repetition? What is the relevance?

According to some commentators, the description of the

Mishkan, especially with its placement before the terrible incident with the Golden Calf, allowed God to safeguard the Jewish People from our own folly. The logic goes like this: there will be moments in history where the Jewish People will defy God to such an extent that they, under the strictures of Divine justice, would merit destruction. By commanding us to build the *Mishkan/Beit Hamikdash,* God set up the mechanism whereby He could destroy stone and wood, albeit precious stone and wood, rather than flesh and blood.

This is a powerful explanation. However, I would rather focus on the enduring symbolism of the *Mishkan,* than on its past utility or function. Additionally, we should examine its meaning and relevance to all Jews, no matter when in history they live.

At the commencement of the project God states "and make for Me a sanctuary **so that I might dwell among (in) you**." (*Shemot 25:9*) The *Mishkan* thus represents not only a Divine home, but the home that we, **within ourselves**, must establish. This home, in all of its incarnations, besides walls, doors, foundations, and supports, contained five major components or vessels: 1) The *Aron* (holy ark, as in Indiana Jones); 2) the *Menorah* (as in Chanukah); 3) the *Shulchan* (table, supporting the showbread); 4) the inner *Mizbeach Hazahav* (gold altar used for incense, except during the Yom Kippur service); and 5) the outer *Mizbeach Nechoshet* (brass altar used for individual and communal animal sacrifices).

• The *Aron* was the repository of the Tablets, the symbol of Torah. Every Jewish home must be centered around and founded on the teachings and values of the Torah.

• The *Menorah* provides light, energy, and warmth. It is also the symbol of human knowledge and creativity. Every Jewish home must have its energy source, both intellectually and physically.

• The *Shulchan* represents the food and nourishment that is essential for life.

• The outer *Mizbeach Nechoshet* represents the sweat, flesh, and blood of toil and commitment. The members of every household must be committed to each other, and be willing to sacrifice for one another.

• Finally, the inner *Mizbeach Hazahav,* one used primarily to offer smoke and scent, represents the intangible, the emotional and spiritual bonds among and between those that create a home — wife, husband, and God.

These ingredients are necessary for the continued survival of our people as a whole, and are equally necessary for the effective functioning of each family unit. Dan and Ora have each already built the foundations for such homes. Having spent time with them this week I know, even if they themselves have doubts and questions, that they have all the necessary tools and blueprints, the blueprints of the *Mishkan,* to build such a holy structure once more. This one will surely be built to last.

TETZAVEH
Clothes Make the Man

Over the weekend, while trying to catch up on some professional and current-events reading, I ran across an article, a humorous piece, in which the writer was trying to predict likely future appointees to the United States Supreme Court based on birth order. Apparently, a scholar from MIT, Frank J. Sulloway, wrote a book, titled *Born to Rebel: Birth Order, Family Dynamics, and Creative Lives,* that analyzed a variety of history makers and public figures in order to derive a correlation between birth order and certain personality traits, drives, and motivations.

In his book, Mr. Sulloway explains that firstborns excel academically and exhibit leadership; they are tough minded, dominant, aggressive, responsible and punitive. Middle-borns tend to be more flexible and to favor compromise, easily seeing arguments from both sides. Finally, last-borns are easygoing, cooperative, popular, flexible, daring, and rebellious.

As the father of six, with a birth order of boy, girl, boy, girl, boy, girl, I have the opportunity on an almost daily basis to view this interplay between birth order and personality development — with an interesting overlay of the differences and interactions between males and females. Effectively we have one set of oldest, one set of middles, and one set of youngest. Neither my wife nor I are experimental behavioralists in the B.F. Skinner mold, but it is sometimes interesting to take a step back and to observe the dynamics of their growth.

Each of our children are being raised with the same parents, in essentially the same home. They attend the same schools, have essentially the same diets and are provided the same recreational and social outlets (age appropriate, of course). My wife and I are careful never to display particular favoritism and we strive to constantly develop their self-esteem. No, we are not perfect parents with perfect children. When necessary we rant, scream, yell, and use other traditional parental discipline techniques (the Iron Maiden the Rack, and the Cat of Nine Tails to name a few), but I believe we employ them as evenly, fairly, and consistently as we can.

So why is the personality of each child so distinct? Why is one more studious; one more playful; one more imaginative; one more artistic; etc.? I can not, and would not try, to answer such questions. I truly do not compare my children. I just thank God for blessing us with these developing individuals.

However, this does not mean that I am blind to their differences. Every so often an event takes place that highlights, and allows us to appreciate, their individuality.

My oldest son, Josh, has all of the aggressiveness and drive of a first born. However, he seems to channel most of it into athletics. Due to his combination of interest and ability, we have enrolled him in a number of activities over the years: indoor soccer at ages five and six, outdoor soccer, basketball, little league, and swimming. He enjoys sports and he has excelled at every level.

Between attending games, carpooling, and assistant coaching, I have spent a lot of time watching children participate in sports activities, as well as observing professional, educated, proper parents like me, display quite a wide range of childlike reactions (classic "Little League Parent Syndrome"). The kids who participate tend to fall into three categories: the children with talent and ability (and unfortunately, huge egos and bad attitude), a.k.a., the jocks; the children who enjoy playing, who try hard, but are destined to be mediocre to average, a.k.a., the rank and file; and the children who sit on the sideline deciphering the patterns in the clouds or digging into the dirt with their cleats looking for dinosaur bones, a.k.a., the daydreamers. Josh is a "jock." Avi, on the other hand, who is four years younger, loves his action figures and his imagination. Thus he has shown the propensity to be more a "daydreamer." Josh loves to play sports. Avi just loves to play.

We were therefore surprised, when Avi declared a few weeks ago that he wanted to play in the roller hockey league at our local Jewish Community Center ("JCC"). Roller hockey requires a broad range of athletic skills. One must 1) rollerblade with some proficiency and stamina; 2) have the requisite hand-eye coordination to maneuver the plastic ball with a hockey stick toward the opposing goal; 3) understand the fundamental concepts of offense, defense, passing, and scoring; and 4) be aggressive. Had Avi asked to play t-ball, basketball, or indoor soccer, I might not have hesitated. However when he asked to play roller hockey, I felt that I needed to be sure that he knew what he was getting into.

To my surprise, he was not only focused on the sport, he had, by borrowing equipment from Josh and one of my nephews, assembled most of the necessary equipment — skates, elbow pads, knee pads, and a helmet. In the face of such determination and resolve, the decision was set; we would let him play. However, knowing Avi, I was still somewhat skeptical that he would play and display enthusiasm when the puck dropped.

The player evaluation and tryouts were held this past Sunday afternoon. These are not tryouts in the traditional "some make the cut, some do not" sense. Every child is assured a roster spot on a team and playing time. This session gave the coaches (other fathers) the opportunity to rate the children so that they could form teams that maintain a certain competitive balance.

I dropped Avi and his friend Steven off at the entrance to the JCC and went to park. I instructed them to go to the locker room and to put on their equipment. I neglected to mention one thing about Avi. He is a cute little kid, emphasis on both the cute and the little. He is among the shorter boys in his class and he is of slight build. My anxiety about this activity heightened as I watched other boys enter the building who were a head and half a torso taller and broader than Avi.

By the time I parked and stopped to talk to a friend in the hall on the way to the gym, Avi had suited up. The skates added some inches of height. The pads on his elbows and knees projected an illusion of added bulk. The helmet with its protective cage added fierceness. The menacing stick with its curved scythe-like blade threatened violence. My cute little boy was a roller hockey player — a gym warrior; at least in his own mind — if that menacing/joyous smile planted on his face while he circled the playing surface was any indication of what he was thinking.

Avi's transformation last Sunday helps us to understand what is going on in this week's portion of *Tetzaveh*. Last week, God described the *Mishkan* and its vessels. The narrative involved a place and objects — a home and furnishings. *Tetzaveh* contains a description of the garments that the *kohanim* would be required to wear while they performed their holy service at the *Mishkan*. God introduces these garments by commanding Moshe "And you shall make holy garments for **Aharon your brother**, for honor and glory." (*Shemot* 28:2).

Why the emphasis on Aharon, as brother of Moshe, rather than on Aharon as *Kohen Gadol* (High Priest)? Additionally, what is the relationship between the eight garments of the *Kohen Gadol* and "honor and glory?" Is the office of *Kohen Gadol* and its function not sufficiently honorific?

Tetzaveh, with God's instructions about the priestly wardrobe, will certainly have relevance throughout the *Mishkan* and Temple eras. Moreover, it will be meaningful in the future when the Temple will be restored. However, upon closer reflection it would seem that God's command to Moshe also took into account the dynamic of the then present moment.

First, Aharon was Moshe's brother. It was inevitable that ungrateful scoffers (like Korach and his crowd) would seek to impinge Aharon's righteousness and fitness for office with claims of nepotism. Aharon thus could not merely function as *Kohen Gadol,* he needed impressive props.

Second, and I believe much more important, Aharon needed the uniform for his own self confidence and peace of mind. As I wrote last week, the Torah portions of *Terumah* and *Tetzaveh* are presented out of chronological order. God related the instructions for the *Mishkan* after the sin of the Golden Calf, which is narrated next week in *Ki Tisa*. Aharon played a pivotal role in that debacle. He actually fashioned the idol. Yes, it was done under the threat of death. Yes, he was trying to stall until Moshe's return. Yes, he was not held culpable for his actions. But, one would think that, on some level, Aharon could not avoid blaming himself for what happened. Aharon, a righteous, spiritual, peace loving man was likely plagued by "would've, could've, should'ves."

God understood how important Aharon's character was to our fledgling nation. He also understood that Aharon supplemented and complemented Moshe's political and moral leadership and teaching. With one gesture, with a set of garments worn intimately on Aharon's body, God was able to restore Aharon's self-confidence and to signal his esteem to the Children of Israel.

Aharon was a spiritual giant and thus we can not often ascribe to him our own more pedestrian reactions and emotions.

Nevertheless, I do not believe it would be sacrilegious to picture him the first time that he suited up in his special garments with a smile on his face — a smile of vindication and redemption, a smile of confidence, a smile of thanksgiving, and a smile of joy.

Avi will never be a *Kohen Gadol* (I am not a *Kohen*) and it is even less likely that he will be the next Wayne Gretzky. Yet, the smile he wears when he puts on his gear and the newfound spirit that pumps him up both speak volumes about the almost magical transformation in his state of mind. In this parent's book, "honor and glory" equate with self confidence and a positive "can do" attitude.

KI TISA
"Fourscore"

A few years ago I read Michael Shaara's book, *The Killer Angels*, about the pivotal and monumental Civil War battle at Gettysburg. I was captivated by the personalities and motivations of the officers, by the mindless heroism of the rank and file soldiers, and by the magnitude and senselessness of the carnage. (By the way, *Gods and Generals* by Jeff Shaara, Michael's son, is an equally powerful Civil War novel.) Within about two months of reading the book, legal business brought me to Harrisburg, Pennsylvania. When I recognized its proximity to Gettysburg, I made sure to set aside time one afternoon to visit the battlefield.

The battlefield itself is part cemetery (with carved monuments erected in tribute to different individuals and units involved in the battle), part museum (with some preserved artifacts and structures), and largely a big empty field surrounded by various hills and some vegetation. If one is not versed in the history of the war and does not know the details of the battle, there is little about the location that would attract and captivate attention. The "real life" scene simply does not match what is pictured in the mind's eye.

On the grounds of the park is a visitor's center. It is there that one can find the images that we of the fully-wired web have come to expect. In our world, little is left to the imagination. There is nothing that happens that we can not get pictures and video footage of almost instantly. When the Civil War was fought there were no movies or videos or audio recordings, and there were few still photographs. Yet at the visitor's center the story and the images of the battle are captured in a large mural that circles a specially designed viewing area that is termed "Cyclorama."

The landscape of the battlefield, the strategic positioning of the fighting forces, the important characters, the fierce fighting, and the tragic injuries and fatalities surround you and draw you in. You stand observing an important moment in the history of our country in a manner both detached and intimate. The work is a tribute to the artist and to his ability to capture the drama of an event that unfolded over the course of hours and days, in one panoramic work.

The Cyclorama works well as a means of capturing the fury of Gettysburg. The landmarks are distinctive, the events self contained, and the scope dramatic. It would be interesting to see such talent applied to capture other events. For example, to the dominant event in this week's portion of *Ki Tisa* — the sin of the Golden Calf.

In one section, the artist could depict Moshe on Mt. Sinai. He could perhaps focus on Moshe as he is descending with the tablets in his hands. Note the look in Moshe's eyes as he becomes aware of the golden calf. Imagine the muscles in his arms tense the split second before he hurls the tablets in protest. Picture the resignation in Yehoshua's gaze as he looks up at Moshe.

Another section would center on Aharon. The artist could capture the desperation and terror he feels as he watches the evil, riotous crowd murder his nephew Chur and coerce him into fashioning the calf. The brushstrokes would freeze the moment that he stands before the calf and proclaims, with equal parts of defiance, anger, fear, despair, and remorse, "this is your God, O Israel, that lifted you out of Egypt."

Curve around the circle and view the malevolence of the protagonists as they clamor for an idol. Over there a man is forcibly taking his wife's rings and bracelets for the project. Over here is a basket full of glittering gold jewelry — piles and piles of stolen gold, a pot of molten gold, gold littering the scene as it is so recklessly abdicated and forfeited.

In one final area, a duplicate, illusory Sinai with a vision of a deceased Moshe. A trick from the master trickster. A picture worth not a mere thousand words, but almost worth the six hundred thousand words of Torah — as a people almost believed and almost gave it all up. Satan tries to convince the Jewish People that they are leaderless. They almost buy into the lie.

Yes, this particular dramatic moment could generate quite a powerful cyclorama.

Other moments, however, do not lend themselves to such pat representation — despite no shortage of dramatic images. It would take more than a single cyclorama, or a hundred, or even a thousand to do justice to an event like the Holocaust. Each victim had and deserves their own moment. Each survivor has their own story.

The Holocaust occurred in a more recent, more contemporary era. We do not need to rely on an artist's rendition, or still photographs, or words from old diaries and journals to witness its horrors. We have film and we have records and we have museums and monuments and we still have some of the eye witnesses — those who were victimized but were able to survive through God's kindness.

This past Friday night, we were invited for *Shabbat* dinner with our friends the Kahns, Benny, Fran and their children. My kids always enjoy visiting the Kahns because of the attention they receive from Benny's mother, Mrs. Kahn. In fact, my little ones do not call her Mrs. Kahn. They instead refer to her as "The Bubbie" — as in "can we go visit The Bubbie?" or "can I sit on The Bubbie's lap?" She is outgoing, warm, soft and round in a pillow-like way and she always wears a big smile. The kids are drawn to her and constantly run over to hug her, kiss her, and ask for candy.

Toward the end of the meal, after the younger children left the table to play, we learned a lot more about Mrs. Kahn. She is a survivor. She hid in a cellar with some of her brothers and sisters the day the Nazis came to round up the Jews of her village. The Nazis took away several of her siblings and their children and they were never seen again. Mrs. Kahn was able to hide in the woods with partisans and avoid to the concentration and work camps.

I could, and probably should, fill in all the sordid details. I should describe how the Nazis swiftly and callously disrupted the lives of this family. But my cultured words would only be a poor substitute for her accented ones. I could not capture the tears that she still sheds. I can not convey the raw emotions that punctuate her version of events. Mrs. Kahn's voice reaches back over fifty years and drags the horrific reality she faced and survived into our comfortable present.

After we returned home and settled the children into bed, I reviewed the portion of *Ki Tisa* several times since I was scheduled to be the *Baal Koreh* (Torah reader) in synagogue the next morning. In my mind, as the words of this portion rolled by, I contrasted the Holocaust survivors, who were lucky to escape all manner of physical abuse and torture with the shirts on their back, with the survivors to the Egyptian bondage, who left similar physical oppression laden with gold and treasure.

As I finished my review, and with Mrs. Kahn's story still echoing in my ears, I was too wound up to go up to bed. I reached down into the magazine rack near my favorite chair looking for something current to leaf through. I pulled out this week's issue of *Time* magazine and almost jumped through the ceiling for on its cover I saw a photograph of the Golden Calf. No, not the one Aharon made, we know that Moshe destroyed it. Nevertheless, it

129

was quite clearly the legacy of that idol. On the cover was a well-recognized symbol, a single large Nazi swastika, pressed out of pure gold.

As related in the accompanying story, during the war the Nazis took everything of value from their victims. They took furnishings, bank holdings, businesses, and personal possessions. They even stooped so low as to wrench gold teeth and silver fillings from their mouths. Pictures in the magazine show piles and piles of gold rings, as well as other jewelry and valuables collected from the Jews.

The thievery and greed of the Nazis was nearly as well known as their brutality. What had been conveniently overlooked or, perhaps, covered up, was the complicity of the Swiss and other nations in providing refuge for these collected valuables. But if their actions in serving as bankers for the Nazis, for allowing them to fund their war effort and to allow the corrupt Nazi leaders to personally profit were not bad enough — these silent partners hid behind the skirt of their own bank secrecy laws to deprive the victims and the families of victims from withdrawing assets that they personally and legally deposited for safekeeping. Thus these victims and their families could not even reclaim what was rightfully theirs and they were prevented from rebuilding their lives more easily.

Now, nearly fifty years later, there is a glimmer of hope that some portion of these billions in gold and currency will be returned to Jewish hands.

I could not help but return to the contrast between the survivors of the Egyptian bondage and the survivors of the European Holocaust. One group got the gold, one lost it. Is there a relationship? Might there be a reason why now, over fifty years after the end of the Holocaust, there is a good possibility that some of the confiscated possessions will be returned to Jewish hands?

Returning to our Torah portion may provide some insight. When Moshe reacts forcefully after the initial shock of the sin, he is forced into an emotional about-face. He must control his own anger and disappointment in order to serve as an effective advocate for continued Jewish survival. God threatens to destroy the entire Jewish nation and to rebuild through Moshe alone because of the magnitude of their crime. Moshe argues forcefully and eloquently, ultimately winning a reprieve for them. This is not, however, a full pardon. God gets in the last word, proclaiming, "and on the day that I make my account, I shall bring their sin into account against them" (*Shemot* 32:34).

The Jews sinned because they were unable to handle their wealth responsibly. God revived their broken spirits and battered bodies with miraculous redemption. When God showered these former slaves with riches, they had no appreciation of the gift. Later, when He asked them for a portion as atonement for the sinful calf, they gave it freely and generously.

The surviving Jews of Europe also emerged broken and battered. They were likewise revived by the miracle that is Israel. But their gold, the gold pictured in heaps and piles as part of the Nazi hoard, remained, quite literally, on account. God kept it on His account, either as interest for that long ago incident or as collateral against a future line of credit. So why is it now being returned?

In the last decade we have witnessed many miraculous events. Scuds fell on Israel with no direct loss of life. The Jews imprisoned in the former Soviet Union were allowed to leave.

Something is most definitely going on. Something cosmic, something miraculous. Are these the footsteps of the redemption? Is the return of the Nazi gold to Jewish hands a sign that we have paid enough for the sin of the Golden Calf? I, of course, await the answer, today — and everyday. *Ani Maamin* (I believe...). However these days my hope and my belief are a lot more focused.

VAYAKHEL-PEKUDEI
Inspiration

The weekly portions of *Vayakhel* and *Pekudei,* which are often read together, are not quite clones of the portions *Terumah* and *Tetzaveh,* they are really more like nearly identical twins. Both sets of portions describe the *Mishkan* and its vessels and the priestly garments. There are few differences between the versions, even on the level of *trop* (cantillation).

Rather than returning to concepts that we explored so recently, I decided to use these weeks to experiment and to deviate from this twisting, yet set, path I embarked on with this book.

In detailing the construction of the *Mishkan,* the Torah also offers us a glimpse into the creative process of the artists and craftsmen. The project coordinator was a thirteen-year-old boy named Betzalel. His chief assistant was Ahaleav. The rest of the team consisted of talented and dedicated men and women. However, their talents and efforts were not sufficient for the task. They needed something extra, something Divine. God acknowledged this when He proclaims "and I will fill him with the spirit of

God, with wisdom and knowledge, and all manner of technical know-how" (*Shemot* 35:31). Their art had to be inspired.

We can understand why this could be necessary for the fashioning of holy objects — such objects represent a merger between the physical and the spiritual. But what about original art — ideas, thoughts, and images that move from the mind or perhaps the soul of the artist onto paper, canvas, cloth, or stone. Can there sometimes be a direct or manifest link between Divine inspiration and human talent? By way of experiment, in order to stretch the limits of possibility, I decided to write an original piece of fiction, to put pen to paper and see what happened. With some trepidation, I hereby present the following original story:

Renaissance

Emerging from the violet lightness, the young man took his place on the large, white platform set on the otherwise barren surface. His appearance, though youthful, exuded untapped reservoirs of courage, confidence and maturity. He was a fine looking young man with penetrating eyes, straight black hair, and a strong body. He stood erect, head slightly bent, and stared into the light.

As the light began to redden, a transformation began. He felt his skin tingle — first on his face, then over his entire body. As if on fire, his hair began to singe and curl. His skin reddened and slowly turned charcoal. Muscles tightened, limbs continued to burn and then the process ended leaving a black lump resembling the lad lying on the white surface.

"Why Dadiv; why today — the day of his initiation?" exclaimed Domana, the saintly looking mother of the now departed lad. There was no reply, there never was.

Esoms broke the silence. As leader and as one of the oldest members of the Colony, his words were always sapient. "We are all here to serve. In His infinite wisdom, the Supreme Intelligence has created us to fulfill His will. We must continue in our drive to perfect ourselves physically and mentally as He has commanded. If we do so, when we depart upward, through the heavenly gates onto the surface, we will be deemed beautiful by our creator and then, if we are worthy, we will be called upon for the ultimate service."

The lump remained motionless as an orange light now began to shine in lieu of the red. A crack, no a straight line, appeared on the surface of the white platform next to the body. A section of the platform moved slightly revealing glistening metal tentacles. The tentacles emerged and wrapped themselves around the body. They lifted the body, they moved it several yards and finally lowered it. They released their grip, retracted, slithered back into the ground and, as the platform moved back to its original position, were gone as if they were never there.

Yellow light descended. From the sides of the platform came swirling brushes. They swept over the form removing much of the char. As they disappeared from view, a transformation in the body was noticeable; it was no longer charcoal black, but light gray — almost off-white.

The people had heard Esoms's words often, words of blind faith. But his words still carried the same impact. After all, what other plausible explanation is there for "life" and "life after departure."

A few of the younger members of the colony contemplated various alternate possibilities; but while Esoms lived, they were afraid to let their ideas surface for hadn't he conversed, face to face, with the Supreme One; hadn't those two bonelike projections been placed on his head as a sign to the people that man's ultimate destiny had yet to be achieved? Besides, who wanted a rebellion?

Green was predominant as a fine white mist was sprayed on the body, quickly hardening to reveal a marble-like surface.

Blue then triggered new movement. A hole appeared, as if from nowhere, in the middle of the platform in an area near the feet of what was once the body. Moments later the hole was not only filled from within, but something began to surface. As movement slowed to a halt, a marble block became a new companion for the lifeless body, a friend with whom to share the emptiness. The body was no longer alone.

Domana had been calmed. She now realized that her son had been called up for better things and bore her loss with grace. Her only concern was how to serve her sovereign; perfecting herself for Him to help fill the void in her life created by her son's departure. Esoms aided her in this endeavor.

Because of Dadiv's departure and the subsequent cancellation of his initiation feast, the people were in a somber and dejected mood. A new tenseness was prevalent in the Colony. One would think that they were waiting for a new sign to reinforce their beliefs and to break the monotony they called everyday life.

As the people rallied together, Chorka, a young philosopher who envied Esom's position as leader of the Colony, jumped to the forefront and began to lead the crowd in a defiant chant. He questioned the origin of the projections on Esoms' head, he questioned Esoms' authority and he then began to question the very beliefs that provided the foundation of Colony life since its inception. Chorka had been bold in the past, but this time he was downright audacious. Caught up in his own emotional rampage he blurted out, "If this supreme intelligence exists — let Him show us a sign!"

As an indigo lightness set in, the dimness of the scene was offset by a blinding light. After a flash of laser light, the marble block was affixed at the base of the now marble-like body of what was once Dadiv. The indigo stage continued as small brushes and chisels polished, smoothed, and pronounced the details of the new statue.

Esoms and Domana emerged from Esoms' dwelling and moved to head off the crowd. Realizing the danger of the situation, Esoms raised his hands in a gesture intended to silence the crowd; surprisingly they were rendered silent. "One may not deliver ultimatums to the Supreme Artisan," began Esoms. "He is temperamental and He is assiduous, but if He is approached in the right manner, as I will try tonight, He may show us a sign of His unlimited power. Return twenty-four hours hence and we shall see who is right."

Esoms and Domana spent the night in quiet meditation and solemn prayer in Esoms' dwelling. Chorka, on the other hand, enjoyed a premature victory celebration amidst a small number, two hundred and fifty or so, jubilant and uplifted colonists. (The preparation of the conflicting parties for the rapidly approaching show-down reflected how each thought it would end.) Would a change occur and if so, would the people really be able to accept it?

The moment of truth arrived. Esoms, with Domana by his side, stood at one side of the Platform of Service — Chorka stood on the other. Moments passed — tension mounted.

"So there, old man," sneered Chorka, "admit defeat."

As the last word left his mouth, the platform began to tremble. An instant later Esoms and Domana were gone from view as if they were swallowed by the platform. Chorka and the rest of the Colony stood in silent awe.

The violet lightness once again emerged. A solitary tentacle appeared and chiseled the word "David" on the base of the statue. As the tentacle retracted, marking the end of the process, two new forms took their places on the platform....

Michaelangelo was not a Jewish artist. However, he had a genius for representing and capturing images and people that form the center of our existence, our Torah. Be it his rendition of the moment of man's creation or the *Akedah* (binding of Yitzchak) in his Sistine Chapel work, or the sculptures of Moshe and David, one can not deny the power of his art. This story is a tribute to some of his most famous statues, David, Moses, and the Madonna, within the framework of the clash and showdown between Moshe and Korach. I thought that this was somehow appropriate since we can understand Korach, who is seemingly motivated by ego, as a man who is seeking expression outside of the new structure and order transmitted through Moshe. The *Midrash* fills in details of the discussions between Moshe and Korach that show that Korach, while being a rabble rouser, still had a flair for creatively challenging the status quo. The message here being that it is the motive behind the challenge (whether or not it is truly *l'shem shamayim* [for the sake of heaven]) that distinguishes creativity from heresy.

I would not assert that God directly inspired Michaelangelo, any more than I would say God planted this story in my mind. But Michaelangelo worked with and used the Bible, at least as he read it, to provide his mind and talent with the raw materials necessary to produce his art. He and I have at least this much in common as artists, as I likewise used elements of a famous biblical incident as a canvas for my imagination. In a sense, this is also the message of the book of *Shemot*.

The book is called *Shemot,* Names. It could have been called *Geulah* (redemption), or *Nisim* (miracles), or "The Birth of a Nation." However the focus is on names — Moshe, Aharon, Pharaoh, Miriam, Yehoshua, Yitro, Yocheved, Nachshon, Betzalel, (we do not really encounter Korach and his rebellious cronies until *Bamidbar,* Numbers), and the six hundred thousand others who were actors — who wrote the story by living it. Without them, the Torah would still have been God's Torah, but it would not have been the Torah of the Jewish people — our Torah. As we say the traditional *"Chazak Chazak V'Nischazek"* (May we go from strength to strength) marking the completion of this second of the five books, may we continue to **live** a greater understanding of the Torah and ourselves.

VAYIKRA
Silence is Golden

In this "Age of Information," controlling the flow of knowledge or perfecting ways to deliver it has become as valuable a skill as dealing with any other precious commodity. Television news teams trumpet the fact that they were able to break a story thirty seconds or a minute before any other station. Tabloids and so-called news magazines spend hundreds of thousands of dollars on exclusive photographs of private celebrity nuptials. Writers and reporters will go to almost any length — using hidden cameras and microphones, paying informers, and even staging events — in order to uncover "a scoop" (something everyone else does not know or has not heard yet). The fact that most of us could not care less, is of no consequence. If a network or newspaper can market an item sensationally, people will feel a need to know.

People are, after all, curious by nature. There is some inner compulsion (otherwise known as a lack of self-control) that forces us to collect and to share secrets. I liken it to the behavior of my youngest son, B.Z., when he manages to extort a dollar from an unwitting relative. He, of course, has no concept of the value of the currency or of the cost of items in the store. He knows, however, that he can use money to purchase candy or soda. Starting with the split second the bill touches his flesh, he begins a nearly relentless assault to convince us to drop whatever it is we are doing and to drive him to our local kosher supermarket so he can buy something with his dollar. Typically, he is unsure of what he wants. However, he is compelled to spend the money and he will make our lives miserable until he can. He is consumed and driven by an inner need to expel the dollar from his care and possession.

Most of us are like that with secrets. If we think one of our family, friends, or co-workers is privy to some choice morsel, some fascinating tidbit — especially one involving another family member, friend, or co-worker — we are willing to whine, cajole, beg, plead, or barter in order to partake of the information. Of course, such measures are usually not necessary because the person safeguarding the confidence is as willing to tell as we are to hear. They are as eager to expel the secret from their lips as B.Z. is to expel the dollar from his pocket, and it moves just as quickly. What greater invitation to broadcast is there than the words "I'll tell you if you promise not to tell anyone else," or some derivative thereof?

The issue becomes significantly more acute when someone reveals to you information of a personal nature "in confidence" and you delude yourself into believing that the information can be used for personal advantage or benefit (I am certainly not referring to illegal insider trading, a la Dennis Levine and Ivan Boesky, on whose cases I worked in my former prosecutorial life). This was precisely the dilemma I faced this week as I wrestled with friendship, ethics, common sense, greed, and self-interest.

The company I work for, like all companies, has its own politics. Some people are in the good graces, others are in the doghouse. Some executives are constantly looking to expand their power and influence, others are in decline, struggling just to hold on to what they have, or think they have. While I am in a fairly well defined professional role with few managerial responsibilities, some of my duties overlap with those of a colleague. I have greater responsibility for certain litigation and administrative matters, Phil is more involved with current transactions and tax planning. He has also been my closest work friend since I started here.

About a week ago, Phil was contacted by a legal recruiter about a position with another Detroit-area company. The job would entail considerably more responsibility than his present position, but the increase in salary and benefits would be commensurate with extra burden. For whatever reason, Phil decided to confide in me about the opportunity and to help him reason through the pros and cons of the new company and his situation. He came to me because I am a friend whose judgement he values and because I faced a similar set of choices when I decided to accept my current position a little over a year ago. We assessed the situation and reached a cautious "keep all the options open" conclusion.

Early this week Phil went for a second interview. This time he met with senior executives of the company, as opposed to his prior meeting with the recruiter and an H.R.-type. He liked what he saw and heard, but was still unsure about his own willingness to make the commitment necessary to the new job, especially when the cost would be to sacrifice much of the precious time he spends with his family. He, therefore, must more seriously weigh his various options, namely: 1) to accept the new job, if offered; or 2) to reject it and maintain the status quo; or 3) to use an offer, if received, to leverage for increased compensation and/or responsibilities at our company.

I am only human. Thus I can not help but to view his good dilemma from the selfish perspective of how does this affect me? If he leaves — will they hire someone new, who will aggressively compete with me rather than complement my position; will I have the leverage to request greater responsibility; or will I bear the

brunt of the ire of management scorned by an ungrateful and treasonous employee who dared to leave? If he stays — will my role
diminish; will good projects be steered his way as part of his deal;
or will I be groomed to assume more responsibility as a hedge
against Phil's next power play?

Inevitably, my thoughts veer toward the one small weapon or
advantage that I have in all of this — information. I know what Phil
is considering, management does not. Can I, should I, breach this
confidence to further my career through subtle manipulation? I am
certainly tempted to pursue my own terms and to deal with the situation proactively rather than as a passive bystander.

Aside from reading the Torah portion of *Vayikra* this week, we
also read the *Megillat Esther,* the Book or Scroll of Esther as a part
of our celebration of the Purim holiday. Not surprising to me was
the fact that my dilemma with Phil was in some ways similar to the
dilemma that Esther faced as she served as queen to Achashverosh,
the king of Persia and "one hundred twenty seven provinces from
India to Ethiopia." She was the favored wife of a powerful king.
She knew that the wicked Haman had drafted a decree and enact-
ed it as legislation with the king's official seal to destroy the scattered and spread *Yehudim* (Jewish People). She was a Jew and may
have felt, deep down, that she could intervene. Only no one else
in the government knew it and she was instructed by Mordechai
(her husband/uncle) not to tell. She had a secret, a powerful secret,
a potentially useful secret — and was forced to wrestle with its consequences on a daily basis.

The Book of Esther is an elaborately crafted work. Every main
character has a doppleganger or mirror image — Haman and
Mordechai, Esther and Vashti, the earthly Achashverosh and our
heavenly King. Likewise, every event has a countering denouement
— Vashti is killed and Esther becomes queen; Haman prepares a
gallows to hang Mordechai and is hanged on it instead; the Jews
are to be exterminated by their enemies, yet 75,000 Jew haters fall

on the very day designated for massacre, etc. But what I find most fascinating is the correlation between the signature behaviors of Esther and Mordechai and the actions of the Jewish People that served as the catalyst for the crisis and near national tragedy. The actions of Esther and Mordechai served to repair two significant breaches of religious etiquette by the Jews.

Our sages discussed what precipitated the events of Purim. (In fact, the Talmud in the tractate of *Megillah* 12a relates a discussion between Rabbi Shimon bar Yochai and his disciples on this very question.) One view identifies the sin as occurring when the Jews bowed down to an idol in the days of Nebuchadnezzar (of the entire nation, only the three prophets, Chananyah, Mishael, and Azariah refused to bow). The other view criticizes their participation in Achashverosh's royal feast — a feast which prominently displayed vessels purloined from the Temple.

The first sin, bowing to the idol, was a very public and symbolic act of desecrating God's name. There was no subtlety or ambiguity involved. Those that bowed symbolically cried "Uncle," thereby abdicating faith in God's supremacy, and acknowledging some other higher authority. However, the Jews of Shushan who rubbed elbows with the political elite ("hobnobbed with the goobersmoochers") sinned in a backhanded, indirect way. The *Midrash* relates that the strictest of Jewish dietary laws were observed in the palace during the feast — kosher meat under the Chief Rabbi's supervision, dairy products from "Jewish Cows," kosher wine with Jewish wine handlers. To all outward appearances the people came merely to pay respects to a king who, in turn, respected their religious traditions. But the king knew, and they likewise knew, what was not outwardly apparent. The king was celebrating what he perceived to be the extinction of the "God of Israel." The Jewish prophets had foretold that the Temple would be rebuilt and that the exile would end 70 years after Nebuchadnezzar destroyed Jerusalem. By Achashverosh's calculations the time had come —

and gone. The lavish party celebrated the perceived inaccuracy of the predictions. Thus, when the Jews themselves came, ostensibly to curry favor with the powers that be, they wittingly or unwittingly were denigrating God and their belief in His promises of their redemption.

The actions of Mordechai and Esther, respectively, represented a *Tikkun* (repair) of these transgressions. Mordechai expressed his beliefs in a very public and confrontational way. When Haman commanded all citizens to bow to him (and to the idol he wore around his neck), Mordechai could have chosen a more cautious path — he simply could have avoided contact with Haman. The words of the *Megillah* lead us to believe that had he done so, Haman might not have been provoked as quickly into setting his trap in motion. Mordechai knew, however, that the root cause for the continued exile was the public, albeit coerced, display of fealty to an idol. The *tikkun* could only come through a similar notorious display — only this time a display of loyalty and of the willingness to sacrifice for God.

Esther's actions were passive (not that leaving her home and family to live in the harem of a Persian king is what one would typically term passive). She had to win a beauty contest, avoid conflict, and keep her true identity secret. The first two were relatively easy, the third, as noted above, must have been excruciatingly difficult — remaining silent while her people were threatened with extermination. Yet, her silence, her feigned indifference, was necessary for the *tikkun,* to remedy the indifference of the Jews to Achashverosh's true celebration. In the end, when the timing was right, Esther was allowed to use her secret to help her people achieve salvation.

Thus, the two national faults were corrected with different personal approaches.

The drama playing out with Phil and his career decision is his private affair. Could it affect me — yes, but it is not my place to inject Machiavellian manipulations. While we are schooled not to rely on miracles, we also must believe that our successes and failures are attributable to God's will. I do not believe that God would will me to betray a confidence and to jeopardize a friend's standing in order for me to advance. Silence, combined with concentrated effort on my responsibilities and performance will give me the clearest and cleanest path to success.

TZAV
Dodging a Bullet

When I sat down at my computer to start this project, I was almost giddy with the possibilities. If my life this year would be anything like last year's or the one before that, etc., I could be assured of a nice mixture of family occasions, professional experiences, noteworthy current events, and a few surprises that would carry me through the year and our Torah. In fact, with great assistance from God, no doubt, I have gone nearly twenty-five weeks without revisiting a topic or straining to figure out what to write about. Moreover, I have been given the chance to explore a wide range of emotions, write different types of pieces, and even venture into fiction.

One thing I have not attempted is to write multi-part entries, or a serial — continuing a theme or event from one week to the next. This is, after all, understandable. My basic "M.O." is to sit down during the week of a particular Torah portion and "to go with the flow" by relating what I am observing or experiencing to that particular portion. I am not a prophet (as my NCAA basketball pool picks will attest) and thus lack the ability to put paper to pen with the prescience necessary to arrange a continuing saga. This week may be the exception, although I continue to pray to the depths of my soul that I am wrong. These are times that begin with fading breaths and which may give soon way to sobbing ones.

Back during the week of the portion of *Bo,* my friends and loved ones faced plagues of suffering. At that time, I briefly and superficially described the ordeal that my mother-in-law was enduring (also discussed in *Beshalach*). In the ensuing weeks we have prayed for her, visited with her, encouraged her, and hoped with her. The family has ridden the roller coaster of her illness and its complications.

I deliberately choose not to write directly about Mom this week because I know that far too soon I will be called upon to reflect on her life and accomplishments and inadequately express what she has meant to us, her children and grandchildren. However, as emotional as we will all be and as hectic and crazy the hours before the service may be — I simply can not and will not think about what form those remarks will take. We have belief. We have faith.

Do I think a cure for cancer will be discovered in the next few hours? Do I think that God will miraculously intervene and cure all of Mom's ailments? Do I believe that *Mashiach* will come today, thus changing all the rules and reversing the ebbing flow of life force?

If my answer to question number three (the *Mashiach* one, for those of you with MTV attention spans) is YES — it can only be YES, as belief that *Mashiach* can come any day is a fundamental belief of our faith — then while there is still life, I must hope for either door number one or door number two, as well. And I must beseech God to provide the best solution.

As an aside, faith and prayer are quite wonderful in times like these. Let me illustrate: While this is all going on, Kim (my wife) is in New Jersey by Mom's bedside — where she has been since before last weekend — and I am home with all six children. Playing Mr. Mom is tough even when Kim is able to anticipate the finite duration of her trips and can plan accordingly by leaving us well stocked with prepared food, clean clothes, and detailed carpool instructions. The sudden downturn that Mom took this weekend, however, caught us all by surprise.

By Saturday night, Mom was very uncomfortable and an infection was seriously impairing her breathing. Early Sunday afternoon, Kim called to tell us to start packing — Mom had floated out of consciousness and the doctors were not having success in restoring her to wakefulness. When I updated my two older children, Josh and Peshie about their Bubbie's condition and solicited their assistance to organize, they first started crying. They then went about the task at hand — packing for the drive to New Jersey. About an hour later we were ready to go.

Kim was supposed to call back to give us an update, to help decide whether we should leave or wait. During the 45 or so minutes while we awaited that call, Josh and Peshie sat with *Tehillim* (Psalms) reciting prayers for their Bubbie. I did not ask or even hint for them to do this. They just knew that such action was appropriate. While the kids were not aware of it, those prayers served two important functions; the prayers helped their Bubbie in ways we can not know and the prayers quite tangibly helped my children cope with a painful situation that we, unfortunately, can not shelter them from. Kim called and told us that, thank God; the immediate crisis had passed. The trip would later be made, but not this day.

With the strain and emotions (the proverbial roller coaster), I feel entitled to ramble a little this week. I know, however, where I want to end up. It will just take me a bit longer to get there. I find writing this to be my way of coping. It is similar, in some ways, to the prayers of Josh and Peshie. These words are an island of escape where I can lose myself in expressive thought. Thus, I want to go off on another tangent and capture another moment involving the phone and my children.

After Sunday's "excitement," we jumped every time the phone would ring. The reports from the hospital were muted; full of appreciation for the time left but seeped in inevitability and resignation. Mom has not been "up to" speaking on the phone since Thursday night, so neither the kids nor I have had the chance to hear her voice and to touch her with ours. We sat helplessly wondering if we would ever again get to speak with her.

Late Monday evening, Kim called from Mom's hospital room just to touch base. All of the other children were in bed, except for Josh, with whom I was studying (o.k., we were watching the end of the Piston's game, on a school night, no less!) As our conversation wound down, Kim asked to speak to Josh. Mom must have heard Kim speaking to Josh and asked for the phone. (Believe me I did not feel slighted or insulted. Josh, after all, is Mom's oldest grandson and the first one to bear the name of Kim's father, who passed away a few months after we were married. Mom, of course, loves all of her children and grandchildren deeply, but Josh has a particularly special place in her affection).

I like to think that Josh is a typical modern American child. He receives a good well-rounded education, is aware of current events, and is capable of causing his share of trouble. But the reality is, his home, school, and the community we are a part of, each shelter him. He, like his friends, have few truly hard edges. They are blissfully innocent about much that is ugly in our world. Josh's innocence was on full display when Kim turned the phone over to Mom.

Despite the pain I knew he was feeling, Josh's face immediately lit up in a smile — one so bright one would think it projected over the miles. The smile gave way to a slightly puzzled look on his face as you could see him trying to decide how to make conversation. He was hurting, but he knew he could not let his Bubbie sense his pain. He wanted to cheer her up, but did not know quite how. He was caught in an awkward situation — one even the most glib and cultured conversationalist would find daunting — and his mind was working to find the right approach.

After the prerequisite "Hello Bubbie," he asked, quite straightforwardly, "How are you feeling?" You should realize that, Mom is on morphine for pain management, is aware of the decline of her condition, and is literally not taking each day at a time, but each hour, as she reaches the limits of her mortality. Yet, she hears this sweet young voice so caringly and sincerely ask "How are you feeling?"

Her brain and body may have wanted to cry out — "I feel worse and more scared than I could have ever imagined!" Yet, she replied with an "I am doing fine" that was much more than perfunctory. For those few moments, despite her pain and her circumstance, while she spoke on the phone with her grandson she was fine.

When Josh completed his "conversation" with Mom, I got back on the phone with Kim. We had a decision to make — should I pack up with the children and head to New Jersey immediately, or should we wait? On the one hand, while Mom's condition had improved somewhat, according to the doctors her end, and thus our inevitable trip, nevertheless, loomed near. On the other hand, it would really not be so bad for everyone to spend some time with her while she is still alert and still very much herself in spirit and awareness. All signs indicated, in blinking neon letters, pack up and go. But we did not leave Monday night or Tuesday, we waited an extra day until Wednesday morning.

I am feeling a bit guilty about the delay. It was based on my decision, made for my own reasons, linked to some extent, to my convenience. Before I describe the circumstances for this day, one must delve into this week's portion of *Tzav,* which, while certainly not justifying my actions, lets me know I am not the only one nor the first one who chose such a poor course of action.

Tzav is very similar to last week's portion of *Vayikra* (which is why I wrote about Purim instead). These portions both primarily deal with the *korbanot* — sacrifices. I do not know who came up with this translation for that word. In my mind sacrificing involves giving up, doing without, or choosing one course at the expense of another. The Hebrew word *korban* from the root "K-R-V" denotes closeness; *karov* means near, *kerovim* are relatives (close family members). *L'hakriv* is to bring near. *Korbanot* are thus not sacrifices but instruments for bringing us closer to God.

If things were going particularly well and a person wanted to show appreciation to God, he could bring a *shelamim* (peace) offering. If a person survived a life-threatening ordeal, was released from prison, or completed a difficult journey, he could bring a *todah* (thanksgiving) offering. When a family made its pilgrimage to Jerusalem on the festivals and wanted to leave a calling card, they brought an *olat r'eiah* (burnt offering of visitation). God, who has no corporeal existence, has no need for the animals offered. However, by enacting this structure of *korbanot,* He gave us an outlet to reach out and to tangibly draw ourselves closer to Him.

Saying "thank you," is rather benign — the person offering thanks typically does not feel estranged from God. Quite the contrary, he or she feels Providential protection. Where *korbanot* get really interesting is when they involve the sinner. Sinners, through offending action, have pushed their selves and their souls away from God. Their holy essences have been tainted. They have disregarded the command of their King — and likely want to run and hide farther away in order to avoid culpability. The *korban* helps to bridge this gap and to realign and balance the Jew and his or her core ideals.

Just as sins come in many different flavors, so do the *korbanot.* They are designed to cleanse the stain and bring the sinner closer to God. If one commits certain sins in an intentional manner for which there is no prescribed punishment, then an *olah* (burnt offering) must be brought. According to many of the classic commentators, this offering also relates to sinful ideas and thoughts. (In a sense there is a nice symmetry here — a sin of thought is atoned for by an offering that is totally consumed — that leaves no physical remnant.) Other sins may require an *asham* (guilt offering) or a *chatat* (sin offering).

Each of these offerings, like most topics in our religion, has rules and subrules, and many layers of meaning. However, I would like to focus on just one aspect of the *chatat* offering. Again, if we move away from translation to the real meaning of the word, *chatat* really does not mean sin, it means error — as in sinning carelessly, inadvertently, thoughtlessly, but not rebelliously or intentionally.

God is telling that there are things in life, like His Commandments, that we can not treat cavalierly. If they really mattered, if we paid proper attention, if we really cared, if we were not distracted, if we did not have other conflicting priorities — then we would not violate or transgress. The *chatat* offering was a reminder for each Jew to maintain proper attention and not to delude his or her self.

Returning to my week of *Tzav,* I owe my wife and mother-in-law a *chatat* of sorts. As word came through the phone on Sunday that we did not have to leave right then and there, and as Monday's report contained no significant change, the wheels in my mind began to turn. You see, on Tuesday afternoon I was scheduled to represent my company in court on a multi-million dollar matter. Over the past year and a half I have reviewed documents, written briefs, interviewed witnesses, and plotted a strategy that, hopefully, was to bear fruit at the scheduled hearing. If, God forbid, the worst had occurred, I doubtless would have been able to obtain a postponement, with the consent of my adversary, the Assistant Attorney General. But this situation was simply too up in the air. I found myself hoping that Mom would hold on, not so much to spare her or the family pain — but so that my employer or I would not be inconvenienced.

Sure, there were plenty of rationalizations — this was less disruptive on the kids and their school work, I had a job to do, Kim was with her mother doing the most good for them both — but the reality is that I should have been there if the situation was as bad as it seemed. Did I, would I, callously, intentionally, vindictively hurt, disrespect, insult, or disregard my wife or mother-in-law? Most certainly not! But circumstances — not being prepared to deal with the kids alone for an extended period, the pressure of the court date, dealing with many intense emotions on both sides of the phone — caused me to take my eye off the ball.

As low as I personally feel about this, at least the week had a somewhat better ending. On Wednesday morning I loaded the car and drove to New Jersey without regard to office matters, vacation policies, or other commitments. When we arrived, all of the kids were able to visit their grandmother — who had rebounded from the crises (which means — *boruch Hashem* [bless God] this will NOT be a two-parter after all) to interact with them lucidly.

However, I got mine — during the drive, as the miles rolled by, I felt increasingly warm and achey and my throat felt like it was on fire. The family doctor in New Jersey diagnosed my affliction as strep throat — which would prohibit me from visiting Mom for another two days (when the antibiotics would kick in). Poetic justice in a sense — I was somewhat glad for the two day delay when the trip was not convenient, now I am forced to wait through a two-day delay when visiting is eminently convenient — with the hospital a mere three minutes away. We should never lose sight of our priorities and we must be thankful that God points the way to reorder them, if we are astute enough to pay attention.

SHEMINI
Batter Up

When baseball was still the "Great American Pastime," this was a very special week; the beginning of a new season. Today football has a better television contract, basketball generates considerably higher merchandise sales, and college championship games have reached near religious significance. Yet, this week still retains some of its magic.

October may be filled with Jewish holidays, but a portion of our attention always seems focused on the last days of a pennant race, or the playoffs, or the World Series. The pathways of my life have deposited me in Chicago while the Cubs collapsed in 1969 and in New York as Mr. October himself (Reggie! Reggie!), won championships with my Yankees in 1977 and 1978. I can still appreciate the balance of offense and pitching displayed by the 1986 Mets and I was present in Cleveland when those perennial doormats, the Indians, finally became a power in the mid 1990's.

The march to that glorious month of October, however, begins in early April — on Opening Day. There was always a certain buildup, leading to the start of the season. First the newspapers covered the Winter Baseball Meetings, where teams met and actually made trades — sometimes blockbuster deals — in order to shake up their rosters and position themselves for a pennant run. Then in February, perhaps a week or two before spring training, the Streets and Smith magazine came out previewing the upcoming season and providing statistics, predictions, and great pictures we could cut out and paste on the walls in our room. In mid-March, we could catch a few exhibition games on our transistor radios as we sat opening our first packs of baseball cards for the new season.

Baseball cards were so different then. First of all, there was really only one major brand, Topps. Second, the cards were not issued all at once, they were issued in various series over the course of the season; each one with its own special cards and a checklist. Third, we did not view them as investments to be put protectively away. They were our own small parts of the game — to throw, toss, flip, and trade. If we disliked a certain opposing player, we might draw a mustache and devil horns on his card. We memorized the fun facts and statistics and we imitated the picture poses.

About a week before the season, the local newspaper began to preview the other teams and players. By this time the weather was finally nice enough out for us to put down the footballs and hockey sticks and to assault the neighborhood with mitts, balls, and bats. As the teams prepared for the season, we began to re-tune our skills.

Finally it was here, Opening Day. The local paper would usually print a special section with the complete team schedule, pictures of the players, and predictions. Sometimes, it might even include a full-page team picture or a poster or two of our favorite star players. We would dig our team caps, jackets, and t-shirts out of the closet and advertise our allegiance — to the team or to a player — not to a swoosh or a stripe!

Opening Day was wonderful because it represented hope. For

one day our team, no matter how poor its prospects truly were, was in first place — albeit tied with every other team. Injured stars appeared to be rehabilitated. The flames of rookie phenoms were still burning, as the league's pitchers had not yet adjusted to their weaknesses. Typically, the best pitcher was on the mound, with the best player lineup in the field. And, of course, everything is a first: the first hit, run, home run, strikeout, double play, and hopefully, win.

This week's portion of *Shemini* is also about Opening Day. It was an opening day that marked both a healing and a fundamental change in the relationship between God and the Jewish People. For the past several weeks we have read about the construction of the *Mishkan* (Tabernacle) and its vessels, as well as some of the sacrificial offerings that would be brought there as part of its operation. As *Shemini* opens, Moshe had essentially conducted "spring-training" for the *Mishkan* for seven days. On each of the days he set it up and took it apart. Finally it is the eighth day, (*Shemini* in Hebrew means eight) the day when Aharon the High Priest and his sons, also new priests, are invited to participate in the ceremonial consecration of the *Mishkan.*

As would be expected, the day is full of pageantry, annointings, sacrifices, and likely lots of speeches. After all, this was a momentous event. This grand opening signified that God truly forgave the sin of the Golden Calf and, according to some commentaries, was actually willing to accommodate the peoples' need for a more tangible way to relate to and worship Him. The notion of worshiping an all-powerful, all-knowing, non-corporeal deity had to be somewhat overwhelming to this nation of recently freed slaves — especially a nation that was exposed to the panalopy of Egyptian idols, as well as to the majesty of the Pharaohs. While certainly not changing His nature, God nevertheless gave His people an opportunity to perceive Him on more intimate or human terms. He now, so to speak, had a house or palace they could visit.

Such intimacy, however, brought with it responsibility and danger, as the other events of that opening day illustrate so vividly.

Things were cruising right along: The *Mishkan* was open for business: Moshe stepped aside so Aharon could perform the duties of High Priest, Aharon and his sons donned their new uniforms (see, *Tetzaveh*); and the Levites sang the national anthem. It was a glorious, holy, and most happy day.

The Torah relates, however, that Aharon's two elder sons, Nadav and Avihu took it upon themselves to expand the ceremony, with disastrous consequences. Now, mind you, Nadav and Avihu were not ordinary people. Aside from being sons of Aharon, and thus two of only five people (aside from Moshe) that were qualified then to serve as priests, they were also respected teachers. According to the *Midrash,* they were the worthy successors to Moshe and Aharon as leaders of the Jewish People. In other words they were not mere enthusiastic, reckless, or spirited adolescents, they were thoughtful spiritual men — true leaders.

Moshe had carefully taught them the rules about bringing sacrifices. They nevertheless sought, out of a passionate desire to serve God, to add their own creative touch. Rather than bringing an offering and allowing a heavenly fire to consume it, they introduced an *aish zarah,* a strange fire. As a consequence, they were, in turn, sacrificed to God, as they were consumed by heavenly fire. (Note, the sages offer many explanations about their sin, if they in fact committed one. I choose to view the incident as it is related in the literal text). When Moshe and Aharon discover the tragedy, two interesting things happen. First, Moshe quotes God as characterizing the deaths as involving *"bikrovai ekadesh,"* ("through those close to me am I sanctified"). Second, Aharon maintains a stoic silence, *"vayidom Aharon,"* ("and Aharon was silent") (*Vayikra* 10:3).

From God's explanation, "through those close to me I am sanctified," it would seem that the deaths of Nadav and Avihu were a preordained component of the Opening Day activities. Why should such a tragedy be forever linked with a joyously historical day?

What message was God conveying with such harsh delivery?

I believe that there are two important lessons to be learned from the events of that "eighth day."

There is a popular comic strip entitled the "Wizard of Id," that is set in medieval times with characters that are stereotypical of that era — a king, a wizard, knights, peasants, etc. One of the main characters is the king — short in stature, big in ego, and short in temper. A running gag in the strip involves various subjects heckling the king, either verbally or in graffiti with the epitaph "the King is a fink!" When such a heckler is actually captured and brought before the king, he reacts with fury, sentencing the violator to prison or execution. Usually, however, the heckler is protected by anonymity.

God is everywhere. He sees and records everything we do. We are always in His presence. Nevertheless, there is a difference between saying "the King is a fink" in the privacy of your own home and proclaiming it in the palace with the king there. If the king becomes aware of a private treasonous statement, he may well punish the perpetrator — but he can delay his response until a more propitious time or he may even give the sinner an opportunity to make amends. But when the act is done in his face in his palace, the response must be immediate and decisive.

Opening Day is supposed to be a happy day. It is certainly not a good day for an execution. Under more ordinary circumstances, even if the action was deserving of it, such punishment could have been deferred to a later date. But when we are so close to God, a higher standard of sanctity applies. With the *Mishkan* in their midst, with God's house so close, the Children of Israel needed to learn this lesson. They had to be shown, in the most graphic of manners, that they would be subject to a higher standard, a standard that no one — even the sons of a High Priest — would be exempted from.

If the first lesson involved increased responsibility or stricter scrutiny (depending on the perspective), the second involved establishing realistic expectations. As noted above, Opening Day at the *Mishkan* was particularly meaningful because it showed that God had forgiven His people for the sin of the Golden Calf and was willing to make allowances for their humanness. This was certainly a fine example of Divine mercy. However, such benevolence could have de-motivated the people from striving for the spiritual heights embodied in the Torah. If God was willing to make allowances for their inadequate spiritual imagination, perhaps allowances could be made for other difficulties or deficiencies.

By sanctifying the *Mishkan* with the deaths of the precious and spiritual Nadav and Avihu, by injecting death on a day of completed atonement, sorrow on a day of joy, impurity in the place of ultimate purity, God was proclaiming "My house, My rules." Or, to put it differently, this *Mishkan* may seem to be a concession to your limitations, but it is not so. This *Mishkan,* like everything else in God's Torah and God's world, does not operate according to man's perceptions, logic, or emotion. It runs by God's. Thus, if the Jews possibly had any lowered expectations, they were quickly shocked back into reality. A meaningful Opening Day, with meaningful and tough lessons.

As I write this, the baseball season has shocked me back into reality, as well. The Tigers had a 5–0 lead going into the sixth inning, and they ended up losing 7–5! A meaningless Opening Day for another meaningless season.

TAZRIA
Dependency Exemptions

Another year, another set of tax returns that are due. Between my own state and Federal returns and the ones I must prepare for various family members, virtually all of my extra time this week will be consumed in the sea of income, deductions, credits, payments, and refunds. I am simply not going to have a lot of time to write, at least if I do not want to take any shortcuts in preparing all of these returns.

This week, for me, is usually somewhat surrealistic. I spend my professional work time immersed in the tax laws. From the time I arrive at my desk until quitting time, I read tax periodicals, review cases, prepare reports, analyze new tax regulations, and respond to inquiries from IRS and state tax auditors. Yet, I rarely prepare or review returns. I may advise what to file, when to file, and how to file — especially with respect to individual transactions. However, the tax compliance process is really not my forte. Thus, I approach preparing my own and my family's returns with as much anxiety, procrastination, and disorganization as most everyone else.

This year, the process is not proving to be quite as cumbersome, which has allowed me to jot down these words, now and then. Taking advantage of the power of my home computer system and utilizing the tax preparation software recommended by our department's resident computer whiz, putting the various returns and schedules together has been almost easy. The program helped me to organize by prompting me for the necessary information, it performed all necessary computations, it informed me which additional forms (which were also in the program) I needed to complete, and it printed everything out, including supporting worksheets for review and filing.

If all that were not enough, the program had some other interesting, and useful features. By pressing a button, I could request that the software audit the returns. This turned up some inconsistencies and typos that were easily corrected, as well as highlighting items that were out of line with statistical averages (for which I have legitimate explanation and proper substantiation). By clicking on another icon and authorizing a nominal payment, the entire return would be filed electronically, expediting the expected refunds. I dare say, the process could almost be termed "fun."

But paying taxes is not fun. Whatever refunds I may receive are only a small fraction of the taxes that I paid and what the government is going to keep. Additionally, there is something intimidating about having to lay out a complete record of your financial affairs for the year. Whatever income, from whatever source, is disclosed. Where you send your children for day care, who cleans your home, where you moved from and to, your charitable giving — all and more — is disclosed. In a sense, almost everything you do counts, in one way or another — and you are responsible, in our system of voluntary compliance, to count it and report it.

The beginning of the Torah portion of *Tazria* also involves counting of a quite intimate nature. After nine long months, when a woman finally gives birth to a child, one would think the only priority would be nursing and caring for the newborn and helping the mother regain her health and strength. Yet, the Torah imposes an unusual set of rules for counting the days until the very woman who "suffered" through it all, can regain her status of ritual purity. If a woman gives birth to a boy, she is unclean for seven days, on the eighth day (the day of the boy's *brit,* circumcision) she is clean. She then counts thirty-three days (a total of forty "unclean days") after which she is obligated to bring certain sacrifices. If she gives birth to a girl, the initial period of ritual uncleanness is fourteen days, after which she counts an additional sixty-six (for a total of eighty, or twice the amount of time for the birth of a male child) and then brings her sacrifices.

Why does the Torah impose this scheme of counting? What message is it conveying? Before we turn to the counting, I would like to address the difference between the birth of a male child and the birth of a female one. As we noted, the period of uncleanness following the birth of a girl is twice that which follows the birth of a boy. Is the Torah somehow signaling that there was something worse or less clean about the birth of a baby girl? Moreover, why does this uncleanness arise in the first place?

To understand this we must understand a little bit about spiritual cleanliness and uncleanness. As a general rule, the highest degree of uncleanness is associated with things that are not alive. A human corpse, for example, is the most "unclean" object in this entire scheme. Certain dead animals convey different types of uncleanness. In contrast, with the exception of human beings, living things themselves cannot become unclean. Similarly, things that grow are only susceptible to becoming unclean when they are detached from the ground. In a simplified sense, life is spiritually clean, the absence of life creates an unclean void.

When a woman is pregnant with a child, she is life plus life — super life. She essentially has two life forces — hers and the fetus'. When the baby is born, she experiences a diminution in that she recedes to the standard one life force. In a certain sense, there is thus a void in her where that second life force once resided. During the transition period, determined by the Torah to be forty or eighty days, this void is filled with the force that thrives in the absence of life — spiritual uncleanness.

This explains the different time periods, as well. A female, inherently, has the capacity to become super life. A male does not. The doubled period of uncleanness after a girl is born, reflects the fact that a larger void of lifelessness is left behind — not the void of a mere life but the void of a life plus the potential to bear additional life.

Let us turn back, however, to the counting. In our life experiences, we encounter two prevalent types of counting. Countdowns and adding up.

When we hear the term "countdown," the image that immediately comes to my mind is a rocket ship — Cape Canaveral, Mission Control, Gemini, Apollo, and Space Shuttles. For others the picture might be New Year's Eve as the famous ball drops at Times Square. School children post countdowns to the end of a school year and the start of summer vacation in their school lockers or in their notebooks. Engaged couples share the private countdown to their wedding day.

In Judaism we have a few countdowns, as well. The entire Jewish month of Elul, with its daily shofar blasts, functions as a countdown toward the Day of Judgement, Rosh Hashana. We count (albeit **up**, from one to forty-nine, rather than **down**) the days marking the time from the Exodus on Pesach to the giving of the Torah on Shavuot. On Chanukah, we count, and mark each of the eight days by lighting a corresponding number of candles.

Similarly, there are times when we account and add up (But remember Kenny Roger's admonition as the gambler, "You don't count your money sitting at the table, there'll be time enough for counting when the dealing is done!"). Tax time is one, in particular, that we are all familiar with. When a person passes away, leaving behind assets, a trustee or executor prepares an accounting before making distributions. Upon divorce, both now-former spouses must list their possessions so that they can be equitably divided.

We also have our Jewish accountings. On the High Holy Days our merits and transgressions for the year are weighed as we are judged for the upcoming year. In order to give the required tithes, a farmer had to determine the amount of crops raised and animals in his herd. Before Pesach, one must identify all of his possessions containing *chametz* (leavening) or identify where it is stored, in order to arrange a legal sale to avoid violating the prohibition against possessing it on the holiday.

The counting of a woman after childbirth is different from these other types. She has already endured her countdown — the truly joyous countdown — until her new child was born. These postpartum days are emotionally anticlimactic, if not downright depressing. This is certainly not a time to total up. It is a beginning, not an end. So why count?

I believe the counting allows the new mother to reinforce and properly focus all or her priorities: Yes, you have a new baby. Yes, there are new demands on your time. Yes, your world has changed. You would not be faulted for losing yourself in the mundane world of diapers, and catching some rest. Still, these are days filled with concerns about holiness, and purity. Or perhaps more metaphorically put, you are still accountable to your **other** partner (and we know God is the parents' partner in the newborn child).

In a sense this is similar to the lesson we learned from the deaths of Aharon's sons, Nadav and Avihu, in last week's portion *Shemini*. When they died on the joyous inauguration day, God sent the message that the world does not run on human expectations and emotions, but on the rules God has established as embodied in the Torah. Their deaths somehow did not signal distance, rejection and impurity, they represented acceptance, closeness, and consecrating holiness.

Tazria adds to this by letting us know is that this is not merely a lesson for extraordinary people (like the sons of Aharon) or for an extraordinary occasion (like the grand opening of the *Mishkan*). This lesson applies to each of us literally from birth. Our lives offer countless opportunities to pause and assess our priorities and direction. Periodically, we need to audit our lives, to amend, if necessary, and sometimes even to make estimated payments. If we are honest in our evaluations, we may avoid serious deficiencies, and be assured of receiving a refund, with interest, after 120 years.

METZORA
Sticks and Stones

It may actually be true that most of what we need to know about life was learned in kindergarten, but some of those lessons were not entirely correct. We must share, play nicely, and treat our teachers with respect. Certainly, a short nap at strategic times during a long day can be refreshing and beneficial. But I want to take issue with one of the venerated maxims of the early-elementary set — "Sticks and stones may break my bones but names will never hurt me." Names, labels, and stereotypes can hurt. Words can hurt.

In a management course that I took a few years back, the instructor showed us a short video; a documentary entitled "The Self-Fulfilling Prophecy." The film described an experiment done in an elementary school classroom. Before the beginning of a particular school year, all of the children were given a series of achievement and IQ tests. Based upon the test results, they were divided into equivalent groups — equal, or as close to equal as possible, in number, gender, intelligence, achievement level, and potential.

The school hired a new teacher to teach the two classes. The principal informed her that one group was comprised of the bright children who were high achievers and the other group was merely ordinary. She was, nevertheless, instructed to follow the same curriculum and to use the same textbooks and teaching materials with both groups.

At the end of the school year, the students took a new series of tests. The group that the teacher thought was brighter scored measurably better on all the tests than the group she considered merely ordinary. The teacher's perception, based on a mere label or name, obviously changed the way she related to each group. During the year, with the teacher's consent of course, a number of her lessons were video recorded. When the researchers analyzed and compared the lessons, they found that the teacher gave more positive reinforcement and encouragement to the brighter group, and displayed less patience for the ordinary one.

The researchers concluded, and my instructor preached, the important correlation between attitude and result — if you think you can do it, you are more likely to make it happen — "The Self-Fulfilling Prophecy." Yet, I saw a subtler, but equally important lesson; when you label or categorize a person or a group, you can effect how they perform and how others relate to them. In other words, names can truly hurt them.

This message was hammered home this week in an incident involving my oldest daughter Peshie (who has been waiting eagerly for her turn to be at the center of a chapter in this book). I could easily rattle off a few pages of how proud we are of her and her accomplishments (look Peshie, if you are going to read this I might as well give you some grief) — however, I will tell you just a few things that you need to know to fully appreciate the situation.

As I have mentioned at least a few times already, I do not rank, rate, or compare my children. This does not mean, however, that Kim and I are not aware of their strengths and weaknesses and the different aspects of their personalities. Peshie is probably the most inherently spiritual of our children. No, she is not a meditating flower child, but she practices our religion and its obligations with maturity beyond her years. When the kids have some free time, she is the one most likely to sit down with a religiously-themed book. In difficult times, like the ones we have faced with Mom's illness, she is the first one to pull out the Book of Psalms and to offer a hopeful prayer. She truly cares about performing our rituals and observances through true understanding rather than imitation. She also takes pride in our religious lifestyle.

Recently, her class completed a unit of Torah study and planned a party to celebrate. Rather than a small scale soda, chips, cookies, and candy celebration, they decided to organize a lunch. Each girl was responsible to bring something necessary for the event — either cutlery, soft drinks, or one of the menu items. Peshie was asked to bring in a tossed salad — apparently a coveted assignment.

Although all the girls in the class come from homes that keep kosher, individual families maintain different standards — from the strictest down to the merely passable. Accordingly, the school has a policy (a wise one at that!) which requires that all food brought in for such events be prepackaged (not homemade). Additionally, it must be certified by reliable kosher supervision. Since we, thus, could not just cut up some vegetables and send them in a bowl or bag, we traipsed off to our local kosher supermarket, One Stop Kosher, to purchase bags of kosher tossed salad.

The next day, Peshie bound off to school, salad bags in hand, to participate in the big party. When she came home, we expected to be regaled with a description of how well the party went and how big a hit the salad was. Instead, Peshie was somewhat quiet and reserved. We sensed something had happened, and gently probed and questioned her to get the full story.

It seems that while the girls were setting up lunch, two of Peshie's "friends" noticed the bags of salad and literally grabbed them from her hands to examine them more closely. These little 11-

year-old *"rebbetzins"* (small R), with their vast worldly experience, had never heard of this particular salad brand. Horror of all horrors, the bag did not have a qualifying symbol on it. They asked, inquisitionally, "Is this kosher? Where did you get it from?"

Peshie responded that the salad was purchased at One Stop Kosher and that every product sold there is certified kosher both by national and local Detroit kosher authorities. Putting aside the fact that these girls know Peshie and how careful she is, and have visited and eaten in our home numerous times — the explanation simply did not satisfy them. They wanted, no demanded, to take the bags to a higher authority, the principal, to make sure that they could be used. (Ironically, the principal's nephew is one of the owners of the kosher supermarket).

The principal viewed the bags, listened to Peshie's explanation, and immediately ruled that the salad was indeed kosher and could be eaten at the lunch. But by that time, the serious damage had been done. Because of mere words, and some actions and attitude, Peshie felt that a barrier had been erected between her and her friends. All of a sudden she was not religious enough, or trustworthy enough, or good enough. Their fervor was directed, of all kids, at Peshie who tries so hard and is so proud of her religiosity. They may not have literally called her names, but the effect was the same. Their words hit her where it hurt most.

I am not going to beat this to death — it was all quickly smoothed over with some phone calls, some apologies, and some lessons learned. Peshie is no worse for the wear. Nevertheless, Peshie and her friends certainly experienced the harsh reality of the power and consequences of what we say to and about people.

This message is at the core of this week's portion *Metzora*. If you simply review the text, it does not seem to make much sense, or have much relevance to us today. The entire portion deals with skin blemishes and discolorations, *tzoraat* (badly translated as leprosy). It describes how to determine if one has the condition; how to treat one with the condition; and how to remove the spiritual impurity. It also discussed what to do when your garment or the wall of your home gets the "disease."

The commentators are quick to explain that all is not what it seems in this portion. First of all, the Torah is not describing the medical condition where your skin rots off. The onset and advance of real leprosy is quite different from what *Metzora* describes. Secondly, *Metzora* describes a ritual process of diagnosis and cure which signifies an ailment more in the spiritual realm than the physical one. Finally, the Torah actually identifies the cause the one time it records a person being afflicted with the disease — when Miriam the Prophet, the sister of Aharon and Moshe, makes a private disparaging remark about Moshe, she is punished with *tzoraat*.

The sages thus explain and conclude that the *tzoraat* described in our portion is a spiritual ailment, with an identifying physical manifestation. At the root of this ailment is one particular type of sin — *lashon hara,* literally evil speech. Under the biblical scheme, when the Jewish Nation was on the high level befitting those with God manifest in their midst, if a person spoke ill of another, whether the words were true or not, God would afflict that person with *tzoraat.* As a result, that person would become ritually impure and was banished from the camp for a period of days or weeks.

Tzoraat provided nice symmetry, or poetic justice. When a person speaks publicly or privately against someone else, that person is displaying a total disregard for society and its individual members. Accordingly, that person must be isolated and removed from social interaction — must be made to feel like a pariah, and receive a dose of their own medicine, before they can return to a normal life.

Merely to banish them would not be enough. Such a person needs to be taught that words can hurt in a tangible way. Thus, the punishment must have a physical side; it must manifest on a corporeal plane, in order to have its full impact.

As Pesach approaches, I have begun to review the laws and literature of that special holiday. In fact, it's more than likely that whatever I write next week will involve this holiday in some way. For some reason, I was drawn to the earlier stages of the unfolding story — the first encounter between God and Moshe at the burning bush and Moshe's first encounter with Pharaoh.

When Moshe asks God for some signs to prove his "bona fides" to Pharaoh, he is told to place his hand inside his garment against his chest, and then to remove it. As he follows this direction, the hand that entered with a normal flesh tone comes out white with leprosy. This is a rather nice parlor trick — but did anyone believe that this could impress Pharaoh or convince him to let the Jews go free?

From what we learned in the Torah portion this week, we can better understand what God, through Moshe, was really trying to show and tell Pharaoh. Their first encounter was all about words. Moshe asked for a respite for the slaves in a very straightforward way — "Let my people go." When by Pharaoh asked to describe God, Moshe again responded with the short descriptive phrase — "I am what I am." We can picture Pharaoh laughing at these mere words — "You want me to do what?" "Who presumes to ask for something so outrageous?" "You speak and I am expected to simply roll over?" On one side Egypt and its mighty Pharaoh, on the other mere words.

When Moshe showed the sign with his hand he was conveying the message of *tzoraat*. Mere words can manifest physically. Mere words can transcend both the physical and spiritual dimensions. Mere words can change reality. Mere words are the beginning of your end. Pharaoh missed the message, or at least chose to ignore it — and we all know how things ended for him!

We do not get *tzoraat* anymore, but we all speak *lashon hara*. We may not get heavenly reminders of the damage we cause, but the damage is no less severe. Names can be much worse than sticks or stones. Can you remember the last time you threw a stick or stone at someone? How about the last time you spoke about someone in a less than complimentary manner? Think about it, since these cases are really not all that different.

ACHAREI MOT
A Different Kind of Seder

Is it harder to stay home for Pesach or to go away? If you stay, there is lots of cleaning and food shopping to do — there seems to be no end to the work needed in the house or the food items that we can not live without, for one week. If you travel, there is cost in time and travel expenses, packing — an especially large issue when the weather is in that unpredictable zone between winter and spring, and logistics — trying to plan in advance how to keep the family occupied, what religious books and other items are needed to enhance the holiday, and making sure everything in the office is under control or suitably covered.

In recent years, I have tipped the scale heavily toward staying home. In fact, Pesach has become the one time when we, the perennial out-of-towners (nearly all of Kim's and my siblings live in the New York/New Jersey metropolitan area) host rather than free-load. I enjoy being on my own turf, praying in my regular synagogue, sitting at the head of my *seder* table, and sleeping in my own bed (rather than a sofa bed or a trundle). This year, however, due to my mother-in-law's failing health, we agreed to travel to New Jersey.

We are all actually quite excited about the trip. We were able to arrange for Mom's release from the hospital so she could come to Kim's sister for the holiday (where she will have a hospital bed, round-the-clock nursing care, and visits from her physical therapist). Mom will be able to attend our *seders* and be able to cherish the participation of her grandchildren. The rest of us will hopefully create a special "Pesach with Bubbie" that the children will remember with a smiling fondness rather than melancholy nostalgia.

The past few *seders* have followed a similar, and unfortunately somewhat less than orderly, three-part pattern. At the beginning the children dominate — between five and ten repetitions of the "Four Questions," the *Mah Nishtana,* (each child wants their turn, and some do it in more than one language — serenading us with Yiddish, French, and Ladino versions), countless insights into the *Hagaddah* text read from sheets prepared by their teachers, and the inevitable show and tell gallery of assorted Pesach-themed arts and crafts projects.

With the steam released from the pressure cooker and the initial burst of enthusiasm spent, the kids settle down. I then take over for part two, leading the charge through the meat of the text. Admittedly, by this time I am usually a little uptight. I want to restore some decorum and to use the *seder* to fulfill my obligation to teach and discuss the story of the Exodus. My attempts to lecture and intellectualize do not mesh well with the kids' expectations. So one by one they drift away from the table to plot how to retake control of the proceedings. Which leads us into part three.

In order to explain this stage, I want you to recall the old "Our Gang" or "Little Rascals" comedies. You know, the ones with Spanky, Alphalpha, Froggie, Buckwheat, Darla, et. al. The most common plot device in that series was for the kids to organize and put on a show. For example, if Alphalpha wanted to raise money for a Valentine's Day present for Darla, they'd put on a show; or if the gang needed money to build a new soap box racer, they'd put on a show; or if they broke a neighbor's window with a baseball and had to pay for it — well, you get the idea.

In a matter of minutes, those sceen kids whipped together, and staged a show filled with musical numbers (centering around Alphalpha and high notes), props, and costumes. People flocked from all over the neighborhood to buy tickets for and to watch the show. And they all lived happily ever after.

Our kids and their cousins, having left the *seder* to the adults, typically gather in the basement/playroom. After a little leg stretching, one of them comes up with the "original" idea that it would be fun to put on a show to supplement the *seder*. Collectively they come up with a plot (usually some variant of a familiar children's tale), determine which songs they know and can sing together, assign the parts, raid the closets to throw together costumes, and collect some props. Although highly spirited, the caliber and quality of their performance — to the extent that there is one between the giggles and critical-sniping ("It's your line, stupid" — "He pushed me too hard" — "I told you I don't know that song") is reflective of their foresight and preparation. In other words its one big "mish mash." Yes, there is value in the fun they have together, but yours truly does not believe this third part enhances their Pesach experience.

In line with my desire to make this year different from all others, I took it upon myself to do some advanced planning centered on the question of how to make the seder more child centered and fun. I found two wonderful suggestions in Shimon Apisdorf's *Passover Survival Kit* and took the time to implement them.

The first involves toys and props — collecting items that would visually and digitally enhance the experience. I decided to start my collection with the 10 plagues. An expedition to the dollar store, a toy store, and a costume shop, provided me with a goodie bag full of the following items:

1) Two red-tinted baby bottles (in the shape of cherry-soda bottles) — when filled with water, the liquid appears red, like blood. When poured out it is clear again;

2) An assortment of rubber frogs (one pack actually glows in the dark), and a drinking cup and a pair of baby booties with "Baby Kermit" on them;

3) Two paper airplanes, shaped like flying bugs (lice) — with an attached propeller, powered by a rubber band (it will be fun letting these fly);

4) Several packages of plastic animals, two huge hollow plastic piggy banks, and some animal-shaped magnets;

5) Two packages of rubber rats (signifying pestilence);

6) Several packages of fake press-on tattoos — instant boils;

7) Eighteen ping-pong balls, that will rain down like hail;

8) A package of neat looking rubber locust-like bugs;

9) Fifteen pairs of "fashion" sunglasses that we will don to plunge into darkness; and

10) Two demonic skeleton-bone swords, a terrifying instrument of a death plague.

These toys will likely precipitate chaos — but it will be fun chaos!

The next idea involved a lot more work, and explains why this week I only have time to write about Passover rather than the upcoming portion of *Acharei Mot*. (To tell you the truth, we have already discussed one of this portion's major themes — namely the deaths of Aharon's sons Nadav and Avihu, in the chapter on *Shemini*. The rest you can catch up with on Yom Kippur, when a large section of this portion is repeated). The kids enjoy putting on a show but are not willing/able, due to time and distant constraints, to prepare anything, be it script or props, in advance. Accordingly, I took it upon myself to write something that would be 1) fun, 2) educational, 3) organized, and 4) easy for them to get right — with a little work. Additionally, I wanted to write something that would allow all eight of the kids, despite their age spread from four to twelve (I decided to exclude YoYo, who is only two-years-old, this year) to meaningfully participate. Here it is, "The Pesach Rap" (Hey, it's my diary and I can include what I want to!) (I have left in the kid's names, designating the parts, to give you an idea about how I thought they would present it):

PESACH RAP

1 (ALL)
Pesach Rap, Pesach Rap
It's time to sing the Pesach Rap
Pesach Rap, Pesach Rap
Let's all SCREAM the Pesach Rap!

It's late on the *seder* night
So hard to keep awake
We'll have to rap so loud
We'll make both your ears ache!

We've asked the *Mah Nishtanah*
We've drunk cups one and two
We've stuffed our mouths with Matzah
As much as we could chew

The time has come for action
To give this night some spice
Let's focus on the fun things
Like frogs and blood and lice

Each one of us is ready
To rap a verse or two
We'll rap it loud and louder
Cause we're each proud to be a Jew

Pesach Rap, Pesach Rap
It's time to sing the Pesach Rap
Pesach Rap, Pesach Rap
Let's all SCREAM the Pesach Rap!

2 (B.Z.)
I'm little baby Moshe
Floating in the sea
Pharaoh killed lots of babies
But he couldn't kill me

Pesach Rap, Pesach Rap
It's time to sing the Pesach Rap
Pesach Rap, Pesach Rap
Let's all SCREAM the Pesach Rap!

3 (Esti)
Miriam the big sister
Watched the baby float
She had to keep him safe
In his little boat

Pharaoh's daughter found him
Gave him Moshe as a name
By the time he was finished
Egypt wouldn't be the same

Pesach Rap, Pesach Rap
It's time to sing the Pesach Rap
Pesach Rap, Pesach Rap
Let's all SCREAM the Pesach Rap!

4 (Avi)
He had to leave Mitzrayim
No time to pack or to be fed
He killed to save a Jewish life
So Pharaoh tried to off his
    head

Moshe ran to Midian
Got a job to tend some sheep
He left Egypt behind him
From Prince to Little Bo Peep

One day a lamb did wander
Got lost by Sinai Hill
Leading Moshe to the burning
    bush
That had to be a thrill

A voice spoke to Moshe
Giving him a simple task
Go to Pharaoh in Egypt
For Jewish freedom to ask

Pesach Rap, Pesach Rap
It's time to sing the Pesach Rap
Pesach Rap, Pesach Rap
Let's all SCREAM the Pesach Rap!

5 (Jordy)
Moshe wasn't quite so sure
How to do this little thing
He wanted some assurance
Before entering the bull ring

He learned to turn his hand as
    white
As a Michael Jackson glove
And he could bring his staff to
    life
As a snake, not some wimpy
    dove

The magicians down in Egypt
Could do these same things
    too
It was now time for those
    nasty plagues
Time to twist and turn that
    screw

Pesach Rap, Pesach Rap
It's time to sing the Pesach Rap
Pesach Rap, Pesach Rap
Let's all SCREAM the Pesach Rap!

6 (Peshie)
Aharon borrowed Moshe's staff
And smacked it on the Nile
It turned to blood so quickly
Dracula would surely smile

Next came lots and lots of
    frogs
Egypt was about to croak
To Pharaoh it was not funny
He wasn't laughing at this joke

The lice came swarming in
Attacking through the air
This was only plague number
    three
It almost seemed not fair

Then the animals went wacko
Worse than that crazy cow dis-
    ease
When the pestilence rolled in
There was little left to tease

Pesach Rap, Pesach Rap
It's time to sing the Pesach Rap
Pesach Rap, Pesach Rap
Let's all SCREAM the Pesach Rap!

7 (Jamie)
Their flesh burst out with boils
Gross lumps of blood and pus
Those boils were so annoying
Pharaoh's magicians made a
    fuss

Hailstones smashed like bricks
Exploding full of mixed-in fire
You would think that by this
    time
Pharaoh'd be ready to retire

By now Egypt was battered
Reduced to piles of rubble
But the locusts came along
Eating any left-over stubble

A week of night then followed
A real nightmare, not pretend
The deaths of Egypt's first
    born
Brought these plagues to their
    gruesome end

Pesach Rap, Pesach Rap
It's time to sing the Pesach Rap
Pesach Rap, Pesach Rap
Let's all SCREAM the Pesach Rap!

8 (Annie)
The Jews were packed and
    ready
Freedom passing through their
    door
No clue about their future
But it wouldn't be a bore

We skipped the Pascal lamb
And the blood they had to
    smear
But we have to save something
To sing about next year

They rushed out to the desert
The dough no time to bake
That's why we eat this Matzah
And this dry potato starch cake

They followed their new
    leader
Till they reached the Sea of
    Reeds
Pharaoh's army tried to lap
    them
And cut them down like
    weeds

Deep water out in front
Pursuing army to the rear
The joy they felt as free men
Gave way to intense fear

Pesach Rap, Pesach Rap
It's time to sing the Pesach Rap
Pesach Rap, Pesach Rap
Let's all SCREAM the Pesach Rap!

9 (Josh)
Moshe said "jump in"
Take a dip in this big pool
They simply wouldn't buy that
These slaves were nobody's
    fool

Finally, a man named
    Nachshon
Believed enough to try
He jumped into the water
And then came out bone dry

The water split before him
Two walls piled up so high
Leaving a dry, wide highway
So they could easily pass on
    by

Pharaoh watched this happen
And said to himself, "Why
not?"
His army followed suit
And got wet an awful lot

The walls crashed down upon
them
Smashing them into little bits
Their bones crushed and shat-
tered
The sea was their burial pit

The threat has now passed
over
Ding Dong Egypt is dead
That's why we have this *seder*
Far better than slavery, instead

Pesach Rap, Pesach Rap
It's time to sing the Pesach Rap
Pesach Rap, Pesach Rap
Let's all SCREAM the Pesach
Rap!

10 (All)
This rap is nearly finished
We've almost reached the shore
But if you'd really like us to
We could sing it all once more

[FOR THE FIRST NIGHT]
Of course, that's why we gather
Again tomorrow night
If we didn't sing it perfectly
Next time we'll get it right

[FOR THE SECOND NIGHT]
That will be a year from now
At a place unlike Mitzrayim
We hope next year will be the
time
We finally gather in
Yerushalayim

Pesach Rap, Pesach Rap
It's time to sing the Pesach Rap
Pesach Rap, Pesach Rap
Let's all SCREAM the Pesach
Rap!

Best-laid plans often go astray. I nevertheless hope this one stays on track and that we all have the healthy, happy, kosher, and memorable Pesach we truly need to recharge our spiritual and emotional batteries.

Post Script: *Acharei Mot* is literally translated as "After the Death." These words turned out to be descriptive of the Torah portion and of our Passover and Post-Pesach week as Kim's mother passed away in the early morning after the second day of Pesach. Our joyous holiday became a period of real *Acharei Mot*. Nevertheless, Mom was with us for the first two "special" days of celebration. She participated in parts of the *seder*, she saw her grandchildren in their fine clothes, and she listened to their spirited renditions of the "Pesach Rap." These days were truly a reward for her efforts and struggles to hold on the precious extra weeks and days of life.

KEDOSHIM
The Delicatessen at the End of the Galaxy

This book is likely not going to be a best seller. However, had I thought things through from a marketing perspective, I might have been able to improve the odds by more carefully selecting my topics and characters. Thank God, I am blessed with a house full of cute, adorable children. Such children and the things they say and do are always popular. Our world is full of celebration — good times like birthdays, Bar and Bat Mitzvahs, weddings, graduations, and tributes to accomplishment. People like to read anecdotes about happy things. Perhaps it would have been wiser to don rose-colored glasses and take a simple "Don't worry, be happy," attitude.

By now, however, I am a prisoner to my format. It has become important, almost obsessive, to relate the most important things that are actually happening each week during this year. "Lucille," we have certainly "picked a fine time" to do this. Yes there have been sweet, precious, joyous moments. But there have also been a seemingly disproportionate amount of hard times. On the heels of last week's sorrow follows tragedy so immense it is almost surreal.

As observant Jews we are prohibited from believing in Tarot cards, palm reading, horoscopes, and their like. In fact, our sages teach that the Jewish People are not governed by mazal (luck or chance). Our national and individual destinies are guided directly by the hand of God. Nevertheless, from the way this week began, I should have seen the storm warnings.

As mentioned in last week's post-script, my mother-in-law passed away during Pesach. Mourning and the holiday can not coincide. Accordingly, Kim, her brother and her sister first began *shivah* (the seven-day ritual mourning period) upon the conclusion of the festival, some five days after the funeral. We decided that the smartest course of action would be for me to return home with our older five children (so that they would not miss a week of school and because they would be easier to care for and keep occupied) with Kim and YoYo remaining in New Jersey.

By now, we are all, unfortunately, equipped to handle Mr. Mom running things. Nevertheless, this meant that the week would start outside of our normal routine and with us separated from the one to whom we wished to provide needed emotional support.

This week also started with Yom Hashoah (Holocaust Memorial Day). There were many articles in newspapers and the weekly magazines discussing aspects of the Holocaust and the television was filled with documentaries and remembrances. While some of the articles and features discussed heroism and courage, most of them recounted the horrors and were shocking and sad. The Jewish community in Detroit held a ceremony that was also sad, but not for the obvious reasons. The ceremony followed the usual formula of speakers, readers, and candle lighters — quite dignified, somber, and appropriate. What was most sad, as noted by an astute reporter in an article in Monday's paper, was the small number of younger Jews, especially children, in attendance.

Then came Monday. We all know what Mondays are like. Bad things do not have to happen on Mondays for them to be disconcerting; they were designed that way. Yet, even Monday can get worse.

The *shivah* observance concluded for Kim and her siblings on Monday morning. They all wanted to ease back into their daily routines and to adjust to a world that they now had to face without either parent. Kim and YoYo were scheduled to return home on an early evening flight. At about three in the afternoon, the phone rang at my sister-in-law's house. On the line was a cousin informing everyone that his sister, Kim's first cousin, was discovered dead in her apartment. Funeral arrangements could not be made until the police and Coroner's office authorized release of her body. Needless to say, we postponed Kim's return.

Kim's now-deceased cousin was a young woman in her early forties. She was sweet, cheerful, and outgoing. As Kim was growing up she had a special relationship with her older cousin.

She never treated Kim as a "pesky little kid." Quite the contrary, she enthusiastically shared ideas, styles, and fashion. When she was old enough to drive, she enjoyed taking her younger cousins to different places. On her wedding day, she asked Kim to help braid her hair and put the finishing touches on her makeup. Her death was sudden, tragic and unexpected. This was a blow that hit all of us, especially Kim, while still numb from mourning for Mom. But if you can believe it, the circumstances were even worse than I have described. As I fill in a few details (I feel that I must restrain myself from getting too personal and too over-dramatic), I think you will understand why I used the terms "immense" and "surreal" to describe the full impact of this tragedy.

In my entry for the week of *Terumah* ("Built to Last"), I introduced you to Dan and Ora. As you may recall, neither of them is a stranger to tragedy — they are both young, they both lost spouses, and between them they have a large number of children to care for. Dan and Ora each possess the strength of character to dig out of despair and are willing to take the steps necessary to rebuild their family lives. God's hand, not fate, has brought them together and they both understand that they are being given another chance at happiness. Dan proposed to Ora on Purim and they scheduled their wedding for this Tuesday night. Knowing how special this couple is and wishing finally to celebrate and to close the door on past sorrow, the families planned a real party; complete with band, flowers, and plenty of food.

The cousin who died Monday was Dan's sister. Since her body was released for burial Tuesday afternoon, Dan, his parents and siblings were forced to begin *shivah,* to begin mourning their sister and daughter, the very afternoon and evening they were to celebrate the light after a long dark night. The wedding was postponed, by necessity. Rather than dancing at a wedding, Dan's family would be in stationary low seats. They would be forced to hold back their tears of relief and joy and to replace them with tears of grief and sorrow.

Sunday's Holocaust memorial service and Tuesday's funeral had two important things in common; 1) at neither event did anyone point a finger heavenward and ask "Why?" and 2) they were punctuated with the *Kaddish,* a prayer praising God and affirming the sanctity of His name that is associated with death and mourning.

Kaddish has the same Hebrew root (K"D"SH) as this week's Torah portion *Kedoshim.* The root K"D"SH means, or represents holiness. In the opening verse of the portion, the Torah proclaims "You shall be holy, for Hashem, your God is holy." (*Vayikra* 19:2). This is quite a high standard. We, the Jewish People, must strive to be holy because our God is. What is holiness? How much do we know about God to be able to emulate His holiness? Is there a definition; are there rules and standards?

The sages, themselves, debate the meaning of this commandment. Some view it in terms of piety; some describe separation and asceticism; some see it as reinforcing core obligations, and still others add a gloss of super-responsibility, setting a standard beyond the letter of the law. I personally favor the classic approach that advises, "sanctify yourself through that which is permitted to you," (avoid gluttony, drunkenness, etc.) a Ben Franklin-esque appeal to the benefits of moderation.

However, especially in light of this week's events, I would like to step away from these interpretations for a moment and focus solely on the word — on the root of the word K"D"SH. Nearly everywhere I turned, I encountered that word:

> During several of the Yom Hashoah tributes, the speaker referred to the fact that millions died *"Al Kiddush Hashem"* ("In sanctification of God's name."). In fact the six million are collectively called *"Kedoshim"* ("Holy Ones");

> The mourners in the family must all now recite the *Kaddish;*

> Going back a week, the last full day of Mom's life was the second day of Pesach. We held the second *seder* on the eve of this day. Instead of reciting the *Kiddush* (blessing over the wine sanctifying the holiday) at the table, I went into Mom's room to chant it for her (while my brother-in-law recited it for the *seder* participants). These were the last moments I spent alone with her; and

> Dan and Ora were to be married. The Hebrew/Aramaic word *Kiddushin* represents an important component of the marriage process and ceremony (when the woman becomes forbidden to all men) and is, in fact, the name of the tractate in the Talmud containing the laws of getting married.

We see K"D"SH ("Holy") in time, in relationships, in joy, and in tragedy. This seems so confusing. Yet it took a silly anecdote, related to me by a friend of the family while Kim was sitting *shivah,* to put my finger on and to achieve understanding amidst this confusion.

Heshy is a big shot in the New Jersey state government. Over the past several years, he has discovered much about our religion that he did not learn growing up in Passaic, New Jersey. Today he fully observes Torah law.

As a young adult, Heshy did not keep fundamental commandments like eating only kosher food or resting on the *Shabbat.* The Jewish community in Passaic was shrinking. There were few in the community that were capable or inclined to enrich his awareness of his heritage. (By the way, over the past 15 years Passaic has enjoyed a renaissance. Today, it hosts a thriving Jewish community with many shuls, schools, *yeshivot,* and other Jewish amenities and necessities). Nevertheless, Heshy identified strongly as a Jew and was quite proud of his heritage

Around this time, a kosher delicatessen opened in Passaic. Even though Heshy did not keep kosher, and even though the food and the decor were not particularly impressive, Heshy enjoyed eating there. "It was not much more than a hole in the wall, and the proprietor was more grumpy than friendly, but I liked the place." He told me. The name of the establishment was Simcha's Deli.

Moving forward a few years, Heshy met his wife to be, Chava, a girl from a more observant background. A few months after they began dating, one of Chava's relatives passed away and she dragged Heshy along to make a condolence call. Heshy had never experienced the environment and ritual of traditional Jewish mourning. He was puzzled by the etiquette of the visit and the strange words that people were mumbling to one another. Chava tried to explain things to him as best she could.

As they were getting ready to leave, Rabbi Levy, a local Orthodox rabbi with whom Chava was acquainted, entered the house.

Politely, Chava brought Heshy over to introduce him to the rabbi. After exchanging pleasantries, Rabbi Levy pronounced the parting words that Jews traditionally exchange when they meet at unpleasant times "May we meet again at *simchas* (joyous events)."

Heshy perked up a bit and replied to Rabbi Levy, "So Rabbi, you like to eat there too?"

Rabbi Levy had no idea what Heshy was talking about. To Rabbi Levy *simcha* meant happiness and good times. To Heshy, Simcha's was a deli in Passaic. The same word had a vastly different meaning to these two men. One said the word and one heard it, but the individual contexts were not even in the same ballpark. But then again, the two men were vastly different, as well, as were their frames of reference.

Holiness is everywhere, just as God is. It is not constrained by labels like good and bad, happy and sad, or dead and alive. It is not limited to certain days or times or places. It is most certainly not the exclusive property of only certain people.

Some years ago, a group of space scientists launched a spacecraft to the cosmos. The ship was designed as a means of communicating the existence of the human presence on Earth to potential extraterrestrial intelligence. The craft contained a basic message of peace and welcome written in different languages. The message was broadcast in different languages and on different frequencies. The craft also contained symbols and pictures illustrating these same concepts. The team that put this together tried to anticipate the different ways the message could be received or understood and attempted to increase the chances that it would be delivered — if anyone or anything was out there that could capably receive it.

In a sense, I believe God does the same thing with us, His children believers, and followers. He wants us to discover the existence and nature of holiness. He wants us to communicate through it. By surrounding us with it and by giving us opportunities to experience its aspects, we ultimately are being spoon-fed a better understanding of God, Himself.

K"D"SH is as far away as the furthest galaxy, but it is also as close as our own hearts and souls.

EMOR
Lawnmower Boy

April showers have brought only May showers — as winter refuses to defer to spring and summer. We are going through a long stretch where temperatures seem to rarely rise even into the 50's and the days are wet and gray. After the long winter, cabin fever has us eager for softball, bike rides, yes... and even a little yard work. Yet here it is, mid-May and we have yet to experience even one truly nice day. But this past Sunday was close.

With a forecast calling for partly sunny skies and with the mercury expected to reach into the 60's, the President of the Young Israel announced our first softball team practice. Our motley crew of rabbis, lawyers, dentists, accountants, doctors, and assorted others gathered on the damp field on a chilly morning. The air was soon filled with the thwacks of ball hitting glove and the pings of aluminum bats. (The grunts, groans, and *kvetches* did not appear until a good half-hour into the practice.) While it is far too early to make predictions or even to present an accurate scouting report, I can confidently say that this season will provide plenty of fun and laughs.

Most of the guys ran out of gas before eleven, which meant I had adequate time before the never-ending carpool to mow the lawn. I have reached a critical juncture with lawn mowing, one that presents a dilemma for which there is no simple or pat answer. On one hand, I have the basic cutting down to a science: 1) we have a mulching mower, so I rarely bag the grass; 2) the mower is self-propelled so it is not difficult to push; 3) both yards (front and back) are rectangular, with few obstacles or irregularities (the only tricky part is the swing set); and 4) Kim lets me borrow her "Walkman" so I get to listen while I work. On the other hand, I have a twelve, soon to be thirteen, year-old son and one of the sacred rituals of adolescence is being entrusted to handle the heavy lawn equipment.

I can remember back when I was that age. My family had just moved from Chicago into a new house in Rochester, New York and I was being traumatized by the experience. We moved in June and my Bar Mitzvah was scheduled for Labor Day weekend. In my mind, the only thing that could be worse than leaving behind all the friends I grew up with, was leaving behind all the friends I grew up with three months before my Bar Mitzvah. After all, few, if any, of my Chicago friends would be able to attend my celebration, and since we moved after the school year ended in Rochester, I would likely not even know any of my future classmates (who my parents had the foresight to invite anyway).

The best solution would have been to ship this "unhappy camper" off to camp. However, the combination of move, new house, Bar Mitzvah, and younger siblings (as in, I, as the oldest, had to help watch them since my parents so busy with everything else) foreclosed camp as a realistic option. I had to "grin and bear it," "take it like a man," "roll with the punches," "make the best of a bad situation" — and extort money for lots of comic books and baseball cards, demand a new bike and baseball glove; and whine until I got a basketball hoop, etc. As these demands mounted, my parents were wise enough to realize that they had to grab this bull by the horns. I needed to be given responsibility, I needed to earn some of the things I was demanding, I needed my time constructively occupied — in other words, it was time for them to put me in charge of the yard.

Now forgive me since I have to work from memory and we moved out of that house over twenty years ago — but, at least in my mind's eye, that yard was huge (so huge, in fact, that the next summer my father purchased a riding mower). To top it all off, the backyard was ringed by tall, thick, leafy bushes — which had become badly overgrown. The mission, which I had little choice in accepting, was defined as follows: 1) mow the lawn (with a lawn mower that was not self-propelled, that did not mulch, and that had a grass catcher that I had to empty about every fifteen to twenty feet), 2) trim the bushes (again, we did not have an electric hedge trimmer. This had to be done with those big oversized scissors), 3) do the edging (a manual edger, not a weed whacker or powered edger), 4) spread fertilizer, weedkiller, insecticide as needed and 5) put out and move the hoses and sprinklers (flowers were not in my contract!).

Yes, I still had time to play ball in the park, read comic books, ride my bike, and prepare for my Bar Mitzvah. However, maintaining that yard took lots of work. To tell you the truth, the task had quite a few benefits. First, I had a good feeling when I completed a task and could remove an item from my mental to-do list. Second, I could tangibly see the results of my labors — the yard looked neater and the grass was greener than when we moved in. Third, I developed a sense of pride in our property and new home — after all I was a stakeholder in the yard. Fourth, I learned what it meant to be in charge of something. Finally, I got to slice up sticks, errant candy wrappers, and other debris with the blades of my powerful machine (kind of like tearing up the road on a Harley-Davidson).

By now you can see my current problem — should I let go of the memories, of this link to my past, of the fresh air and exercise, of this responsibility — and pass the torch (or in this case, the lawnmower) on to my son so that he can learn its valuable lessons?

Before we turn to this week's portion of *Emor* and its directive on this very subject, I choose to defer to another of this week's events. On Wednesday night I attended a lecture given by Rabbi Adin Steinsaltz. For those few of you who may not have heard of him (after all, he's even been featured in *Time* magazine), Rabbi Steinsaltz is one of the leading Jewish scholars of this century. He has spent the last twenty years translating the Talmud into Hebrew (it is written in Aramaic) and separately into English (for Random House Publishers, no less). He has written many books on mysticism, religious thought, sociology, philosophy, and science.

The topic of his lecture was "Are We One? — Truths and Myths of Jewish Unity," a topic that is of great interest in light of the inflammatory remarks directed recently by a group of Orthodox rabbis at Conservative and Reform Jews. I arrived early, clutching one of his books in my hands, hoping for a brief conversation and an autograph.

When I entered the room I saw him standing with one of the local Detroit rabbis. Fortunately, there was not a crowd hovering around him. Sensing a clear opportunity, I headed straight for him. I stood respectfully until acknowledged, and then held out my hand in the traditional *"Shalom Aleichem"* greeting. As he responded, I mentioned to him how I had attended when he addressed my law school class fifteen years earlier and that I was glad to have this opportunity to meet him again. With sincere humility he turned to the other rabbi and said, "Isn't it remarkable how someone remembers me after so many years?" It was as if he was unaware of his own fame and notoriety. He was genuinely happy that someone, someone he did not even know, remembered and appreciated his efforts of long ago. For men like Rabbi Steinsaltz, they may get "bigger" but they remain rooted in their core selves.

Rabbi Steinsaltz's lecture was simple and direct. He did not try to dazzle us with his grasp of the nuances of Jewish history, he did not quote an array of obscure rabbinic sources, and he did not engage in the mental gymnastics of philosophical speculation. He presented the family as a workable model for the complex inter-relationships between Jews and supported his premise with examples from within our own common experiences.

I am not going to repeat or summarize his talk. However, I did gain some measure of comfort from the notion that examining particular and specific relationships such as those between brothers, or between parents and children, or between man and wife, can provide important and useful models for understanding the universal relationships among groups of men and between man and God. If, through these weeks, I have ventured too far into the realm of the personal and particular, I nevertheless believe that the underlying Torah messages can still be applied far more broadly and have now had this lesson reinforced by the renown Rabbi Steinsalz.

The portion of *Emor* is, for the most part, a universal portion. The core of the portion is occupied by a march through the cycle of Jewish holidays. All of the biblical holidays, including the *Shabbat,* are discussed, as well as the forty-nine day *omer* period between Pesach and Shavuot. Quite interesting is the fact that the Torah presents the command to light the *menorah* (candelabra) in the *Mishkan* (Tabernacle) immediately after discussing the holidays. According to some commentators this is a hint referencing the holiday of Chanukah that would be added by the Rabbis in the Second Temple era.

The portion of *Emor,* however, opens and closes with concepts that are more specific. At the beginning of *Emor,* God tells Moshe to convey to the *kohanim* (the priests, descendants of Aharon) a series of specific rules of conduct that apply only to them. These rules run the gamut from hygiene and appearance to suitable marriage partners. At the end of *Emor*, the Torah returns to historical narrative and relates an incident involving a Jewish child (Jewish mother, Egyptian father) who curses God; a capital offense. The noteworthy aspect of this incident involves the fact that it was a case of first impression. While God had given Moshe and the Jews the Torah with its rules and punishments, they had never before been called upon to carry out this aspect of their responsibility. They were being asked for the first time not only to uphold the law, but they literally had to kill for it.

My dilemma this week is about mowing the lawn, a significantly less important responsibility — despite any proclivities toward slicing things with yard equipment that I may have expressed before. The guidance I needed is to be found in the portion's second verse. "Say (*"Emor"*) unto the *kohanim* the sons of Aharon and you shall say (*"v'emarta"*) unto them..." (*Vayikra* 21:1). God's instruction to Moshe is redundant — "say and say." The classic commentator, Rashi, explains that this particular redundancy teaches an important lesson — "To enjoin adults with regard to minors" (*"L'hazhir gedolim al haketanim"*). Adult *kohanim* are commanded to see to it that *kohanim* who are minors learn the rules and avoid ritual impurity.

The entire scheme of Torah education, of preparing a person for life, is built on this concept — parents must take the lead in teaching their children. Do I want to abdicate my yard chores? Not really. Is it beneficial and meritorious for my son to learn the skills and be given this type of responsibility? Certainly. Then I have to teach him and give him the chance. Similarly, as he approaches the age of *mitzvot* (fulfilling Torah commandments as a Jewish adult at age thirteen), I have to be more aware of what he needs to know. I can not simply take for granted that he will intuit or comprehend the rituals and laws that have been ingrained into me through years of compliance and commitment and through the teachings of my parents.

BEHAR-BECHUKOTAI
The Golden City

Time, as we all know, is a very precious commodity. Each day is a true race against the clock, as we try to accomplish all that we can. We have to find time for our ritual obligations, for our families, for our employers, for community work, for recreation and relaxation, and for our necessary personal needs (eating, sleeping, bathing, etc.). As we struggle to prioritize, we develop our own personal rules that guide us through most days and most usual situations.

As an observant Jew, much of my dance card is already penciled in. On every *Shabbat* and Jewish holiday, my beliefs require that the secular and mundane be pushed aside. Every morning begins with certain rituals and blessings and a period of prayer. Every day ends with additional prayers and psalms. There is also another part of my day that is usually spoken for, the time I spend studying Torah.

Our sages recommend (require) that we set aside time each day for such study. The descriptive expression for this is *Likvoa Itim L'Torah* (to set aside time for Torah). The word *likvoa*, literally, has a more specific meaning than "to set aside." It implies a more permanent form of establishment — to block out a certain time each day, or specific time on certain days each week so that there can be consistency and priority. For example, if I establish 12:00 P.M. to 1:00 P.M. on Tuesday as a designated Torah study time, I avoid various conflicts wherever possible — I will try not to schedule meetings away from the office, or to accept a squash match at that time on that day.

Scheduling Torah study time becomes even more important when you study with someone else. Self-study is certainly important. Studying with a teacher or mentor is of even greater value. However, the most meaningful and lasting learning comes from the refinement gained by studying with a partner. Two heads are not simply better than one. The separate individuals are able to grow and develop because of the experience of studying in tandem with another.

Even after the completion of my formal, institutional, Jewish education, I have always tried to set aside a number of hours each week for this mode of study. Over the years I have been fortunate to find partners that had the skill, background, and commitment to complement my needs (as well as the temperament to be able to put up with me). In certain ways a good study partnership is like a good marriage — over time the partners understand each other's styles, they learn to communicate more and more effectively, and they often reach a level where they are able to anticipate the other's arguments and explanations. When one finds a good study partner, one works to keep the momentum going and tries to keep the interest level high.

Going back the last ten or so years, I have had some excellent partners. However, real life finds a way to intrude. Thus, two previous partners moved for job or family reasons and I changed locales myself moving to Detroit. Each move leads to the search for a new partner.

I was able to find a new study partner within a few weeks of arriving in Detroit because I made it a priority. The rabbi of our Young Israel gave me a few suggestions and one, in particular, was a good fit. Yossie is a doctor who is completing a fellowship before he returns to practice medicine in Jerusalem. He arrived in Detroit nearly three years ago with his lovely family. Yossie studied in several fine *yeshivot* in Israel before he went to medical school, so studying with him has been a good challenge. (It has been an added bonus that his children match up well in age with mine so that our families have developed a nice friendship, as well).

All good things must come to an end — Yossie's program concludes at the end of this week and he is returning to Jerusalem with his family. The end of this partnership is certainly bittersweet. On one hand I am sorry to see a friend and his family leave and I face the uncertainty of establishing a new study relationship. On the other hand, Yossie is doing what most of us merely hope and pray for. He is going to make a life for himself and his family in Jerusalem, our holy city. For Yossie, this is not a shallow *"l'shanah habaah b'Yerushalayim"* ("next year in Jerusalem"), this is here and now. Coincidentally, next week we are celebrating Yom Yerushalayim (Jerusalem Day) which commemorates the liberation of the entire city during the Six Day War in 1967.

Kim teaches in one of the local Jewish day schools and has been placed in charge of coordinating a special assembly to celebrate this day. With a copy of my "Pesach Rap" in hand (see, *Acharei Mot:* A Different Kind of Seder), she asked if I might be able to compose something in honor of Jerusalem. As my mind was on that Golden City anyway, I agreed (not that she would have taken no for an answer). At the insistence of my wife, I digress to present *Yom Yerushalayim:*

> Yerushalayim, our heart and our soul
> Yerushalayim, rebuilding is our goal
> Yesterday and tomorrow, full of God's glory
> We celebrate today, by sharing Her story

(1)

Here is the story in words that rhyme
Of a place that is beyond space and time
Every jew is linked to this holy city
Even if her tale has not always been pretty

From Avraham our father to Mashiach the king
Yerushalayim is a part of almost every Jewish thing
The First Temple was built there, the Second one too
And the Third one will be there before all is through

(2)

Avraham saw a special place from afar
A place that glowed brighter than any star
He traveled there to offer his son
Our nation was born before he was done

In the end Avraham did not have to kill
Instead, he sacrificed a ram on that hill
The sound of the *Shofar* was first heard then
And its sound has rung out again and again

(3)

Our father Yaacov ran to get away from His brother
He received Yitzchak's blessings thanks to his mother
He stopped at a place to catch up on his sleep
Even with a pillow of rocks, his slumber was deep

In Yerushalayim he had his amazing dream
A ladder with angels who played on his team
This was a place of vision and prayers
Where he met God and learned that He cares

(4)

To Egypt first, for a 400 year stay
After we returned, there was still a delay
Until David was king the city was quiet
He crowned her as capital in a joyous dance riot

He Sent for the *menorah* and the holy ark
Yerushalayim would no longer be kept in the dark
But God told David he would not get it all done
The real building job was reserved for Shlomo, his
   son

(5)
Shlomo the king, the wisest of men
Drew the designs with papyrus and pen
He built the Temple as a spiritual center
A place of service for all Jews to enter

Yerushalayim was up, the rest of the world was down
The city had the holy Temple as its crown
For over 400 years the *Shechinah* was present
But when the Jews finally strayed, things got very
   unpleasant

(6)
Bavel and her armies came and destroyed
The *Kohanim* found themselves unemployed
Our people were exiled, in total distress
Yerushalayim in rubble, one very large mess

They waited 70 years for the darkness to end
In the middle with Haman they had to contend
The son of Queen Esther gave his permission
Building the Second Temple became an important
   mission

(7)
With Ezra to lead them many did return
So much to rebuild, so much to relearn
They tried to restore the Temple back to normal
But with some holy objects missing, it was a little less
   formal

The second was special, but it was not like the first
And before long the Greeks brought out their worst
The Jews gave in to some foreign vices
So soon there was another terrible crisis

(8)

With Mattityahu to lead them, a precious few
Showed the rest how to be a good Jew
They fought the Greeks, their gods, and their pigs
This time the littles beat up on the bigs

They won back the Temple, but the *Menorah* was
    dark
Barely enough oil to light with a spark
In the city of miracles, a city of lights
One day's supply burned for eight nights

(9)

Yerushalayim stood for two centuries more
Those years were hardly ever a bore
Jews simply weren't nice to one another
Free hatred, not love, pitted brother against brother

A people strong together was falling apart
No longer a body that beat with one heart
The Romans burned and slaughtered, leaving little
    behind
For the next 2000 years, exile would not be very kind

(10)

Yerushalayim was desolate, a plowed over field
Foxes ran through it, the land would not heal
The *Shechinah* in exile, our *Mikdash* broken stones
But better a building than all Jewish flesh and bones

Turks and Crusaders claimed her for a while
The Arabs filled her with graves and garbage piles
We could not get near, but we would not forget
Each day with our prayers, we cried our eyes wet

(11)

Out of the Shoah came a remaining spark
They arrived in Yisrael hoping to make their mark
To revive a people too long without a homeland
To live in a city David and Shlomo once planned

They were not ready for war, but this did not matter
With God on their side, the enemy did scatter
Jews returned to Yerushalayim in a country of their
    own
Yet the Kotel remained with the arabs on loan

(12)
For nearly twenty more years, Yerushalayim was split
So near yet so far, just another little bit
Then in 1967 the arabs got bold
Jerusalem divided became Jerusalem of gold

Israel was not run into the sea
God led her armies to a great victory
The attacking arab armies were cut down to size
Yerushalayim the holy city was the war's biggest prize

(13)
For over thirty years all of Yerushalayim has been in
    our hands
We've restored much of her beauty, grown gardens in
    her sands
Her streets are now filled with the sounds of kids
    playing
The result of our many, many years of real praying

But our Return is still not fully complete
The hold of this exile we have yet to defeat
A mosque stands where holiness should be
The *Mikdash* rebuilt is what we need to see

(14)
Eliyahu will soon ride in, *shofar* in hand
The blast that it makes will sound through the land
Mashiach's arrival will be shown on TV
As will be the appearance of holy temple number
    three

> Avraham, Yitzchak, and Yaacov will bask again in her
> glow
> David and Shlomo will help make her grow
> Every word of our prayers will be used as a brick
> Every tear that was shed, will heal what was sick
>
> Yerushalayim, our heart and our soul
> Yerushalayim, rebuilding is our goal
> Yesterday and tomorrow, full of God's glory
> We celebrate today by sharing her story

As I finished writing this poem reflecting on the meaning and history of Jerusalem and as I thought about how lucky Yossie is to be returning there to raise his children. I began to wonder — Why do I pray toward Jerusalem each day, and sing of a desire to return, and proclaim a hope of gathering there next year — while I live firmly rooted where I am? I have picked up and moved my family before, Yossie is moving his now, why don't I just go?

The answer is, as difficult as this to admit, that my faith is deficient. I know that God provides for my material needs and the needs of my family. I certainly know that He will provide us with what is necessary whether we live in Detroit, London, Hong Kong, or Jerusalem. I even know that our standard of living, what we own, and where we live is a product of God's grace, not my abilities.

As seen in the final two portions of *Vayikra, Behar* and *Bechukotai,* this lack of faith has been a root cause of Jewish exile since biblical times. In fact, one could say that inadequate faith in God's ability to provide for our material needs is incompatible with any notion of residing in the Holy Land.

At the beginning of *Behar,* the Torah describes the laws of the Sabbatical and the Jubilee years (*"Shemitah"* and *"Yovel"*). The basic cycle of years is quite similar to our weekly work cycles. Six days we work and on the seventh (*Shabbat*) we rest — six years we cultivate the fields of the Land of Israel and in the seventh (*"Shemitah"*) they lie fallow. These two shorter cycles are fractals of another, larger cycle. After seven cycles of seven years (forty-nine years for those of you without a calculator) the land is given additional time off, the fiftieth year, called the Jubilee year (*"Yovel"*).

In our era and country of plenty, which is part of a worldwide economy with nearly endless seasons for growing produce, this may be hard to picture — but during the Sabbatical and Jubilee years the economy in Israel, which was agrarian, simply halted. No plowing, seeding, irrigating, harvesting, etc. No produce markets, no commerce, and no exports. Everything stopped because of the command of God and because of His promise to provide.

This may have been manageable during a regular seven-year cycle. However, what do you think people went through the Jews' minds as the Jubilee year approached? They not only had to "rest" in the forty-ninth year, but in the fiftieth, as well. Add in the work necessary at the beginning of the fifty-first year to restart things, and you have nearly three years where the Jewish people did not work the land to provide for their needs.

If I told you that the Torah required us to walk away from our jobs for two or three years at a time, your first questions would likely be "what will I live on, how will I support myself?" The Torah, which does, in fact, make such a demand, provides the following guarantee in connection with these questions: "If you will say: What will we eat in the seventh year? — behold we will not sow and not gather in our crops! I will ordain My blessing for you in the sixth year and it will yield a crop sufficient for the three-year period. You will sow in the eighth year, but you will eat from the old crop; until the ninth year, until the arrival of its crop, you will eat the old" (*Vayikra* 25:20–22).

Imagine, the bounty of the sixth year will be sufficient for the entire nation for the three-year hiatus! Realize what an amazing promise this is. In a sense, God's reputation is visibly on the line — as the sixth (forty-ninth) year passed, the Jews would, as guaranteed in the Torah, see a threefold increase in their crop yields. If not, they and the rest of the world would be able to question the veracity of the Torah itself.

God thus called upon the Jews in Israel to have this faith. Presumably they should have followed the game plan and witnessed how the bounty of the sixth year carried them into the ninth — end of story. However, if this positive reinforcement was not enough to motivate them, we find in the portion of *Bechukotai* the consequences that would flow from ignoring the *Shemitah* and *Yovel* cycles. The Torah lists verse after verse of curses, plagues, and exiles that would be the quid pro quo of disobedience.

As the curses reach their crescendo, and as the Torah describes a desolate land with ruined cities, God proclaims "The land will appease its *Shemitah* years during all the years of desolation, while you are in the land of your foes; then the land will rest and it will make the *Shemitah* years appeasing" (*Vayikra* 26:34–5).

In commenting on this verse, Rashi, with 20-20 hindsight, provides the historical background for this prophetic warning. The 70 year Babylonian exile corresponded to 70 years of *Shemitah* and *Yovel* that the Jews violated between the time they entered the Land of Israel through the destruction of the First Temple. Despite visible, tangible reward, and despite the strongest of Divine threat, the people still could not muster the faith in God's ability to provide for their material well being. Ultimately, without this faith, the Holy Land is unable, perhaps unwilling to tolerate our people.

By living where I do, namely outside of Israel, I regretfully, if unintentionally, signal a lack of faith in God's ability to provide for me and my family. Until I am able to overcome this deficiency, Israel is no more ready for me than I am for her; perhaps even less so.

I wish Yossie and his family all the best and I hope that my study and association with him has moved my *emunah* (faith) a few steps closer to that boarder separating "heck no" from "what the heck" — between provincial cowardice and pioneering courage. In the interim, as I continue to pray toward Jerusalem each day, I must be sure to throw in an additional prayer for God to help me to overcome this resistance to move toward Jerusalem. All in all, instead of entering the Holy Land, and helping to speed the rebuilding of the Temple and the restoration of the services detailed in *Vayikra*, I remain entrenched *bamidbar* ("in the desert"), which just so happens to be the name of the fourth book of the Torah that we will explore, with God's continued help, over the upcoming weeks.

BAMIDBAR
The Burning Flag

It is June, summertime. The name of this week's portion is *Bamidbar,* which means "in the desert (or wilderness)." So naturally our topic is... ice hockey. Professional hockey is an acquired taste. Of the four major professional sports, it is the one we played least as kids. Additionally, most of the good players were not (and still are not) American athletes. For years Canadian born players dominated the sport. This made it a relatively hard sell to us provincial Americans.

Hockey is an interesting blend of graceful skill, physical and sometimes violent effort, and individual and team strategy. I developed my appreciation for the sport while following the great New York Islander teams of the early 1980's that won four consecutive championships. The "Miracle on Ice" at the Winter Olympics in Lake Placid — a U.S. Gold Medal — only served to further heighten my love of the sport.

If living in the New York/New Jersey area provided a feast of hockey action — a smorgasbord of Islander, Rangers, and Devils games, Cleveland was truly a hockey desert — lacking even a high minor league team until our last two years there. Sure, it was fun to take an occasional trip to Pittsburgh, Buffalo, or Detroit to catch a game, but these were soulless events — watching a game without having a rooting interest is like eating a hot dog without mustard and sauerkraut — a part of the experience is missing.

Our move to Detroit brought me back to a real live hockey town. (In fact local fans call Detroit "Hockey Town".) During our first year here, the Detroit Red Wings set a record for the most victories by a team during the regular season. Alas, they lost in the playoffs. This year they conserved their efforts and paced themselves to peak for a championship run. This team is less flashy, but more focused, more patient, more disciplined, and more successful. As I write this, they are in the Stanley Cup Finals, playing for the league title.

The city is Red Wings crazy. Wherever you turn there are signs and banners bearing the team logo and encouraging slogans. People in stores and offices are wearing Red Wings sweaters, t-shirts, and sweatshirts. Then, there is the one item that seems to have become the biggest symbol of Detroit's pride in its team — car flags. These are small fire-red flags (maybe 8 in. x 8 in.), emblazoned with a white Red Wings logo (a winged-wheel), that are attached to a plastic pole that, in turn, is designed to clip onto a closed car window. I would guess that about one in every four or five cars in the city are currently sporting these flags.

To my wife's amusement ("Please tell me you didn't spend $10 on that." — "I won't, I spent $15."), I purchased a flag and playfully affixed it to my car. When I drove up to the house, the kids ran out, pointing to it with big smiles and said things like "Wow, you got one!" It was as if by putting this flag on my car, I had done something special for them.

To my amusement, the flag is really noticed. When I stop at a red light, drivers next to me flash a thumbs up. In the parking lot at the office, several co-workers inquire about my thoughts and insights about the playoff series. By placing a red colored piece of fabric affixed to a small plastic rod to my car, I have, somehow, become a member of this club or family of Red Wings fans. It seems so silly, so trivial, yet it is real.

The tangible effect of the symbolism of flags is actually one of the themes of *Bamidbar,* this week's Torah portion. The portion does not have much of a story line and it contains little in the way of law that has relevance to modern Jewish life. In previous weeks, the Jews left Egypt, received the Torah at Sinai, sinned with the Golden Calf, and were forgiven. They then spent some time building the *Mishkan* (Tabernacle), learning about its functions, including when to bring the various sacrifices, and they were instructed on the different facets of holiness.

Now, approximately a year after the Exodus, it is time for them to prepare to enter the Holy Land. In *Bamidbar,* the Jewish Nation does some of the things one would expect a group of over two million people, in transit and in transition, to do. First, they had to take a census. They needed to know what their potential military strength would be for the expected battles against the Canaanite peoples (I purposely choose to ignore the fact that such strength was basically irrelevant, as their battlefield successes would be the result of Divine providence, not superior force). Next, they needed to properly organize their camp for proper defense and for orderly travel. Finally, they needed to be told how to care for the *Mishkan.* Accordingly, the Torah sets forth the individual roles of the *Leviim* (Levites) in handling the *Mishkan* during the period of transition until a permanent Temple could be established.

I initially had trouble understanding one procedure set forth in the portion. In describing the configuration of the camps, the Torah states: "The Children of Israel shall encamp, each man by his flag according to the insignias of their father's household...." (*Bamidbar* 2:2). God thus commanded the Children of Israel to display flags.

Various commentaries debate the precise number of flags; with opinions ranging from four (one for each of the tribal groupings) to twelve (one for each tribe) to a large, unspecified number (one for each family). Additionally, there is some debate about their design. However, there is no debate about their role — they comprised a significant element of the organization of the camp. However, there seems to be no explanation about their function. What was the purpose of these flags? This question becomes even more compelling when we consider that apart from this reference, they do not, historically, appear to have any ongoing vitality or relevance.

I would like to suggest two possible motives behind the Divine command regarding the flags. The first involves military tactics and the second the evolution of a family into a nation.

Have you ever seen an old-fashioned war movie — perhaps a Civil War or World War II picture? If you have, you will likely be able to recall a point in the film where the good guys are being battered by the enemies and are barely holding on. But, they have their orders, they must take that hill (or hold the fort). They face the battle with their flag hanging high. As the tide turns against them, it starts to falter and drop. Suddenly, some courageous soldier grabs the flag from the wounded bearer. He boldly raises it to its full glory and leads a final charge to victory.

In war, people kill for the flag, fight for the flag, and die for the flag and what it represents. No matter what else has happened, if the flag is still on display, the enemy has not won ("the rocket's red glare, the bombs bursting in air gave proof through the night that our flag was still there"). Knowing this, the soldiers guarding the flag will risk all to protect it.

God knew what Jewish history would be. We were destined to live under the dominion of dozens, if not hundreds, of flags through the ages. We had to be shown true flags, flags of Torah and flags of holiness, so that we would never waiver in our loyalty. Symbolically, we were taught never to let our beliefs fall.

On the other hand, the flags may well have had a more temporary function — to pull families together to form tribes and ultimately to form a nation. As slaves, these people had little responsibility or control. Their discrimination into family units, with flags to proudly rally around, meant that they had identity — they were each somebody, not something.

As I described above, look how people in Detroit have rallied around flags bearing the logo of a sports team. Strangers wave to each other, smile at one another, and exchange pleasantries. Civic pride has increased. People have pulled together, albeit temporarily, because of a common rooting interest.

A related group of former slaves with a flag to rally around were now a family entity. Groups of families could, in turn, rally around the tribal flag and experience a pride of numbers and developing power. In time, the twelve tribes, once settled in their own land, could unite under a common flag of nationhood — be it the flag of the Davidic dynasty or the blue and white flag of more recent vintage. Viewed this way, the flags could almost be viewed as training wheels leading to political unification.

The flags have led the way after 42 years, to a Red Wings championship. The flags of support and pride are now the flags of victory. Maybe the Jewish People will be lucky enough, after nearly 4,000 years, to see the flags waving in a parade heralding a return to the glory of the past.

NASO
Teacher's Pet

This week has been a blur. Right smack in the middle was the holiday of *Shavuot,* the celebration of *"Matan Torah,"* the receipt of the Torah from Hashem on Mount Sinai just seven weeks after the Exodus (see, "*Yitro:* Little Miss Sunshine"). With the holiday taking up two full days, the other days have become a mad scramble to prepare for it, while trying to keep up with the demands of work in the office.

This was the kind of week when I was severely tempted to take off an extra day, and to call in with the "blue flu." Apart from our busy schedule, the weather had finally turned nice. As I sat at my desk glancing briefly out of my office window, I daydreamed of sitting under a tree with a pitcher of iced tea or lemonade, a pad and pen, and a few good books. Then I noticed the following item in that morning's paper:

> It was anything but a normal last day of school for Keith Morency. On Wednesday, Morency became the

first student in the Northville School District to have
perfect attendance from Kindergarten through 12th
grade. He's never been tardy either. Morency, 17, completed his 2,353th day by attending class and doing a
television interview. On Friday, he will receive an
award during graduation ceremonies.

Can you imagine that — Kindergarten through 12th grade, thirteen years of school, without once being absent or late?

This was a significant enough achievement to halt any thoughts
about a day of hooky from the office. But as I thought even more
about this achievement, I became downright uncomfortable, reli-
giously uncomfortable.

When we received the Torah as a nation at Sinai, we accepted
many obligations. Some commandments only apply to certain
members of our people (like the *kohanim* or *leviim*), or only apply
when certain historical conditions are met (like having a Temple in
Jerusalem or having a reigning Jewish monarch descended from the
ancestry of King David). However, the bulk of the practice of nor-
mative Torah Judaism is of the day by day, or week by week, or
year by year variety.

We are obligated to pray three times a day (extra times on
Shabbat and holidays); to recite the *Shema* at least twice a day
("When you rise up and when you lie down"); to don *tefillin* (phylacteries) every day (except *Shabbat* and holidays); to recite certain
blessings every day; to set aside time for Torah study every day, etc.

We work six days and on every *Shabbat,* we rest. Every year on
Pesach we clean out the *"chametz"* (unleaven) from our homes and
hold our *seders*. Every Succot holiday is welcomed in our own *succah* huts and with special prayers punctuated by waving the four
species (*lulav* [palm branch], *etrog* [citron], *hadasim* [myrtle], and
aravot [willow]). And so on and so forth, et cetra, et cetra, et cetra
(apologies to Yul Brenner — Lou Diamond Phillips will never be

the King of Siam in my eyes).

Have I missed reciting the *Shema* in the last thirteen years? Have I been late for services at synagogue during that time? Have I ever missed a day of wearing *tefillin?* Was there a *Shabbat* when I was ill after an operation causing me to sleep through it and its rituals? The answer to these and other equally embarrassing questions is yes — as I am sure it is for most of us — we are not perfect saints devoid of the slightest blemish or taint — even if accidental and out of our control.

Imagine, however, after 120 years (otherwise known as the end of our days) standing before the Heavenly Court and being asked to explain all the discrepancies in my religious track record — but I was sick; but my flight was delayed with my *talit* and *tefillin* in my checked baggage; but I stayed up all night working on a brief and slept through the time for morning prayers; but it was below zero and there was a foot of snow on the ground and I did not want to walk to shul and back;...

The lights will dim and a movie screen will roll down. A picture will appear on the screen — a picture of seventeen-year-old Keith Morency. A voice will boom — thirteen years, never absent, never late — not for the service of God, not to fulfill *mitzvot,* not to fill his soul with holiness, but for school! HOW DO YOU PLEAD NOW??!!?!

A similar message is conveyed in this week's Torah portion of *Naso*. At 176 verses, it is the longest of all portions. However, the length is somewhat deceiving as the last seventy or so repeat the same information, using the same words, over and over again.

The end of the portion discusses the dedication of the *Mishkan* and the offerings that the *Nesiim* (Princes) of each of the tribes brought. While the Torah describes the gifts as *korbanot* (sacrifices), they were, in actuality, a combination of items — some of which were offered and some of which had practical use. The offering of each Prince was identical. However, rather than simply giving a sum total or listing one Prince's offering and explaining that all of the others were the same, the Torah lists each and every gift separately, describing each individual component.

We know that the Torah does not contain extraneous material. In fact, the description of some important laws is so sparse that it could be termed almost cryptic (e.g., while the Torah sets forth the general prohibition against working on the *Shabbat,* the rabbis had to employ rather complex exegesis in order to define the 39 prohibited categories). Why then is the description of the gifts repeated over and over again?

The answer brings us back to Keith Morency. While genius, creativity, individuality, and originality are admired and celebrated, consistency and reliability have value, as well. Each day, each Prince's gift could have been different — a reflection of the differences between the twelve tribes themselves. In fact, it could have been somewhat like the Miss Universe pageant — where each contestant dresses in a costume designed to represent some unique aspect of her country. Or perhaps there could have been twelve days of "Can you top this?" with each Prince setting out to outdo, outspend, outshine the other.

Instead, they brought identical offerings; the same offering on every one of the twelve days. However, each Prince added something special — his own attitude. The gifts of day five were brought with the same enthusiasm as those on day one. The ones on days seven, nine, eleven, likewise the same. The purpose of the repetition is thus to tell and to teach us that the gifts were, in all ways, truly the same.

It is easy to get excited about the *seder* on Pesach, we do it only two nights a year. Oh, how we look forward to dancing on Simchat Torah — a once a year pleasure. But praying every day and studying every day and fulfilling all the other regular obligations requires focus and true greatness.

God's *Mishkan* was inaugurated with consistency. The hallmark of the service within it was measured regularity. We may not be able to face every day with the fresh enthusiasm, the sheer joy, of the new and exciting. However, we can try to face every day as a Prince — burdened, yet privileged.

BEHA'ALOTCHA
Secret Decoder Ring

When I was eight or nine years old, I remember bothering my parents to buy a new pair of Keds sneakers for me. A star athlete did not endorse these sneakers. They did not have heels or soles that lit up when you ran. They did not have air cushioning, springs, or gel-cells. The sneakers I wanted were plain old Keds — with a level, waffled, rubber sole, a blue canvas upper, and white cotton laces.

So why did I want these shoes? What made me exaggerate the pain caused by my current "too small" shoes and to peel some rubber from the toe guard to make them look more worn out? It was the secret agent kit that I would receive with my purchase — the very kit several of my classmates already carried.

For those of you who may not remember, let me describe the kit. Picture a small blue plastic rectangular box, about the size of the top digit of my adult thumb. One side of the rectangle was embossed with the "Keds" logo — the word "Keds" in block letters. The other side of the box had a small circular hole it its center. The

217

hole was filled with a removable plastic lens that functioned as a magnifying glass. Under the plastic was a piece of paper that was backed with foil, like a Wrigley's gum wrapper. Per the instructions, a secret agent could signal with this by reflecting sun light off the foil to someone else awaiting such a flash.

The box was split on one side and hinged on the other — in other words it could be opened. On one side of the inside of the box was a small piece of cardboard (backed by the foil visible from the hole) which was imprinted with the letters of the alphabet, together with the corresponding dots and dashes of Morse code. The other side of the box had a built in clicker — a mechanism incorporating a small piece of flexible metal that would emit a loud clicking sound when pressed. An operative equipped with the code and the clicker could send messages to one conversant in Morse code and receive messages from another properly equipped agent.

The shoes lasted far longer than my interest in the code kit. But my interest in codes merely lay dormant — and it sneaks up on me when I least expect it.

The Torah is full of codes; word codes, letter codes, number codes. In *"Bo:* The Three Bad Wolves," I mentioned the concept of *Gematria,* the system of utilizing the numeric equivalent of the Hebrew letters to derive matters both important and trivial. When we received the Torah, we received the written "Five Books of Moses," but we also received an oral tradition of interpretation and exegesis. Our sages teach that God "looked at the Torah and created the world." This means that the Torah, as blueprint for creation used by our eternal G-d, contains everything that was, is, or will be. In fact, in *Ethics of the Fathers* (5:26) the sage Ben Bag Bag is quoted as saying, "turn it and turn it for everything is in it."

These statements can be viewed in one of two ways — as metaphors or as being fully accurate. The metaphoric approach is reflected in the very book that you are reading. This year I have been searching for connections between my life and the words of the weekly Torah portion. This is not magic or metaphysics. The Torah was, of course, not written only for me and only for this year. Any one of us could (and should) find practical, useful, and concrete meanings and connections in the Torah every day and week of our lives. That is, in part, why the sages instituted the reading of the Torah portions on a weekly basis in the first place.

However, throughout the ages there have been a select few with the ability to enter the words of the Torah on an mystical level and to extract almost prophetic inspiration from those very words. In the past, this has been the province of the spiritual and kabalistic or, as in the case of the *Gaon* from Vilna (Rabbi Eliyahu of Vilna, 1720–1797), the purely brilliant. Recently, however, the ability to recognize the code has emerged from the realm of the mathematical and scientific — augmented by the capabilities of our computer age.

Late last week I read three articles, one each from *Time*, *Newsweek*, and the *USA Today*, reviewing a new book, *"The Bible Code"* by Michael Drosnin. In this book, the author, a journalist who has written for the *Washington Post* and the *Wall Street Journal*, claims that the letters in the text of the original Hebrew Bible, "reveals events that took place thousands of years after the Bible was written... In a few dramatic cases it has foretold events that then happened exactly as predicted." Needless to say, I was hooked. I wanted this book like I wanted my Keds secret agent kit. I went out and bought the book — whose subject matter is especially appropriate in light of this week's Torah portion. (I need some time to finish the book, so I am detouring to the weekly portion, before I come back and give you my thoughts about Mr. Drosnin's work).

The portion of *Beha'alotcha* is almost three separate portions in one. In fact, as we will see, it is demarcated as such. The first part is a continuation of the story line of the past two weeks. In *Bamidbar* the Jews were counted and their camp configured. In

Naso, the counting of the *Leviim* was concluded and their individual family roles set out. Also in *Naso,* the Princes of the tribes brought their offerings, marking the inauguration of the *Mishkan* and its first twelve full days of operation. *Beha'alotcha* begins with a description of the lighting of the *menorah* by the high priest, and continues with additional details about the *Mishkan* and the camp, and the commandment regarding fashioning the trumpets (which were used to signal the movement of the camp and coordination of the army, and to mark the celebration of certain days of holiday and rejoicing).

According to the commentators, at this point, a little over one year after the Exodus, the Jews were fully prepared to enter and conquer the Land of Israel.

However, before proceeding, we encounter something very unusual in the text of the Torah itself. The narrative is interrupted by an enlarged and inverted letter, the Hebrew letter *"Nun."* The text continues for two verses, *Bamidbar* 10:35-36, and then we encounter the second enlarged, inverted *"Nun."* The two verses framed by the *Nuns* describe the procedure for moving the Holy Ark. When the Ark begins its travels, say this. When it is once more placed at rest, say that.

As we pass these two verses, we move on to the third section of the portion, one that signifies an abrupt change of gears. The narrative continues with a description of the Jews as "complainers, evil in God's eyes." (*Bamidbar* 11:1). They miss "the good life in Egypt." They feel suffocated by Moshe's leadership. On the very doorstep of destiny, on the eve of the fulfillment of their promises and dreams, the people stumble backwards. They fall so far that, as we will see in next week's portion, *Shelach,* they will forfeit their right to the completed redemption and they will perish during a forty-year period of desert wandering.

In this my week of codes, the Torah portion presents an unusual one, the two inverted *Nuns.* What is their function; what do they reveal; what have they shown us; what will they tell us?

On the basic level of textual understanding, the *Nuns* represent a change of direction. Literally from the creation of the world, until this moment, Jewish history had been one relatively straight, chronological path leading to the establishment of the Jewish People — the keepers of the Torah — in the Land of Israel. However, because the people were not ready, God pushed the pause button. These *Nuns*, and the verses they frame, represent that pause.

A famous commentator, Rabbeinu Bachya (Rabbi Bachya Ben Asher, Spain, 1263-1340) notes that the two *Nuns* here each represent the numerical value of fifty. If one counts back fifty paragraphs in the Torah scroll from this paragraph, the landing point would be *Bamidbar* 2:17, which speaks of the *Mishkan* on the march. He thus notes that from the standpoint of context these two verses actually belonged over there.

A more mystical approach focuses on what the letter *Nun* represents. As described in the Talmud, *Nun* often represents *n'filah*, the fall of Israel. In this text, God is revealing two disasters, the destruction of the two Temples, one by the Babylonians and one by the Romans. However, the very words of the verses in this section, dealing with God's vengeance against our foes, and the return of the multitudes of Israel, soften the harshness of the prophecy by foretelling the ultimate redemption and return. The fact of this redemption is thus likewise foretold here.

Perhaps the timing of our final redemption could be ascertained through proper analysis. Nevertheless, while there are some secrets that are for us to learn and understand, there are clearly others for other eras, other times, and other minds.

In a sense, this is the thesis of the *"The Bible Code."* Mr. Drosnin suggests that the Torah has different levels for different times and technologies. For thousands of years B.C. (Before Computers) it has functioned, and was intended to function, as a source of law, ethics, and guidance. In our modern era, however, thousands of years after the Torah was given, mankind, according to *"The Bible Code,"* has the capability of deciphering the code and learning what it is that God (or according to Mr. Drosnin, a member of some more-advanced species) planned or expected to happen in our history.

I am not planning to summarize completely a 264-page book here along with the complex theories of Dr. Eliyahu Rips of Hebrew University. You can read the book or attend an Aish HaTorah "Discovery" seminar on the Torah Codes. However, the system can be described, in brief, as follows:

The ability to decipher the hidden messages is dependent upon the computer's ability to scan all of the letters of the Torah and to apply a "skip code" — taking every 10th, 57th, 2,086th or any other nth letter to search for a key word. When it finds the word, it rearranges the entire text of the Torah into an array whose length is the same number of characters as the skip pattern. Finally, the program scans the letters within the reconfigured array diagonally, vertically, backward and forward for other words related to the key word.

The results are incredible. Utilizing this procedure, and testing for statistical accuracy, Mr. Drosnin "found" direct references to the stock market collapse in 1929, the Kennedy assassination in Dallas, the San Francisco earthquake, the Gulf War, and the Rabin Assassination (complete with date, city, the name of the assassin, and the number of shots). Some of this later information was supposedly found in advance of the event, but the heeded warnings were ignored.

I can buy into some of the research (it has withstood peer review from statistical scientists), and it is certainly fascinating to see some of the information mined out of the Torah text. However, I begin to get uncomfortable when the focus turns from locating to predicting. If God intended us to know precise details about the future, one would think He would reveal them either directly (prophecy) or through an intense mystical or analytical Torah study approach — no gimmickry or automation. Thus, when actual predictions are asserted, like an atomic holocaust in Jerusalem in the year 2,000, or the start of World War III in 2,007, etc... I worry about how the Torah will be perceived.

Our Torah is eternal. Everything is in it and can be found in it. The path to such enlightenment, however, is by toiling to understand it and not using it as a secret decoder ring. Yes, it contains codes — like the code in *Beha'alotcha,* but the Torah is far more important as a roadmap to understanding God, than as a guide to history, past, present... and future.

SHELACH
Designated Hitter

As we enter the fourth week of *Bamidbar,* identified by some as The Book of Numbers, here are some numbers for you: 13–7 and 9–2. These are the scores of the first two victories of our Young Israel of Southfield Softball Team over the likes of Conservative powerhouses Shaare Tzedek and B'nai Moshe. I do not think that the Yankees (or for that matter, even the Tigers) have much to fear from our more lucky than good crew. However, winning is preferable to the alternative.

We play in a league here in Detroit comprised of area synagogues and temples. As the only Orthodox group represented (with one rabbi at shortstop and one in right-center, no less) we recognize a responsibility to comport ourselves in a manner that is consistent with the values we aspire to in our religious lives. We are competitive, and tempers can flare in the heat of battle, but we try to be vigilant against lapses of conduct or language that could reflect poorly on our chosen religious lifestyle. This may seem somewhat self-centered; after all — a game is a game, a player is a player — why should we think that our actions are subject to closer scrutiny than any other team's? The not so simple answer is because they are, much the same as Jackie Robinson knew that he was being held to a different standard — that's just human nature.

In reality, our experiences on the field have been comfortably routine — good games with teams looking to have some fun on summer Sunday mornings. What I am truly surprised by is the reaction I have encountered from some within the Orthodox community to these games. Some is really too broad a characterization — I should have said the reaction of one particular individual who felt it was his responsibility to inform me just how much he disapproves of any interaction with Conservative or Reform Jews.

Now we are not speaking of participating in their services, adopting any of their religious standards, or in any way approving of their interpretation of what the Torah requires of us. We are talking softball, on a neutral field, no less. We may disapprove of their direction, but they are part of our family (see, "*Emor:* Lawnmower Boy"). True, the history of Olympic sports has shown us that sports and politics can overlap (Berlin, Munich, Moscow, etc.). However, you must believe me when I say that these games are utterly devoid of any theological posturing, beyond crouching in the batter's box.

It is interesting that I was confronted with this divisive rhetoric during the week of the portion of *Shelach,* which relates the tragic story of the spies who were sent to scout the Land of Israel. Just one year removed from slavery, the Jewish People were poised to enter their new homeland. However, because ten of the twelve spies brought back a bad report, the people became discouraged — despairing of God's ability to deliver on His promise to give them the "land of milk and honey." In the end, God punished them by declaring that, although their children would enter the land, they themselves would perish during a forty-year period of wandering through the desert.

The ten spies who returned with the negative assessment were great men, at least when they left on the mission. Somehow, they became corrupted — be it from the influence of what they witnessed in Canaan or be it from an accentuation of their own fears, insecurities, and other emotional scars from the years of harsh bondage in Egypt. In the end, the why was almost irrelevant. An entire generation would perish because of those ten men. There were likely few more despicable villains, at least in terms of ultimate consequence, throughout our long history.

Nevertheless, in the Talmud we find that this infamous group provides the source for one of the most important mechanisms in our system of ritual. The Talmud states that a *davar shebikedushah,* certain holy ritual practices (such as public prayer or reciting the seven blessings for a bride and groom) require a *minyan* — a quorum of ten adult (over age 13) Jewish males. When the sages inquire as to the source or reference for this number — incredibly, the answer leads to the group of ten bad spies. How can it be that we look to these villains, these deliverers of national tragedy as the source of unity and holiness?

Without examining this too deeply, the answer involves the fact that there are powerful spiritual forces that are or can be called into play when ten Jews unite for a common goal. Ten men were able to cause calamitous destruction, but ten likewise can reach spiritual heights, can rebuild temples, and can change the world.

During a softball game, ten men are deployed in the field, in contrast with the nine of baseball. Part of me would like to tell my narrow minded, but perhaps well-intentioned friend not to start up with such a *minyan.* All kidding aside, he should be reminded that the men on that field are fellow Jews, they can be counted in a *minyan,* and they do have a vast capacity for channeling holiness. The balance between loving them but disapproving of their chosen path is fine. In fact, there are times and places where the contact can be benignly positive and avenues of understanding can be established. These games will not likely change anyone, they are not supposed to, but I believe they can reinforce some of our common national bonds.

Working with those bonds, to strengthen commitments to Torah, was the focus of the rest of my week. As Dinner Chairman of the annual banquet of Machon L'Torah, Jewish Learning Network of Michigan, I was called upon to assist a major fundraising effort for an organization dedicated to bringing and teaching Torah to those Jewish souls that express even the slightest interest in learning more about the Torah. In the weeks leading up to the event, our committee made hundreds of phone calls for sponsorships, ads, and ticket purchases. As the evening approached, we fine-tuned the program and sweated the details of room layout and seating arrangements. I exercised my prerogative as Chairman and Presidium member to request the privilege of introducing the Director of the organization and a tireless teacher of Torah, Rabbi Avraham Jacobovitz, who we lovingly call Rabbi J.

I choose to present an excerpt from this introduction for a number of reasons: 1) it will provide some insight into who the other two spies were, the ones that resisted corruption; 2) it explains what makes a real teacher of Torah, a real rabbi, unique; and 3) it will give me a further opportunity to express my admiration for Rabbi J and his work.

> Our sages ask, how did the two who did not join in, Yehoshua and Calev, remain steadfast? They explain that while in Israel on the scouting mission, Calev traveled to Hevron, to the burial place of our forefathers Avraham, Yitzchak, and Yaacov, to pray for their assistance. These prayers and the merit of our fathers protected him.
>
> Yehoshua, on the other hand, received a special blessing from Moshe when Moshe changed his name from

"Hoshea" to "Yehoshua" (which means "God will save you"). This blessing served as his shield. Yehoshua was Moshe's disciple. Moshe thus acted out of his responsibility, as a teacher, to protect his student.

We live in a world where the values and ideals of Torah are under constant assault. Many, even many who come from families that formerly observed our traditions, wander away. Only a small number, in *Shelach* one out of eleven, have the fortitude of a Calev to proactively handle religious obligations on their own. Most of us are like Yehoshua — students: students who need guidance — students who need a teacher who cares enough to protect us even if he cannot always be there to intercede directly. Yehoshua, the great prophet and leader, was saved only because he had such a caring teacher.

We in the Machon L'Torah family are likewise blessed with such a teacher and leader. Rabbi J is such a teacher. I cannot begin to count the number of times we had to reschedule meetings and discussions — not because of a conflicting class or family commitments — but because one of his students, one of our Machon family, needed his time for a personal matter. Rabbi J, the teacher, not only educates and guides, BUT HE CARES!

Thank God, the dinner was a success, financially and creatively. As I looked out at the crowd of supporters, I wondered whether next year, or the one after that, some of the seats will be filled with people whose first exposure to my way of thinking was between the white lines. Then again, who am I kidding — no one will likely be moved to such fundamental change because of softball. Yet, when Mashiach comes and instead of a banquet hall I gaze out over the courtyard of the Holy Temple in Jerusalem — guess what? All of those competitors will be there.

KORACH
Two Jews—Three Shuls

In late December every year, without fail, the newspapers (pick any paper, any city) run an article that quotes an array of psychological experts who describe the increase in the number of suicides and reported cases of depression around the secular holidays. While society around them dons its party hat, many lonely people are sent deeper into their own personal darkness. Some feel the pain of missed loved ones. Others experience rejection and abandonment. A few despair of their ability to meet the financial burdens brought about by overspending. What a fascinating contrast — sorrow triggered by the merriment and the joy of others.

Every year, during the week of the Fourth of July, I am forced to face some of these darker emotions. For the rest of my family summer is a great time, the best of times. The school year ended sometime mid to late June (remember, my wife is a teacher so she is off, as well), the weather is nice, and every day is filled with fun. All the while, I sit imprisoned in my office cell.

Then, it gets worse for me. In each of the past ten years (ever since we moved to the Midwest from the bosom of the family in NY/NJ), during this first real week of summer, I am asked to load up the whole crew and drive them to my in-law's summer home in Bradley Beach, NJ — where they stay for six to eight weeks. This is the price I must pay to ensure that my children experience their aunts, uncles, and cousins. This is the pound of flesh my wife extracts for my audacity in moving her away from all that was familiar and comforting.

Their summer is one of vacation and rejuvenation. For two months their days are filled with endless ball games, walks and bike rides along the boardwalk, visits to amusement parks, ice cream, swimming, and visits to the library. There is no shortage of playmates and companions for the kids — nearly thirty assorted cousins, under the age of thirteen, live within two blocks of the house. They may not truly appreciate how special these summers are now, but as adults they will look back on them with the embellishment of time and realize that these summers were part of the golden age of their childhood.

Contrast this with my summer. I sit home, abandoned, in a dark, lifeless home. The energy that pulses around me throughout the year — the laughter, the noise, the conversation, the stories (and the crying, whining, and *kvetching*) is six hundred miles away. I write, read, study, work, eat, sleep, and live — all by myself. Yes, I do have those all too short visits, every other weekend, to sustain me — as well as the nightly telephone calls, but these do not begin to compensate for the emptiness. The withdrawal is too sudden and too complete. (Do you all feel sorry enough for me yet? Do you hear the violins playing sad soulful music?)

All kidding aside, I manage, as does the family, to survive these summers. Sometimes the separation wears on me, but we more than make up for it when we are together in Bradley Beach — a lovely place to be this time of year. Whatever we need to enjoy the summer is in close proximity: There are kosher restaurants, grocery stores, and bakeries nearby; lots of family and friends live in the area; it is right on the coast — so the climate is nice; and it has not one, but two Orthodox synagogues within convenient walking distance.

The two synagogues are quite different in character. They both have nice facilities and have been in the city for many years. However, one is Ashkenaz, attended by Jews of Eastern European descent and the other is Sephardic, with members descended from immigrants from the North Africa and the Arab countries, like Syria, Iran and Iraq. While both are traditional, the custom and rituals of the services significantly different.

My family and I are of Ashkenazic descent. As such, for the first fifteen or so years that we visited Bradley Beach in the summer, we attended services at the Ashkenaz synagogue. The rabbi is a learned and gentle man. Most of the seventy or so summertime residents and visitors who attend services are Kim's relatives or long time family friends. However, the synagogue is run by the year-rounders. These people number about 15-20, and for the most part are elderly.

The Sephardic synagogue in Bradley Beach, for many years, was an outright mystery to me. Because I do not follow those customs, I never had occasion to attend, or even to step foot in the building. It was never even a real option for a change of pace. However, two years ago, the congregation hired a young, energetic rabbi, who really enjoyed teaching the children in the community. On *Shabbat* afternoons, the synagogue began to offer a youth program where the rabbi would study Torah with the children and entertain them with stories. We began to attend these programs and we got to know the rabbi and some of these Sephardic members of the community.

Several weeks later, "The Incident" took place at the Ashkenaz synagogue. On the *Shabbat* of "The Incident," I had, in fact, read the Torah for the congregation and chanted the *Haftorah* (supplemental reading from a book of the prophets that relates thematically to the weekly Torah reading). Joshua, my oldest, then ten, spiritedly led the singing after the *Musaf* service. Avi, then six, wanted in on the action, so he asked if he could put on a *talit* (prayer shawl) and ascend the *bimah* (dais) to help lead the chanting of the concluding song, the *"Adon Olam."* (Master of the World) (Now realize, the congregation sings this song at the very end of the services and after all the announcements. The hour is late, the *kiddush* (collation) and refreshments beckon in the social hall, and most of the men are standing to fold and to put their *talitot* and prayer books away and to engage in all the conversation they attempted to bottle up by remaining relatively quiet during the service. Additionally, the child leading the song essentially is heard for about two notes and one word before everyone else joins in and drowns him out with their voices.)

Avi was actually pretty excited since this was the first time he had mustered the courage to stand in front of such a crowd, albeit with his older brother by his side. We of course said yes and offered words of encouragement.

Avi was dressed for services the way a typical six-year-old would be dressed in the summer (at least any typical six-year-old dressed by my wife and mother-in-law — who are more aware of children's fashion designers than the editors of Vogue are of women's style). He had on a pair of slacks, a coordinating button-down short-sleeve shirt, and was wearing dress shoes (not sneakers or sandals). His hair was well groomed and was topped with a large blue-velvet yarmulke with an embroidered design around its bordering rim.

As he cautiously sang out the "Ah" of the word *"Adon,"* the elderly president of the synagogue stood up and yelled "halt!" He proclaimed that Avi could not be allowed to continue to lead this song and should be removed from the *bimah*... because he was not wearing a suit or sports jacket.

If I may digress for a moment, many synagogues, like the synagogue in Bradley Beach, have standards or rules of conduct for those wishing to participate in or to lead the service. Some require the wearing of hats. Some, like Bradley Beach, require jackets. Some require both. These rules are grounded in respect for the service and congregation and are generally intended to apply to adults leading the important or operative parts of the service. They are not typically applied to children leading a concluding song!

Avi was shocked, and I was livid. How dare this man embarrass a child (embarrass anyone for that matter) who only wanted to join in and sing? How dare this man take it upon himself to disrupt the service and its decorum, in the name of upholding them? How dare this man start up with my Avi?

I rose from my seat, walked up to the *bimah,* took Joshua and Avi by the hand, and walked away proclaiming, "Don't expect me to step foot in this asylum again" (or something to that effect — I have been assured by others that I did not use any expletives or threaten anyone with physical violence). Starting with the afternoon services that day, and continuing for the rest of that summer, and the next, we did not return, despite the pleas of our friends and family (sadly, neither the rabbi nor the offending president, ever chose to get involved to smooth things over).

In reality, the switch was not that hard. In many ways I like the Sephard synagogue better, especially once I got used to the service. The rabbi was far more dynamic, the membership was much more accepting of and accommodating to the children (even giving toys and treats to those who attended the services and programs), and the refreshments were better.

However, as we return to Bradley Beach for another summer, I am faced with a dilemma. The Sephard rabbi has moved on to another congregation, taking away the biggest incentive for remaining there. Additionally, in light of my mother-in-law's passing, this will likely be the last summer that we will spend extensive time in New Jersey, so the nostalgic part of me wants to experience things that contain more of the good memories of the past. Thus, I am tempted to return to the Ashkenaz synagogue. On the other hand, part of me is stubborn and feels that I am somehow giving in, losing the war after two years of battling. How should I decide?

This dilemma closely parallels the story line in this week's portion of *Korach*. As the plot unfolds, Korach, a *Levi*, is not satisfied with the status quo. Moshe, his cousin, is the political leader. Aharon, brother of Moshe and likewise a cousin to Korach, was appointed high priest. Aharon's sons got to serve as *kohanim*. A younger cousin received the appointment as Prince of the Tribe of Levi. Korach, himself, is wealthy (having recovered Yoseph's treasure during the Exodus), is a scholar in his own right, and displays leadership qualities.

He gathers a group of followers, including the delightful Datan and Aviram, and questions the right of Moshe and Aharon to lead. "We are all holy people," he shouts. We, likewise, have the right to call the shots. Things start to get ugly.

Moshe, as you can imagine, is beside himself. He has, with God's assistance, rescued these people from bondage, taught and given them the Torah, supervised their organization into a nation, overseen the building of the *Mishkan,* and helped to assure that they were provided with their physical needs for food, drink, and shelter. Let us also not forget that he has successfully pleaded their case and rescued them from the annihilation of Divine wrath after the sin of the Golden Calf. Yet, in the worst case of "what have you done for me lately" in recorded history, Korach tries to rally followers to depose and reject Moshe and his teachings and choices.

Moshe turns to God for advice on how to handle this rebellion. God proposes a little "contest" to establish who represents His word and the best interests of the Jewish People. Whoever believes that they represent the truth of the matter, is instructed to take a pan full of incense and to stand in a certain place at a certain time. God will signify His choice of the victor by sending forth fire and accepting the offering from that man's pan. The loser (or losers) will all perish.

Now picture this. All the Jews know that Moshe can speak with God directly, that he has never been wrong regarding God's words, and that he has coordinated miracles and events far bigger than this face off. In other words, Aharon is as close to a sure thing as the morning sunrise. In contrast, Korach has no track record, his companions are certified troublemakers, and they are told that no matter who wins — there will only be one "panhandler" left standing. How is it then that Korach and two hundred and forty-nine others (one man, On ben Pelet, stayed home — because his wife was smart enough to get him drunk and hung over) could arrive at the appointed time and place "ready to rumble?"

The answer is they were so supremely stubborn that they were blinded even to this obvious path of destruction. They were swallowed by the earth because they were unable to swallow their pride. Sure, there are times that it is important to take a stand. But, there are plenty of times where taking the stand, or more accurately holding the line, quickly loses its significance. Needless to say, when the consequences of maintaining the position begin to outweigh any benefit, it is time to make a graceful, strategic, retreat. A dead soldier cannot fight tomorrow's war.

Looking back, I am upset and disappointed with what happened in the Ashkenaz synagogue — nearly two years ago. But I will not gain anything by remaining stubborn - I may even lose something precious. So this *Shabbat,* barring unforeseen circumstances — like the grand opening of a third shul — I will casually reenter the synagogue, sit in my old seat, and act like nothing ever happened.

CHUKAT
Stones and Sticks

Technology has radically altered the way things are done in the workplace over the past thirteen or so years of my professional career. When I first started out, as a trial attorney for the IRS, I either dictated or hand-wrote the required correspondence, pleading, brief, or memorandum and gave it to my secretary. She (or he) in turn, typed or transcribed my rantings and scribblings into a draft document and returned it to me. With red pen in hand, I carefully reviewed this work, striving to include all stylistic, substantive, and editorial changes and corrections. The secretary would then type a final version with the required number of carbon copies (in the IRS there were yellow, pink, blue, and white copies that went into different types of files or to different offices).

Secretaries in our office did not have desktop computers or word processors (although the office had one Wang word processing system, with a specially trained operator, for use on major litigation projects). They had electric typewriters with no memory capacity (it was a cause for celebration when a few new machines came in with four pages of memory). We made corrections with liquid paper corrective fluid and these had to be made on all copies separately. If a document needed extensive correction or revision, the secretary retyped it, from scratch (although occasionally we would get lucky and could get away with redoing a page or two), often resulting in a slew of new errors.

The process was slow, cumbersome, annoying, and inefficient. However, because we did not have electronic mail, desktop computers, or even easily accessible fax machines the pace was slower. Additionally, because alterations often meant retyping from scratch, both attorneys and reviewers were careful not to change things for change's sake.

As the years rolled by, the secretaries each received PCs with full-featured word processors. In time, each attorney had a computer in his or her desk. For some, this meant near independence from administrative help, as they preferred to type and prepare their own documents and avoid outside interference. Others, like me, jumped in part way — using the computer as a research tool, a communications device, and for spreadsheet programs, but still preferring to let the secretary handle most document creation.

Several years ago, during yet another secretarial change-over, I realized that I could not remain so dependent on the administrative help — the flow of my projects got interrupted far too often resulting in unnecessary deadline pressure and stress. Accordingly, I forced myself, two finger typing style and all, to master the nuances of our word processing software. From that time forward, I have been operating in a nearly independent capacity from my secretary, relegating to her, for the most part, only ministerial functions like making copies, preparing mailing labels and the like.

Toward the end of last summer, my then current secretary left. After a succession of temporary replacements, the department hired Donna (not her real name). The hiring process took longer than usual because of a fundamental disagreement over the qualifications and skill level of the candidates. One side advocated hiring an experienced, seasoned assistant, who would be of particular value, with both legal typing and organizational skills, if and when we became embroiled in litigation. The other side stressed that since most of the professional staff was well versed with the software applications and had become accustomed to doing much of what had traditionally been secretarial for themselves, we should hire a person of lower experience and ability so as not to risk putting a capable person in a position that would often not be challenging. Less experience, and thus less dollars, won.

Donna is pleasant enough and does try hard. However, her lower skill level results in many harmless and some not so harmless mistakes. This in turn, means that we have to expend more time and effort at the start of projects — to assure that the instructions are fully understood, and at their completion — to affirm that all instructions were carried out correctly. I could go on and on with examples of how her lack of attentiveness, initiative, and organization, have interfered with the smooth flow of our work. Getting up on that soapbox, however, will not accomplish anything.

There is, of course, another side to this story. Not Donna's side, per se, but Donna's side as viewed through the eyes of a soap opera writer. Donna had just returned to the United States from abroad with her three-year-old son shortly before she arrived to work here. She was recently divorced from a U.S. serviceman. She came to Detroit, where her family lives, to escape this bad marriage and to try and start over. She arrived without a job, without a place of her own, and with only a few belongings that she was able to ship back here. To make matters worse, her ex-husband was already delinquent in the required alimony and child support payments.

She was fortunate to find a job, an apartment, and a daycare provider — an important triangle of support (a three-legged stool). However, these co-dependent elements began to interfere with each other, especially when exacerbated by other pressures (like those exerted by the ex's refusal to pay). Her son was not happy at school/day care — which led to behavioral issues and clashes — which led to the need to find a new care provider. A potential new care provider was not conveniently located to home, which led to a search for a new apartment. The increased rental cost and higher day care cost led to increased financial pressure. All of these distractions, led to a decreased level of performance (from a level that was, at best, tolerable) that legitimately raised questions about her continued employment. She is "treading on thin ice," "hanging on a thread," has "been read the riot act" by management. The "straw that breaks the camel's back" could be the "next one down the pipe."

And then came this week. We are concluding negotiations with the IRS on a number of tax issues involving millions of dollars. I have been working extremely hard on an issue where the legal authority did not seem to favor us. After digging through old cases and reexamining the facts of the transaction, I discovered an approach that would, at least, provide some negotiating leverage. Partly because I sometimes think more clearly when I write things long hand and partly because I write faster than I can type, I sat down and wrote a 50 page (25 pages typed) position paper and asked Donna to type it so that I could circulate it for comment — to get a reality check on the strength of my arguments.

After several days (far longer than it should have taken), Donna handed me a draft. Without exaggerating, this was the worst piece of typing I had ever received in my life. Quite a number of sentences and paragraphs were missing. Fonts and tab codes were messed up. Many words were misspelled (and she supposedly "spell-checked" it). Before I could begin to edit the analysis, I had to correct the draft. In order to correct it, I had to compare it with my original draft, line by line — a process that took several hours that I really did not have to waste. Needless to say, I was fuming. The question soon became, was I upset enough and was Donna interfering with the efficiency of my work enough for me to take affirmative steps to have her replaced? I had to take a step back and balance my professional needs and the good of my employer with Donna's abilities (and our realistic expectations thereof) and her situation.

For some, this decision would have been a "no brainer" — simply dispose of one part and replace it with another that should be as good, or hopefully better. Not to give myself a pat on my moral back, but I do try to conduct myself in all aspects of life by Torah ethics. Thus, notions like "judging others favorably" and "judge as you yourself would expect to be judged," flashed in front of my face like neon signs.

Fortunately, I was able to find a quick fix in this week's portion of *Chukat*. This portion is one of the more varied and interesting in the entire Torah. It contains the laws of the Red Heifer (I will not try to explain it, even King Solomon did not fully understand), the deaths of Miriam and Aharon, the incident of the rock (more on this later), some good battles, and the fiery and copper serpents. What is perhaps most interesting (though I am not going to digress) is the fact that the "action" in the portion of *Chukat* takes place 38 years (give or take a few months) after the narratives in *Shelach* and *Korach*. Essentially, the Torah has fast-forwarded and skipped over the experience of the Jews in the wilderness in those intervening years.

The guidance I received this week was from "the Rock," not the movie, the professional wrestler, or the insurance company, but a rather infamous biblical incident. While the approximately two million Jewish men women and children wandered in the desert, God provided for their needs in a variety of ways; manna fell from heaven to feed them; the clouds of glory surrounded them providing shelter and protection from the elements and from potential threats to their security; their clothes miraculously grew and remained fresh and in good repair; and their water source was a special well.

The well dated back to the time right after the Exodus. The Jews needed water, so God instructed Moshe to strike a particular rock with his staff and water flowed, as if from a bottomless well. The rock/well (not named Norman) accompanied them during their sojourn through the desert. However, in the 40th year, when Miriam died, the well dried up.

The people were not particularly pleased with this turn of events. They gathered around Moshe and complained and protested rather vociferously. Moshe was now 119 years old, he had watched the previous generation, the generation of the Exodus, die out because of a similar lack of faith and stiff-necked nature. He had little patience or tolerance for such behavior.

He turns to God for guidance and was instructed to gather the people in front of "the rock." When all are assembled, Moshe and Aharon merely have to speak to the rock and it will give forth water. Moshe, gathers the people, lifts his staff, and hits the rock twice — after which abundant water flows.

As a result of this action, God chastises Moshe for not following His directive and for missing an opportunity to sanctify His name. Even worse, God punishes Moshe by decreeing that he will not lead the people into the Holy Land. The great leader, teacher, *tzaddik,* Moshe, who faithfully led, protected, taught, and served for nearly 40 years, is humbled because he hit "the rock" instead of speaking to it!

Obviously, this story has a lot more to it. The commentators and the *Midrash* go a long way toward filling in the blanks. However, I would like to remain on the surface level and to view this as representing the consequences of one simple action. Moshe faced a frustrating situation — he was disappointed in his charges and he saw his life's work, the establishment of the Jewish People in their homeland, in dire jeopardy. There were two ways for him to deal with the situation — softly — talking, coaching, teaching — or harshly — hitting, rebuking, belittling. God instructed him to try the less confrontational approach. After all, this was a new generation of Jews who did not experience oppression but rather were nurtured by Divine grace. Moshe, however, fell back on the old ways. He thus damaged their self-esteem and hastened his own departure.

Perhaps down the road I will have to play the heavy and take a sterner approach. However during this week of *Chukat* I will speak to the rock rather than hit it (verbally, or course). If I, and the other attorneys and professionals, invest a little extra time, explain things more clearly, temporarily lower our expectations and allow extra lead time, then maybe Donna will make it, after all.

BALAK

What You Don't Know...
May Hurt You

This had to happen sooner or later. I am just glad that it took this long. I am floating through a week in which absolutely nothing of note is happening. The family is away in New Jersey, so the children are not around to inspire me. The biggest case that I was working on in the office just settled, so I am in that lull between the excitement of completing an old assignment and developing a "full steam ahead" commitment to a new one. Thank God, we have not encountered any tragedies — our close friends and family are healthy, alive, and for the most part, content. Likewise, there is nothing special to celebrate — no births, weddings, Bar or Bat Mitzvahs, anniversaries, birthdays, new jobs, retirements, etc. The world seems so calm and quiet that even this week's newspapers have been as sparse and thin as I can remember.

Things may actually be quiet. However, this may only be a brief calm interlude. Many events and actions that soon might or will affect us are fermenting away from the glare of our attention. We glide through our lives blissfully ignorant of the forces that swirl around us. Certainly, we have enough to deal with without an Oliver Stone, conspiracy laden, world-view. Yet, at a moment's notice previously unseen forces can impact us and cause everything from minor inconvenience to tragedy or from simple pleasure to full scale celebration.

Here are a few examples of what I mean:

Bill is sitting at his desk doing his usual good and conscientious job. At that moment, totally unknown to Bill, his boss is meeting with the corporate comptroller, who mandates a 50% reduction in the departmental budget — Bill will soon be history. Alternately, the comptroller informs Bill's boss that the department will be expanding and that there will be several new opportunities for promotions — Bill is about to receive new responsibilities and a raise. In both scenarios Bill is the same achieving, hard working, loyal employee. However, based upon conversations and decisions of which he is unaware, his professional life is about to change, for better or for worse.

Jim drove his car through a deep puddle in last month's flash flood. Some water splashed on a vital engine part and began to corrode it. Jim is driving around, going about his business, yet day by day the unseen decay wears through the part. On the morning of an important appointment, he turns the ignition and the car simply does not start. A steady, unseen force has just interfered with his plans.

Brian is trying to secure the last remaining spot on the traveling soccer team. He is competing against Eric and Mark, and is clearly the better player. At the end of the practice, before the coach announces his final decision, Eric's father, having comes straight from work and still wearing a suit, comes running out to the field, waving to his son. Coach, a small business owner, recognizes Eric's father as one of his major customers. Without a word or a nod exchanged,

Brian no longer has a roster spot. Instead, Eric is on the team.

I am old enough to realize that while this week may be quiet, there is no way to possibly gauge how important it may, some day, turn out to be — or not be. I am equally ignorant of tragedies averted and missed opportunities. From a theological prospective, what am I to make of such forces?

This also happens to be one of the major themes of this week's portion of *Balak*. The portion opens with the Jewish Nation on the move toward their promised homeland shortly after they vanquished the mighty Emorite kings, Sichon and Og. These kings were among the most aggressive and feared in the region. Yet, with God's help, the Jews swatted them away like flies.

Balak, the king of Moav, astutely observed that he would not stand a chance if he got in their way. If the Jews could obliterate Sichon and Og, his nation would cease to exist, even if it combined forces with neighboring Midian. As he called together a leadership conference to discuss defense options, he quickly dismissed the possibility of military engagement. Balak was wise enough to realize that the Jews' prime advantage, their most potent weapon, was spiritual; or from his vantage point — mystical and magical. Any possible winning strategy against them would have to incorporate such elements — they had to fight fire with fire. Balak and his council decided that their best alternative would be to hire a prophet/sorcerer named Bilaam.

We are aware of certain physical laws of nature. There are likewise spiritual laws. Among these spiritual rules is the concept that God keeps or allows a certain balance in the world between the forces or powers of good and those of evil. This is necessary in order to preserve mankind's freedom of choice. If the righteous were the only ones that could call upon spiritual forces to accomplish the supernatural or miraculous, over time most people would choose to believe in such clearly superior power. Thus, God has allowed wicked people to practice the so called "Black Arts" — sorcery, magic, witchcraft, necromancy, astronomy, etc.

This is not the "X-Files" or the "Twilight Zone." I refer to practices that are catalogued in the Torah and discussed in the Talmud and in *Midrashic* sources. Thus, if Moshe had the ability to split the sea or to hold the sun in its place in the sky, there had to be an evil counterbalance — someone with equivalent powers. Similarly, if Moshe had superior prophetic abilities, there had to be someone else, an "anti-Moshe" of sorts, who could access similar lines of Divine communication. That person was Bilaam, the non-Jewish sorcerer/ prophet.

Bilaam was the master of the dark side (Darth Vader to Moshe's Obiwan Kenobi). He knew how to curse a person and to cause tangible damage. He knew how to deceive others into following and supporting his distorted ways. Thus, when Balak decided that he needed a "secret" weapon in his war of stealth against the Jews, he turned to Bilaam.

Balak sends messengers to Bilaam and ultimately offers him a fortune if he will successfully curse the Jews and deter them from their march of conquest. Despite God's initial admonition to pass up the contract, Bilaam accepts. With much fanfare and hocus pocus — building altars, changing locations, offering a great number of animal sacrifices, Bilaam tries to curse the Israelites three times. Each time, however, God places other words into his mouth — first words of advise and observation, later words of blessing.

Perhaps most interesting thing about this whole incident is how it made its way into the Torah. Was it historically significant? Maybe. Was it important to record these prophecies about the Jewish people, as well as other nations of the world? Yes. But no one was present to witness the unfolding story. Neither Moshe, nor any other Jew, witnessed or heard the council meeting between the elders of Midian and Moab, the negotiations with Bilaam, or the curse attempts. How is it that it came to be recorded with such precise detail in our portion?

The answer is that God communicated what happened to Moshe and dictated that it be included. Once included, the words became part of the Torah and not unsubstantiated hearsay or the ranting of wicked fanatics (which explains why the opening words of Bilaam's blessing — "How goodly are your tents O Jacob, your dwelling places O Israel" [*Bamidbar* 24:5] have been incorporated into our daily prayers — to show that they were not the words of an evil man, they were holy words from God). God deliberately left Moshe out of the loop while the story unfolded to illustrate that we are often faced with threats that we may well be oblivious to and that we must rely on Him to safeguard our security and best interests.

The portion of *Balak* thus shows us that our faith is rewarded. Sometimes it is difficult to picture God — to know whether He is listening to our prayers, to perceive whether we truly matter to Him. We may not see Him, feel Him, or hear Him. But we, like the Jewish Nation in *Balak,* are also truly unaware of much of what happens around us, even events with the potential to change our lives. If you can accept and understand the existence of these unseen forces, it is not so great a leap to appreciate the One who helps us to navigate through them.

PINCHAS
Death and Taxes

A few years back I attended a week-long tax seminar in Jacksonville, Florida. I was thinking of that seminar because it occurred around this time of year and I remember the arrangements I had to coordinate with the local Orthodox rabbi both for *Shabbat* and for the Ninth of Av (the solemn day of national fasting and mourning to commemorate the destruction of both Holy Temples in Jerusalem) which is coming soon this year, but which fell during that week in Jacksonville. The instructor at one of the sessions, a tax lawyer for the IRS, walked to the podium to introduce herself. She mentioned that since her husband was a mortician, their friends had nicknamed them "Death and Taxes."

Death and taxes are said to be among the only sure things in life. One does not ordinarily think of them as being interrelated — i.e. if one is dead, one no longer needs to be concerned with taxes. However, this week placed me smack in the middle of two situations where death and taxes both played prominent roles.

I do not keep my job (tax lawyer) a secret, and those that know my professional background are aware that I spent a few years working for the IRS. For the past ten years, I have worked exclusively as in-house corporate counsel. Thus, I have not represented individual clients (and generally cannot without my employer's consent), and I have not been remotely involved with the IRS's collection side. Yet, once or twice a year I will field a call from one of our local rabbis (on behalf of a member of community), or from a Jewish organization, or from a family member asking for help out of a mess that they often created themselves.

Their facts patterns are quite similar — they fell behind on tax payments, their accountant made a mistake, or they forgot to include some income on their return, and now the IRS wants to collect and has a lien on their property (which is mangling their credit). Over the years I have extricated schools, synagogues, assorted relatives, and even a *Mohel* (person who performs ritual circumcision) from the clutches of the IRS. In some instances, we were able to make corrections that greatly reduced the liability, in others we were able to negotiate a compromise, and in one case, we were at least able to negotiate a payment plan that everyone could live with.

Whenever I successfully wrap up one of these cases, I walk away with the satisfaction of knowing that I made a difference, that I used my skills to effectively help someone when they needed it most (since I do not accept payment for these services, it's the least I can walk away with). Nevertheless, there is some emptiness that also creeps in at this time. After you traipse through someone else's financial affairs, especially their dirty laundry, they tend not to look at you quite the same anymore. Yes they are grateful, but you are a reminder to them of the mess they created, of the disaster that almost brought them down. Sometimes you lose a friend by helping that friend.

Early in the week I was pulled aside in shul by one of my friends. He explained that his father, a man in his mid-seventies, had somehow generated a significant liability for back taxes and that the IRS was applying heavy pressure. My friend feared not only for his father's finances, but for his health, as well. With a liability in excess of several hundred thousand dollars hanging over his head, and with no apparent ability to pay, the stress on him personally and on his wife was extremely dangerous.

I agreed to do what I could. I met with my friend's parents, tried to assess the cause of the problem, examined a variety of documents, and decided on a general approach toward a solution. To make a long, and otherwise tedious, story short, I was able to negotiate a rather minimal payment plan (virtually token payment) and the Revenue Officer consented to halt all further collection efforts, at least as long as my clients made all the scheduled payments in a timely fashion. There is more work to be done here, but the most pressing problem has been alleviated.

The end of the week brought a "death and taxes" problem of a much more intimate nature. As I wrote earlier, my mother-in-law passed away three months ago. She left behind an estate and a will to direct how it should be distributed. This week, her children and their spouses met with Mom's lawyer to discuss how the estate would be administered and how the estate taxes would be paid. At this meeting we learned that she owned some shares of a family business and that it would, thus, be necessary to arrange a meeting with other members of the extended family to better understand how to deal with this wrinkle.

Since Kim and I are the only non-New Jerseyites, we are not as readily available as everyone else involved. So meeting number three this week was hastily arranged. To be honest, we approached the meeting with a good deal of apprehension. It is one thing to sit down and talk with uncles, cousins, and siblings at a joyous occasion, at a family picnic, or just during a visit. It is quite another to talk about matters that have a direct financial impact on everyone. I have seen brothers stop talking for years over who should have picked up the tab at a restaurant; I have seen a child, a grown successful professional with a family of his own, turn his back on his parents because he was not given something he felt entitled to; and I have seen a wedding called off and a young couple broken apart over who should pay for the extra guests at the celebration. Our discussions would likely move in to quite dangerous areas of trust, fairness, and would be layered with healthy doses of family history, tradition, and "how things have been done." Thankfully, the discussions were amicable and we all moved in the direction of simplifying many of the complexities (this is basically jargon for — this is all private family business and while it was an important event and thus something I needed to write about, I am certainly not predisposed to reveal anything but the sketchiest details about the situation and what took place).

Interestingly, but, of course, not coincidentally, a similar "family" discussion took place in this week's portion of *Pinchas.* The beginning of the portion deals with the aftermath of Pinchas' zealous action of killing a Jewish prince and a Midianite princess in quite a violent, and aggressive manner in order to halt a plague caused by the immorality of the Israelites. The end of the portion sets out a detailed list of the special communal sacrifices associated with each regular day and holiday during the course of the year. The middle, is what really drew my attention.

In *Pinchas,* the Torah, for the second time in the book of *Bamidbar,* details a census of the number of Jewish adult males. The census here lists the major families of each tribe, as well as the population of each tribe. The Torah itself (*Bamidbar* 26:51-53) explains that this census had a unique purpose. The data assembled would establish the basis for dividing the Land of Israel among the Jewish People. Each tribe and each family was allotted a portion. These portions were further subdivided and distributed to the adult male members of each tribe. The size of these portions was dependent, to a large extent, on the number of people that were to be accommodated — based upon this counting.

When the count was finished, five women posed a unique question to Moshe. The five women were sisters — the daughters of a man named Tzelaphchad, who, as they represent, died in the desert for reasons other than participation in the failed Korach rebellion. Tzelaphchad did not have any sons, no male heirs. The women thus asked Moshe what was to become of his portion, of their family portion, in an inheritance scheme identified solely with adult males.

Believe it or not, Moshe did not know. He had to approach God directly with the question. God proclaimed that the women were absolutely correct. Under the circumstances, their father's portion should be preserved. Thus, he established a full set of inheritance rules, which include a provision for a transfer to a daughter in the absence of sons.

As I reviewed this entire exchange, especially in light of my recent experiences, I was quite puzzled. Why should those women have cared what happened to their father's land? First of all, they were still in the desert — the Land of Israel had not been conquered yet. This property was not the family farm or the place where they were raised. Second, the women, presumably, were married or likely would get married some day. Accordingly, their husbands would be receiving similar portions from their own families anyway.

We see from their actions and their passionate defense of their rights, just how important these matters are to people, even if there is not complete rationality. For some, the motivation is pure financial self-interest. Yet others feel a need to preserve family heritage or the family name. The death of the loved one can give life to buried prejudices, petty hatreds, and greedy opportunism. If we are able to follow the lead of these women and remember at all times to bring and to keep our "Judgement before God" (*Bamidbar* 27:5) then perhaps we can continue to preserve many important lifetime relationships, rather than to squander them.

MATTOT-MASEI
Fare Wars

I love fare wars. That may not be an entirely accurate statement. Usually I am rather indifferent to fare wars. Several times a year, because an airline is trying to establish itself in a new market, or trying to grab larger market share, or trying to fill excess capacity on certain routes, it will price tickets to certain destinations at an outrageously low level (as compared to regular fares). Within a day or so most of the other airlines that service the same markets will match the fares — that all stay low until someone finally raises them. This rise, in turn, is the signal for all the others to likewise raise fares to pre-fare war levels, and above.

Through the duration of the fare war, a traveler can get a real bargain if he or she just happened to need a ticket to the blessed destination. However, this means little to the person who planned and booked a vacation months ago, or scheduled some event or convention and made necessary airline reservations way in advance. In other words: why should I care if I could travel to Phoenix for $69 each way or to Indianapolis for $39 each way? I have no need to travel to those cities, and would likely not go if they were giving tickets away for free.

This week, however, I do love fare wars because for once I was able to take advantage. As I mentioned a few weeks ago (see, "*Korach:* Two Jews — Three Shuls") the wife and kids are vacationing in New Jersey and I am "home alone" (lower case). This separation is alleviated somewhat by the fact that I generally travel to be with them every other weekend. Much as I would like to go every week, it would have been rather costly, and somewhat extravagant, to purchase eight round trip fares. Even with the luxury of being able to make the requisite advanced purchases and seizing upon the opportunity of a late spring sale, the cost of multiple air fares quickly adds up.

Since I enjoyed a weekend visit last week, I expected to spend this weekend at home. However, Friday morning, during my drive into work, I heard a commercial on the radio announcing service to Newark by a brand new airline at an introductory fare of $49 each way. The fare was being offered until next Monday for travel through next Thursday. My mind immediately associated this, with the term FARE WARS. As soon as I got to my desk, I called down to corporate travel to inquire whether there were any flights departing early that afternoon with available space and at the special price. Not surprisingly, there were, on another major airline, no less. Next, I had the travel agent check for a late Sunday evening return. My luck held, there was a seat Sunday at 6 P.M. at the discount price. "Book 'em," I exclaimed joyfully. Hence, a mere five hours later I was on my way for a bonus weekend.

As a brief aside, all of these airfare gyrations reminded me of a comedy routine I once heard from George Carlin, or maybe it was Dave Barry. Regardless... the gist of the bit centered on questioning why the computer industry is constantly driven to create machines with increasingly greater memory and computing capacity. The answer suggested was that the demand for greater capacity is dri-

ven by a little publicized FAA (Federal Aviation Administration) regulation. Apparently, the airlines are required, by Federal regulation,
to determine and charge a different fare to each and every passen-
ger on every type of flight. A same day round trip is different from
a round trip with an overnight stay, and different from seven, fourteen, or twenty-one day advance purchases, and different from
flights with a Saturday night stay, and different from a trip origi-
nating on a weekend or holiday, etc. I know, as I write this, it does
not seem quite as funny. I guess that's why Messrs. Carlin and Barry
are famous and successful comedians and I am so far an unpub-
lished author of whatever this is that I have been writing since last
October.

Returning to the trip, much as I treasure all time with my family, there is a price to pay — besides the airfare. I made the trip last
week, as regularly scheduled. The trip this week was a bonus. Next
week, I am scheduled, once again, to depart for a regularly scheduled, advance purchase weekend. All told, this is a stretch of three
weeks of packing and unpacking, being neither here nor there. In
a sense I am a real "Nowhere Man," (or more appropriately "A
Traveling Man"). My home does not feel like home, because the
family is away. While I am certainly welcomed most enthusiastically in New Jersey, I feel that I am somehow intruding on everyone
else's vacation.

In reality, this traveling is but a mild inconvenience. It may even
be, though I admit this reluctantly, a welcome change of pace from
the monotonous routine and rhythm of the rest of the year. Living
in and out of a suitcase for three weekends does not begin to compare with the hassle and trauma of a relocation. Believe me, I have
been there.

During my life, I have lived in Kansas City, Chicago, Upstate
New York, Northern Georgia, Jerusalem, Manhattan, Northern New
Jersey, Cleveland, and Detroit — which averages out to a move
every four years. Each move was occasioned by what at the time

seemed like a compelling reason — a new job, an educational opportunity, the need to try something different, etc. The moves of my childhood were based on my parents' decisions about what was best for them and the family. Decisions about the moves I precipitated were hopefully made with similar reasoned judgement.

Every step along the way has its own place in my memory and makeup. I have encountered many different people, some in more than one time and place. Each city or region has a unique pace and style. The constantly changing landscape provided many experiences, both good and bad, that have shaped the person that I am.

Whenever one settles in a new community, one quickly finds out that there are two types of people; the natives and the transplants. The natives have been in town their whole lives (we are talking post-World War II lives — even today, over fifty years after the destruction of Jewish communal life in Europe, there are survivors who established new lives in America, many of whom arrived with their young children who were born in the Displaced Persons Camps). All the rooms and fixtures in the shuls and schools are named after their parents and grandparents, they went to school with every major or minor celebrity in town; they are part of a tangled, nearly incomprehensible, web of family interrelationships; and they are very snug and secure about their role and sense of belonging to the fabric of communal life (in other words, they were here long before you, and expect to be here long after, so, as long as you do not wear out your welcome, you are tolerated as a welcomed guest).

The transplants are anyone not considered to be a native by the natives (although being related to a native often qualifies one more readily for native status). Some transplants have lived in their community longer than they have lived anywhere else, they have even raised their families here. But for some reason or another (probably because they have always considered themselves to be New Yorkers and have pined for the bright lights like Ava Gabor on

"Green Acres") they have never crossed over the line to earn the native moniker.

As a perpetual transplant, I have a certain affinity for other transplants and embrace the benefits of such a nomadic existence. On the other hand, I can appreciate the security and sense of belonging inherent in native status. Though considering the Jewish historical experience of constant exile and upheaval, it is perhaps oxymoronic that there could be a Jew who considers him or herself to be a native, with its accompanying feeling of smug security, anywhere. (Not coincidentally, this week is the middle of "The Three Weeks" — a period of serious reflection about the root causes of the exile that culminates on the Ninth of Av — a day of national religious mourning and lamentation over the endless stream of massacres, pogroms, exiles, inquisitions, expulsions, and Holocausts over the past two millennium. This period serves as an annual reminder that until Mashiach comes and God declares an end to the exile, no Jew will ever be a native, even in the Land of Israel itself.)

Throughout the years and all the moves, I have never paused to ask "Why?" Why have I lived in these different places? Why have I, and my father before me, moved so many times, when we know so many, including other close relatives, who have remained stationary virtually their entire lives? Even more perplexing to me, however, is the associated free will v. predestination question — are these moves the products of our choices and decisions or are we merely windup toys placed on a bordered path that we will follow without deviation?

The answer to this question can be found in the second of this week's two portions, *Masei*. (The first, *Mattot*, discusses vows and oaths, various battles with ancient nations — including the division of spoils, and the request of the tribes of Reuven and Gad to receive their portion in the fertile Jordan River Valley, outside of Israel proper, as they perceived it as a better place to graze their flocks). The word *Masei* can be translated as journeys. The first part of this portion sets out a complete itinerary of the travels of the Jewish People during their forty year sojourn in the desert.

They began their trek at Ramses in Egypt on the 15th day of *Nisan* (now known as the first day of Passover) in year one. The Torah records all of the intervening travels and encampments, forty four in all, until they stood at the end of the fortieth year "in the Plains of Moav by the Jordan at Jericho" (*Bamidbar* 33:48) poised to enter the Land of Israel.

As an aside, although there are over forty travels mentioned, do not think that God unduly burdened them after His decree that they wander for forty years. Fourteen treks precede the decree and eight more occur in the fortieth year after the death of Aharon. Thus, in the remaining thirty eight years, we find that they traveled less than twenty times.

A few of the destinations have particular significance; we know something of what took place there (e.g. Marah, where they complained about the bitter water and God sweetened it by hurtling a tree into it). However, the vast majority of the locations are essentially meaningless — Libnah, Rissah, Tahat, Abrona, Mitkah, etc. Perhaps a few archaeologists or historians can identify these locations. Maybe some scholars or linguists can tell us what the names of these locales mean and whether there is any significance to them. What little I know about these journeys can be summed up in two broad statements:

1. The Jewish People chose, using their own free will, the conduct that resulted in their being condemned to wander in the desert for forty years; and

2. Their wanderings, though rarely explained, were not random or a product of the people's choice. Each leg of the journey was undertaken only upon God's direction. Whenever and wherever they stopped, they

stayed for a reason — there was something they had to learn, something to experience, something to do. Every encampment added something to their development as a nation.

These principles answer my questions, as well — our direction in life is very much a product of our personal choices. We can choose a religious or a secular lifestyle, we can choose the type of environment we maintain in our homes. We can choose between doing what we think is right and what our instincts tell us is wrong.

Nevertheless, the consequences of these choices may well be directed by God. In His infinite wisdom, God knows what we need to learn and experience, in order to reach our chosen goals. He knows the people we must connect with, the skills we must have, and the challenges we must face in order to complete our life's journey.

On a macro level, this analysis may help us to put the past 2000 years of the *galut* (exile) experience into perspective. While comprised of millions of people living over the span of many generations, God relates to Israel as one body, one collective entity. We are His bride, His queen, His treasure. We, today, are the same nation that left Egypt, received the Torah at Sinai, and entered the Holy Land. We, today, are the same people that witnessed and mourned the destruction of two Holy Temples.

As a nation we made choices, and continue to make choices. We chose to proclaim "We will do and we will listen," when God asked us if we wanted His Torah. Likewise, we are the people that self-destructed with self-hatred before the Roman Empire. Much the same way that God determined the course of our journeys in the wilderness, He continued and continues to do so as our nation sailed throughout the often rough waters of its history.

As we complete the Book of *Bamidbar,* which should more accurately be translated as the Book of "The Wilderness" or "The

Desert," during this time of national mourning and sorrow, may we draw comfort from the lesson of *Masei,* that this exile is not random and that God is guiding our often convoluted path — to lead us to the completion that He knows we will gloriously achieve.

DEVARIM
The Mourning After

During the course of my legal career, there has been little over-lap or conflict between my professional activities and my religious beliefs. There have been some "near misses" — I have had to excuse myself from Friday afternoon meetings that drifted toward evening; I have had to request that a hearing date be rescheduled because it coincided with a Jewish holiday; and as a government attorney I was called upon to prosecute several cases against my coreligionists (including one person who was a prominent member of the synagogue that my Bubbie attended). However, these two important aspects of my life are usually neatly compartmentalized. I cannot recall a situation where I had to resolve an inconsistency between the two systems in order to decide how to act.

When Adam sinned in the Garden of Eden, God cursed him by requiring that he toil and labor for his sustenance. In other words: work is work, it is not designed to be fun, rewarding, or interesting. However, if we are lucky, it sometimes can be. One of the nice things about my job is that I am periodically given the opportunity to apply my skills in areas that truly interest me. If you have been reading along with me this far, you might have surmised that I have more than a casual interest in sports, entertainment, and in my religious heritage. Since my employer owns interests in a number of sports franchises, in several of this country's most successful entertainment venues, and in a growing number of Israeli ventures, some of the routine lawyering I do gets spiced up by context. A few examples:

- A routine employment tax issue involving the treatment of certain bonus payments was much more interesting because it involved reviewing the contracts of a prominent professional athlete.

- An income tax issue involving proper accounting methods for certain types of revenue became a lesson in cash flows and marketing strategy for rock concerts.

- Structuring payment of a corporate gift to a major Israeli educational university provided wonderful networking opportunities within international Jewish institutional circles.

The project that I have worked on over the past several weeks was one of these high interest projects for me — as it involved forming a number of new corporations and partnerships in connection with a new major enterprise to be undertaken in Israel (once again client confidence forces me to be purposefully vague about the nature of this endeavor). This was a classic legal campaign/operation involving lots of documents, lots of lawyers, lots of opinions about how to do things, and little actual time within which to get it all done. Additionally, the transaction involved principals in several countries, necessitating drafting, revising, and translating into different languages. Of course, our ability to communicate and to exchange documents was hampered during the project by a strike called by workers in a major Israeli telecommunication company. As we overcame hurdles, and as the parties moved toward overall agreement, the time came for us to set a closing date.

I am a bit down the food chain on this project, so I did not participate in the conversation/negotiation about when the deal would close. However, when I was informed by my vice-president of the proposed date, I became faced with an interesting religious/professional dilemma — the date selected corresponded with a notorious day on the Jewish calendar — the Ninth of Av; otherwise known as *Tishah B'Av*.

The sages of the Mishnah catalogue five catastrophic or tragic events that occurred on *Tishah B'Av:* 1) While the Jews were in the wilderness, the incident with the spies took place, marking this as the day that God decreed that all adults over age twenty would perish rather than enter the Land of Israel; 2) the First Temple was destroyed by the Babylonians; 3) the Second Temple was destroyed by the Romans; 4) the city of Beitar fell as the Romans stamped out the last embers of the Bar Kochva revolt; and 5) the Romans literally plowed Jerusalem under (*Taanit* 4:6).

History tells us that a vast array of other atrocities have befallen our people on *Tishah B'Av.* For example, the expulsion from Spain in 1492 began on that day. The special book of prayers and lamentations recited on *Tishah B'Av* is filled with testimonials regarding pogroms, crusades and other persecutions that took place on this day. The day is so inauspicious, that the sages caution us, as a matter of Jewish law, to avoid litigation, the conduct of important business, the commencement of construction projects, or the embarking upon a new endeavor from the first through the tenth days of this month of Av (some opinions advise us to avoid the entire month).

While I mentioned that the new venture that I was assisting was an Israeli project, I neglected to mention that nearly all of the parties involved, from investors to proposed management, are Jewish. When I realized that this important undertaking was scheduled to commence on *Tishah B'Av,* I felt an obligation to counsel my clients — or at least highlight the issue and to leave it to their judgement. On the other hand, I did not want to lose credibility as a serious professional over something that others may perceive as a fanatically superstitious concern.

Rather than bringing it up at a larger gathering, I decided to explain these concerns directly to my vice-president. He is, likewise, Jewish and, while growing up, was quite close to his grandfather, who he described to me as being strictly observant. Thus, while he is not particularly involved or interested in religious observance or practice, he does have some background and sensitivity.

I explained the significance of *Tishah B'Av* to him and presented my case for setting an alternative closing date. He shook his head at me and gave me a grin that said, "and I thought I had heard everything." But he agreed to take responsibility for changing the date (which he did). However, before I returned to my office, he shook his head and asked, "Why do we have a day to mourn events that took place thousands of years ago when we just experienced the Holocaust in our century?" He observed that during the Holocaust, Jews were slaughtered on every day of the year. Thus he questioned why the rabbis did not require us to observe some form of commemoration on a daily basis. He also inquired about what we, in fact, do to remember the Holocaust.

While I attempted to answer his questions, I realized that a baseline understanding about the interrelationship between the historical *Tishah B'Av* and the relatively recent Holocaust can be gleaned from this week's portion of *Devarim.* One must realize, at the outset, that there is a close connection between the portion of *Devarim* and *Tishah B'Av.* Regardless of the year (leap year v. regular year) or the breakdown of the weekly portions (sometimes two portions are combined and read on a single week), the portion of *Devarim* is always read on the *Shabbat* before *Tishah B'Av*. The most common explanation for this is that the most important topic in *Devarim* is the recounting by Moshe of the events of the first notorious *Tishah B'Av*.

Let me set the scene. As *Devarim* opens, Moshe stands before the Children of Israel in the Jordan Valley, on the first day of the twelfth and last month of their forty year sojourn in the wilderness. In one month, the Jews will enter the Land of Israel. Within that month, Moshe will reach the end of his life — and he knows it. Moshe has led this nation since the Exodus. He understands the need to review, reflect, admonish, rebuke, caution, and inspire. Much of the Fifth Book — the Book of *Devarim* — is a monologue in which Moshe prepares himself and his people for the cutting of the umbilical cord that has bound them together.

Yet, the people he stands to address are truly a new generation, except for two, Yehoshua and Calev. The men and women that Moshe helped to liberate have all perished in the wilderness. Their children, who have been raised and nurtured by Moshe and the Torah in a miracle laced environment, will be the ones to embark upon the fulfilment of Divine promises in the Holy Land.

After a few introductory remarks and a brief discussion of the leadership structure he is leaving in place, Moshe launches into a comprehensive retelling of the incident with the spies. (As a brief aside, one of the nicknames for the Book of *Devarim* is *Mishneh Torah,* literally a repeat of the Torah. Most of the stories, teachings, and commandments contained in its portions are recapitulations of material found elsewhere in the Torah. The greatest importance of this book, from an exigetical standpoint, stems from the differences in wording, information, and nuance between the versions. The sages of the Mishnah and Talmud derived many of the laws grounded in the Oral Tradition by detailed textual comparison.)

To refresh your memory, in the second year after leaving Egypt, the Jews were poised to enter Israel. A decision was made to send in scouts (one from each tribe) on a forty day mission to report about various physical and strategic matters concerning the land and the forthcoming plan of conquest. Ten of the twelve spies returned with a discouraging report, which in turn caused the people to despair as to their immediate future and God's ability to deliver on His promises to them and to their forefathers. The people literally cried about what they perceived to be their dismal fate all through that night. As punishment for this national breakdown, God decreed that the adult population will be doomed to die in the wilderness during the course of forty years of wandering (one year for each day of the scouts' mission). The sages in the *Midrash* explain that God made another, more far reaching, decision that day. Since the Jews cried all through that night, for no good reason, God proclaimed that in all subsequent years they and their children would be given many reasons to cry. That night and day was *Tishah B'Av.*

(The *Midrash* actually describes that on *Tishah B'Av,* during each of the forty years, the condemned adults left their tents and went into the outskirts of the camp. Each would dig a grave and spend the night in it. In the morning a certain percentage of the people — that year's allotment of fatalities, simply would not rise. *Tishah B'Av,* thus, immediately went from bad to worse.)

In many ways, the spy episode was a defining event in Jewish history. Certainly for the Jews in the wilderness, it virtually established their fate and existence. One would think that Moshe would have discussed, debated and analyzed what took place almost ad nauseam. How is it that he waited nearly forty years, until his final days, to address the issues and the event? (And, though I choose not to go into it any more deeply, there are quite significant differences in the account of this incident in the portion of *Shelach* and the one in *Devarim* — let's save that one for homework!)

I believe the answer lies in the magnitude of the tragedy. For

Moshe and the people that he led out of Egypt, there was no more calamitous event than this Divine punishment. The people would perish and, as their leader, Moshe himself would likewise perish before the mission, the journey, and the objective were completed. The hurt was too great and the consequences far too intimate to allow for reasoned reflection. Only with the maximum distance of the remaining years allotted to him and the sobering reality that his end was near, was Moshe — the greatest, holiest, most saintly, and most humble man who ever lived, able to address the real tragedy and perhaps, only then, because it was necessary as part of the completion of the Torah.

One could assert that a piece of each day should be devoted to remembering and reflecting on the Holocaust. At the very least there could be a specific day, established with its own liturgy and ritual to mourn Hitler's victims. But this tragic event is too close to us. The wounds are still fresh. Many who experienced the horror still live in our midst.

There may come a time (though Mashiach will hopefully come sooner than then) twenty years from now, or fifty, or a hundred — when a group of rabbinic leaders may choose to establish such a day. (Yom Hashoah has become an accepted day of Holocaust commemoration. However, the rabbis have not officially marked it with special services or observances. It is in an undefined area between secular and holy treatment.) But then again, they may choose never to do so — fully understanding that the Holocaust was just the latest wave of retribution, tragedy, and calamity emanating from that first *Tishah B'Av*.

Rabbis speaking about *Tishah B'Av* often close by expressing the sentiment that we should merit to see the day that God fulfills His promise to transform *Tishah B'Av* from a day of mourning into a day of celebration. It is hard to imagine how God will fulfill this promise. Yes, He can bring about redemption and rebuild the Holy Temple, but how could we erase the suffering and pain of the victims who perished over the course of thousands of years? The answer may well be perspective — at the proper time we will understand what the reasons were, we will understand the necessity for, benefit of, and method of Divine action, and we will be consoled.

VA'ETCHANAN
Chief Cook and Bottle Washer

Rabbis — can't live with 'em, can't live without 'em. For centuries we have depended on them for leadership, guidance, and instruction. Yet, when the message is unpopular or when the individual self interest of a congregant intrudes on communal need, the rabbi can quickly became a victim or pawn of political machinations. In *Ethics of the Fathers* we are advised to "make for yourselves a Rav" (teacher, leader), yet we are warned, "to despise leadership."

As the rabbi of a congregation in New Jersey for four years, and rabbi of the branch of a large congregation in Cleveland for six years, I can write much about the rewards and frustrations of the vocation. In some ways it is far more difficult to be a rabbi in these modern times than at any time throughout our history. I am not referring to external forces, the challenges and temptations of modern life or the love-hate relationship with our co-religionists. I am talking about the skill set for the position and the expectations and demands, as unrealistic as they may be.

To begin with, today's rabbi must receive training and an education. In terms of the scope and complexity of the material, the years of committed study, and the required competency level, a full course of rabbinic study is as complete as any other professional track — be it medicine, law, business, engineering, etc. (of course none of the lawyers, doctors, businessmen or engineers in the community care to recognize this fact, preferring instead to believe that they have become "educated" while the rabbi was merely "learning Torah"). Next, he must be willing to sacrifice his time and, to some extent, his family in order to fulfill his commitments to the community. Finally, he must have the strength, patience, and wisdom to toil for a countless number of masters.

If this were not enough, today's rabbi must also be:

1) A teacher — he must be capable of preparing talks on everything from science and creationism, Jewish mysticism, biblical criticism, prayer and meditation, legal and medical ethics, etc., etc., etc. In other words — on anything and everything, in virtually any discipline, as long as it relates to Judaism (which really means everything!!!).

2) An orator — whether giving prepared or impromptu remarks, the rabbi must be smooth, entertaining, witty, amusing, moving, relevant, and interesting — if he is not, someone will be sure to tell him so.

3) A writer, editor, and publisher — whether writing an article for the local Jewish paper, pursuing scholarly research, or producing the synagogue bulletin, the rabbi must make use of these skills.

4) Marriage/family counselor/Ann Landers — A rabbi is called upon frequently to intervene or to assist congregants and others who face any number of personal problems. Sometimes, his job is merely to listen or to refer the person to another professional. Sometimes, he has to get very deeply involved.

5) Fund Raiser — both for synagogue projects and for other

charitable needs.

6)Producer/Director — The rabbi has much control over the tone, content, and pace of the daily, *Shabbat,* and holiday services.

7) Judge/Arbiter — The rabbi is constantly called upon to answer questions of Jewish law. He must have a basic mastery of the sources, a good library, and the sense to know when to consult with a more expert scholar.

8) Social Director/Youth Director — In many congregations the rabbi is looked to as a source of ideas for synagogue programming both for the adults and the youth.

9) Principal — If the congregation has a Hebrew School or an established adult education program, the rabbi will often find himself responsible — even if there is other staff.

10) Justice of the Peace/Bar Mitzvah Coach/Grief Counselor — A rabbi can become very involved with the life cycle events of his constituency — he is always expected to be there and to be able to do and say whatever is appropriate.

11) Psychic Healer — While it is equally incumbent on all Jews to visit the sick, this has become an almost expected part of the rabbi's job.

12)Public Relations/Community Relations — The rabbi is often the most visible symbol or representative of his membership. People like to see their rabbi participating in community events — be it Federation committees, or giving an invocation at the state legislature, or participating in the mayor's Holocaust committee, or doing a local television or radio talk show, etc. (Except, members also want their rabbi to be available for their needs whenever they arise.)

13) CEO — A rabbi is often looked to as the leader. He must motivate, administer, praise, rebuke, and essentially manage his congregation so that they can meet their religious and organizational goals.

Indeed, this is only a partial list. But I think you get the idea.

The expectations are, or can be, almost superhuman. Most rabbis may be able to wear a few of these hats competently — but is it realistic for anyone to be totally proficient in all of these roles? The reason that I am thinking so much about the role and responsibilities of the rabbinate this week is because much of the week was spent engaged in things rabbinic. During the first part of the week, with my "synagogue board member" hat on, I attended two meetings — one originally scheduled, the other a needed follow-up — called to discuss the contract of the rabbi of our synagogue. (I am not going anywhere near the issues, personalities, contract terms, dollars, or any other aspect of these meetings!) The rabbi's current contract expires later this year, and in the ordinary course, the board must meet to determine how best to balance the needs of the shul and the rabbi. These discussions certainly highlight how difficult it is for the modern rabbi to effectively serve and how little people understand about the scope of his overall duties and responsibilities.

One thing that I have noticed when the issue of a rabbi's tenure is discussed (not, however, during this week's deliberations) is how those members who have leaned most heavily on the rabbi tend to lead the charge that may result in his ouster. Maybe it is the couple whose marriage was on the brink of collapse and with whom the rabbi spent hours and hours. Or maybe it is the parents with the son who had a serious substance abuse problem, who the rabbi took under his wing and convinces to get real help. Or maybe it is the member who lost his job and needed discreet financial assistance in order to keep his family from losing everything. Dependency gives way to gratitude, which gives way to unease (because there is no way to repay the kindness, to satisfy the imagined debt), which gives way to discomfort (as the member views the rabbi as a reminder of the misfortune), which gives way to distance, which gives way to dislike, which ultimately leads to the unfortunate action of a person rejecting the very individual who was there when they needed him most — the lifeline over time has been transformed into a skeleton in the closet.

Rather than getting lost in synagogue politics and the rabbi/congregation dynamic, I will abruptly move on to the week's other rabbinic episode. A few weeks ago, I was talking to a friend in Cleveland, a former congregant, who was originally from Detroit. He mentioned to me that his cousin in Detroit was actively trying to establish a new Orthodox congregation in an outlying suburb. The fledgling shul had achieved a critical mass of families to sustain weekly *Shabbat* services and they had just acquired a piece of property on which to build, if they continued to grow. They have not yet engaged a rabbi to service them, so my friend asked if he could give his cousin my phone number — figuring that I might be inclined to offer them some guidance and perhaps spend some time with them.

To make a long story short, with my family away for the summer and with me home alone for a few weekends, I agreed to a brief tenure as guest rabbi. This entailed delivering a few sermons, teaching some classes, and getting to meet some new people. It had been nearly two years since I assumed the pulpit in formal capacity. As the first *Shabbat* approached, I experienced a mixture of eagerness to teach and to inspire, and some anxiety over whether I would connect with the crowd. In the end, it was a rewarding experience; I felt that I had made a difference as to how these people enjoyed their *Shabbat,* how they would approach the upcoming holidays, and, perhaps, I helped them to understand that their growth as a community may well be dependent on hiring a rabbi who can guide them appropriately.

(This little foray of mine back into rabbinics also provided me with another example of how quick and inaccurate the community gossip mill is. This past *Shabbat,* I officiated for the first time, as a guest, at the shul in the suburbs. On Wednesday, at board meeting I was attending, one of the other board members publicly asked me (not in jest) if what she heard was true, that my family and I were moving so that I could assume the rabbinic position there.)

Functioning effectively as a rabbi is thus like riding a roller coaster. There are highs and there are lows, although it seems as if the highs result from patient, steady effort while the lows hit suddenly and abruptly.

We see this illustrated rather graphically in this week's portion of *Va'etchanan*. Moshe is continuing the monologue that he began last week in *Devarim*. It is the last week of his life and he has been reviewing the major events, both good and bad, that have marked his tenure as leader. His main goal is to give perspective and to provide the new generation with a push in the direction of what is right and just. At the close of *Devarim*, he described the battles in the Jordan Valley over the Amorite kings, Sichon and Og, that marked the beginning of the Jewish conquest of the Holy Land.

As you may recall (see *"Chukat:* Stones and Sticks"), Moshe "sinned" by hitting the rock instead of speaking to it when the people demanded water. As a consequence, God "punished" Moshe by decreeing that he would not enter the Land of Israel with his people. Emboldened by the initial conquests near the border of Israel, Moshe dares to hope that perhaps God had rescinded the punishment. He turns to God in prayer and supplication — crying, begging, and pleading to be able to experience the "Good Land."

Instead of accepting these prayers, God becomes angry (Rashi explains, that God was not angry at Moshe. Rather His anger was directed at the Jewish People because they had essentially caused Moshe to suffer this punishment) and says *"Rav lach, al toseph daber elai od badavar hazeh."* ("It is too much for you, do not continue to speak to me further about this matter") (*Devarim* 3:26). There are two aspects of this verse that relate directly to our discussion of the rabbinic persona. Moshe had faithfully served God. He was the emissary to Pharaoh, the teacher of Torah, and the shepherd to a flock that wandered forty years in the wilderness. During his tenure, he withstood virtually every challenge to God's authority. He repeatedly saved our nation from its own folly. Now, literally on the top of the mountain, within clear sight of the width and breadth of the land, he is cast down abruptly to the bottom — prevented from accomplishing the final goal.

Can any possible explanation be given to justify how Moshe is being treated? Yes, Moshe, himself, provides it. He states that God got angry at him because of the Jewish People — which can be explained either 1) that he committed the fateful act in order to respond to their complaints and needs or 2) that since his initial flock forfeited their right to enter the land, he was obligated, as their captain, to go down (remain) with them. Either way, we see that the fate of a rabbi, a leader, is dependent upon his followers — for better or for worse.

In order to appreciate the other aspect, or message in the verse, I want to return to two of its words *"rav lach"* ("It is too much for you"). These words can be literally interpreted as "rabbi for you." (The Hebrew word *rav* also means rabbi). During the course of his pleading, Moshe may well have requested to be released from his obligations of leadership — to be treated as an ordinary Jew. But God answered him *"Rav lach,"* — "You are a rabbi — this is your role, this is your duty, this is who you are." The demands on a rabbi can be unbearable — absolutely maddening. Complaints can be inconsistent and contradictory. Disappointments can outweigh success. However, those who choose to call themselves rabbi and who choose to serve in that capacity are defined by the occupation, and bound by its obligations.

Not coincidentally, Moshe recounts the giving of the Ten Commandments in the portion of *Va'etchanan.* The second set of tablets was the one that Moshe fashioned with his own hands. They contained or represented the laws that he faithfully taught the people for forty years. The placement of the Ten Commandments in

Va'etchanan communicates that despite his disappointment at being left behind, Moshe, so to speak, would have the comfort of knowing that in a significant way he would be going forward with the Jewish Nation. Through the words of the Torah that he transmitted, he would be providing teaching, guidance, and leadership not for one or two generations, but until the end of time. Even though his physical being and existence would end in a few short days his legacy would endure.

This, ultimately, is what any rabbi can rely on. The people, the personalities, the situations, the successes, the failures, the joys, the misery — are all temporal, all situational, all merely the blink of the cosmic eye. The Torah that he lives and teaches, that he brings into people's lives, and that he represents is what truly has lasting meaning for any rabbi, and for that matter, for any Jew.

EIKEV

The Shechinah Knows

On most days my morning routine is pretty much the same: wake up, shave, shower and get dressed, go to synagogue for some study and morning prayers, drive carpool for the kids, go to the office, and collapse at my desk for about ten minutes with some tea and the morning paper.

When I lived back East, the routine was somewhat different because the transportation was different. Instead of driving around for an hour or so each morning, I was able to commute — to sit on a packed bus and train with a lot of cranky people. In some ways this mode was more stressful — I was dependent upon schedules, there was little control over climate (especially on those cold winter days when I had to bundle up to stand and wait for the bus, which was as warm as a sauna when I entered — what a "Catch 22." If I layered less clothing on, I froze outside. If I dressed protectively, I would swelter inside), and getting a seat was often the result of blind luck.

On the other hand, those commutes had their advantages —

well, one in particular, that may be unique to New York/New Jersey — they afforded me the opportunity to read the morning tabloids, the *New York Post* and the *New York Daily News,* which may be loosely described as newspapers (the *New York Times* and *Wall Street Journal* were just too difficult to maneuver in close quarters and were not much fun to read!).

For those of you not familiar with these rags, I mean papers, let me give you a brief description — in the basic order that I perused them (meaning from back to front). The papers are generally sixty or so pages (depending on the number of advertisements). The back quarter to third is the sports section. These papers give comprehensive coverage to each one of the New York professional sports teams — analyzing (usually in the form of second guessing and criticism) virtually every significant play in each game, bandwagon jumping (when applicable), and trying to instigate controversy — between the players themselves, between the players and fans, between the fans and the team — whenever possible. Following several pages of classified ads and stock listings, is a small business section. Then comes entertainment (movie, play, and book reviews, and profiles of upcoming performances and concerts), followed closely by the editorial pages. Passing the editorial we head into the section containing the "hard news:" state and local, national, and international (most of the "stories" consisting of a paragraph or two, at most). After a brief interlude at the gossip pages, we reach the first 8-10 pages of the newspaper — unabashed sensationalism.

These pages are typically filled with any combination of the following:

• Overkill coverage of the dominant world event. For example, if Congress passed a bill there will be descriptions of the new law, text boxes and graphics, pictures of the key legislators, side stories about the back room trading, and a variety of quotes and opinions of those both for and against;

- Crimes and disasters: Plane crashes, earthquakes, terrorist bombings, bank robberies, murders, fatal car crashes all get the full treatment. They are always accompanied by large headlines and lots of photos, the more graphic the better; or

- Anything in the news that is remotely related to sex: A political sex scandal, the breakup of a prostitution ring, allegations of marital infidelity among the rich and famous, or harassment or abuse in a workplace or school setting. There is no limit on what deviance and depravity can be described and/or illustrated in the name of news (and certainly, there is never a thought given as to the impact of the stories and the coverage on the lives of real people).

As the years passed, and the sensationalized stories of what we choose to accept as belonging to the far fringes of our "normal" and "moral" lives blur, we become somewhat calloused. Nobody that we know or are related to seems to ever visit the world depicted in these screaming yellow pages. The actors and actresses in these dramas are either far up the ladder from us (the O.J. Simpsons, and Versaces, Clintons, Dick Morris', and the Woody Allens) or they are far below us (crooks, and drug addicts, and hookers). We therefore approach this material as voyeurs, smug in our solidity, safety, and morality.

As I arrive at the airport in Newark each Friday on my weekend visits with the family, the first thing I do, even as I make my way through the terminal to meet my wife, is to stop at a newsstand and to purchase copies of the *Post* and *Daily News*. The Detroit newspapers are rather bland. I must admit, it is fun to see the world, occasionally, through kaleidoscope-colored rather than rose-colored glasses. And besides, they have much more comprehensive sports coverage.

Usually, I zip through those first eight or so sensationalized pages. But, this week, as page eight of the *Daily News* passed before my eyes, I did a double take. Staring out at me, in a photo that covered about a quarter of the page, was the face of Abraham

("Sandy") Alter — a lifelong friend of my wife's family (they rode on the same school bus in grammar school) and one of my brother-in-law's best friends. The caption under his picture read "Victim: Long stitched-up cut shows on Abraham Alter's face as he describes how he was slashed on W. 47th St. after confronting youths." The page's headline read: "Slashing attack in midtown — Ethnic slurs & a razor."

I read through the story in the *Daily News* (which I will relate shortly) and turned to the *Post.* Flipping through quickly, I found a picture of Sandy's slashed face on page 12. This caption read: "Scars of Hate," Abraham Alter shows the horrific gash down his cheek left by the vicious and senseless attack." The *Post's* headline for the accompanying story proclaimed: "Teen slashed man in face 'because he's a Jew': cops."

The following account of this incident is based on the two articles and my conversation, later that day, with my first cousin, who was present when the incident occurred.

On Thursday evening, Sandy, my cousin, and another friend met for dinner at a kosher steakhouse in midtown Manhattan. After they finished, they went to a nearby parking garage to retrieve Sandy's car, a new Chrysler Sebring convertible (ironically, Sandy purchased this car only a few weeks earlier since his prior car was stolen and the thief killed in it during a shootout with the police). They tarried at the garage a few minutes longer than otherwise, since they noticed actor Ron Silver, in line waiting for his car and stopped to schmooze with him.

After leaving the garage, they stopped the car at a red light on West 47th and Broadway. Six teenagers started yelling ethnic slurs at Sandy and his two passengers, all of whom were wearing yarmulkes.

"*@!! Jews. You get the cars and we gotta walk."

Sandy turned toward the group and asked, "What do you want from the Jews? Why are you talking about Jews like this?"

The teens approached the car and Sandy got out, fearing that he would be attacked and recognizing that he was a sitting duck in the convertible. Before he could even react, one of the youths, a fifteen-year-old girl, slapped him twice in the face and then cut his right hand with a razor blade. After she stepped back to survey the damage, she lunged again, slashing his face. The seven-inch gash required several hundred stitches to repair. Because the blade nicked an artery, the medics had to cauterize the wound to prevent Sandy from bleeding to death.

(Filling in some details that were not reported — and trying to give credit where credit is due — my cousin immediately dialed 911 on the car phone and the New York Police responded within 30 seconds. Additionally, plainclothes officers apprehended the group of teenagers within about five minutes of receiving their description, except for the slasher herself. After a brief interrogation, the other teenagers gave up the name and address of the slasher, who was picked up at her home in the Bronx a few hours later. During this incident, the New York Police lived up to their reputation as New York's finest.)

The teens were charged with assault and criminal possession of a weapon. The District Attorney is considering whether to include bias or "hate-crime" charges.

Sandy's wife Debbie summed up everyone's feelings in one of the articles when she stated that she was most upset that "you can't wear a yarmulke without being attacked for being a Jew."

I saw my cousin in shul, down the Shore, the next morning, on *Shabbat*. He looked visibly shaken and he was exhausted, having been kept up by the police most of Thursday night/early Friday morning in order to identify the perpetrators in a series of line-ups (Sandy was in the hospital, so the other two witnesses spent most of the night with the police). He was called up to the Torah so that he could recite the traditional blessing of thanksgiving to God for delivery from harm.

When he spoke of the incident and its aftermath, two words stood out as the description unfolded — fear and terror. A pleasant evening of dinner with good friends degenerated into one of terror. A carefree respite near the end of a long week resulted in facing the fear of death. He doubted if he, or Sandy, will ever be able to walk anywhere confidently without having to glance back or to size up everyone within their field of vision. In other words, they have been damaged by destructive fear.

Fear plays an important role in this week's portion of *Eikev,* as well. However, in it we encounter a different kind of fear — an important, required fear.

As *Eikev* opens, Moshe is continuing the monologue he began in *Devarim.* While psyching up the Children of Israel for their upcoming conquests, he also tries to help them avoid future pitfalls. He also tries to counsel them to avoid the mistakes of the past — which he illustrates by recounting the incident of the sin of the Golden Calf. At the conclusion of this incident, God asked Moshe to fashion the second tablets. Moshe describes this process, as well.

Not wishing to sound frivolous or irreverent, but at about the middle of the portion, I get this mental image of Moshe speaking and the people beginning to fidget. After all, there is just so much moral direction one can listen to in one day, especially when it is punctuated by less than pleasant, if not embarrassing, historical precedents. Taking this further, I see Moshe noticing this and deciding he needs to regain everyone's attention. He pauses and says — look I've been going on and on with this for ten chapters already and I've got quite a ways to go. I would really like you all to pay attention, as my words are meant to guide you through the centuries and millennia. But for those of you with short attention spans, I am going to boil it all down to one sound bite — "Now, O Israel, What does Hashem, your God ask of you? Only to fear God, your God, to go in all His ways and to love Him, and to serve Hashem, your God, with all your heart and with all your soul" (*Devarim* 10:10).

Rabbi Chanina, in the Talmud in the Tractate of *Berachot* (34b) states that this verse proves that: "Everything is in the hands of heaven except for fear of heaven." Which means that while God controls, guides and influences everything else in the world, He allows man himself free choice with respect deciding whether to "fear God."

Fear of heaven is not the fear of a victim or potential victim, or of hate, or of nightmares, or of insecurity, or of the unknown and alien. It is a fear of awareness. This fear comes from understanding the consequences of actions, of knowing before whom we stand at all times, of knowing what is expected — even when we fall short because of our own humanity. This fear is grounded in our obligation to live up to the standards of our forefathers, in our commitment at Sinai, and the responsibility of chosenness.

But such fear is not a simple matter of fear itself. It is the advance guard of love. The discipline it brings, the boundaries it establishes, and the conduct it engenders all bring us closer to, not farther, from God. This aspect is what is truly difficult to master and to explain. When we fear someone or something we try our best to avoid the source. We hide, withdraw, and sometimes even run and flee from the object of our anxiety. But when we learn to fear God, when we understand the hows and whys of this fear, and when we affirmatively choose to fear Him, we are drawn closer and closer into His loving presence.

Who knows what fear lurks in the hearts of men? Not the Shadow, rather the *Shechinah* (Divine Presence)! The *Shechinah* knows!

RE'EH
Peaks and Valleys

At the beginning of this week's portion of *Re'eh* (how's that for a switch, for once I am discussing the portion first and then moving back to real life) Moshe continues his monologue by discussing the blessing and the curse that will be placed before the Jewish People. If they listen to God's commandments there will be *berachah* (blessing), if not, *kelalah* (curse).

This, of course, is rather standard fare. In fact, near the end of *Eikev*, read last week, we find the text of the second paragraph of the *Shema* prayer (*Devarim* 11:13-21) that tells us some of the good things that will happen if we follow God's word and some of the bad, if we do not. Moshe does not seem to be breaking new ground here!

Yet, there is something quite different about this *berachah* (blessing) and *kelalah* (curse). It is not necessarily the words themselves that prove unique, but the setting. Moshe describes that "it shall be when God, your God, will bring you to the land... and the blessing will be given on *Har G'rizim* (Mount G'rizim) and the curse on *Har Eyval* (Mount Eyval)" (*Devarim* 11:29).

Nothing more is mentioned about these blessings and curses in *Re'eh*. But if we skip ahead three portions to *Ki Tavo,* we find a command from Moshe regarding the event. In *Devarim* 27:11-14, Moshe dictates that six tribes, Shimon, Levi, Yehudah, Yisaschar, Yoseph, and Binyamin will stand on *Har G'rizim* to bless the people and that the other six, Reuven, Gad, Asher, Zevulun, Dan, and Naftali, will stand for the curse of *Har Eyval.* The Talmud, in the tractate of *Sotah* (3b) explains that six tribes ascended one mountain and the remaining six the other. The *kohanim,* some of the *leviim,* and the Holy Ark were situated in the valley between the two mountains. The *leviim* would first turn to *Har G'rizim* and relate one of the blessings. They would then turn toward *Har Eyval* to express the corresponding curse (the blessings and curses are set forth in the portion of *Ki Tavo* — each blessing for observance had a corresponding curse in the event of transgression). After each blessing and curse the people jointly said "Amen."

Why did the people say "Amen" to each curse? Why did God split the tribes, designating some on a mountain of blessing and some on the mountain of curse?

This week my family and I stand between two mountains. One that appeared at a distance to be a mountain of curse and one that appears, unequivocally, to be a mountain of blessing. This past Sunday, the day after we read the portion of *Eikev,* we gathered to dedicate and unveil my mother-in-law's tombstone. Next Sunday, the day after we will read *Re'eh,* we will be together, please God, with family and friends in celebration of my son Joshua's upcoming Bar Mitzvah. Two Sundays — two mountains of emotion. One mountain is awash with dread, tears of sadness, pain, and perhaps curse. The other mountain is bathed in anticipation, tears of joy, pride, and hopefully much blessing.

Both of these events flow from God. The time of birth and the time of death are His to control. For one loved one, the mission, whatever it was, had been completed. For the other, that mission is just coming into focus. What is a blessing? What is a curse? Who is blessed? Who is cursed?

Ironically, the remarks that I composed to deliver at the unveiling, our so-called "cursed" event, focus not on *kelalah*, but on *berachah*. In tribute to my mother-in-law and to further illustrate this blurred line between blessing and curse, I present these remarks:

As you all know, when Mom passed away four months ago, we were not allowed to eulogize her fully because we were celebrating Pesach. The words I used that day conveyed a sense of loss but they could not describe the magnitude of that loss or give insight into the many special characteristics and deeds that made her the person who meant so much to all of us.

So today I am going to beg your indulgence, I am going to speak a bit more about her than one might otherwise at the dedication of a headstone — in part because she deserves it and in part because we need to pay appropriate tribute to her life and memory.

In yesterday's Torah portion of Eikev we read a powerful verse: "And now O Israel what is it that your God asks of you, only that you fear God, your God, walk in all his ways and love him and serve Hashem, your God with all of your heart and all your soul." The Talmud in the tractate of Menachot derives an important law from this verse, one that impacts the conduct of our daily lives and provided a goal or focus for the structure of our daily prayers:

"R' Meir used to say, a person is obligated to recite one hundred blessings every day as it says 'now, O Israel what is that Hashem your God asks of you?'"

What does this verse have to do with 100 blessings?

Rashi, on the Talmud offers one cryptic answer, "read it as 100" — read the word MAH (what) as MEAH (100) — of course the word MAH (what) appears many other places and we do not read it as MEAH (100)? Rabbi Boruch Epstein in his commentary, the Torah Temima, explains, that the true connection between this verse and the one hundred blessings is that fact that the verse has 99 letters,

*100 letters less one, in it, thus "read it as 100" means "read 100 let-
ters." The blessings that we give to God can never truly be adequate
for what He gives us — but He treats it as complete. Similarly, we do
not always appreciate the blessings He gives us — wanting more,
looking to tomorrow and not appreciating today. Yet all of His blessings are "read it as 100," 100% complete.*

*When we had Mom, we had and we received complete blessing
— Mom for us was 100 daily blessings in who she was, what she
stood for and what she meant. I mentioned before that I was going
to ask your indulgence — this is where I take it — as I read to you
the list of 100 blessings that Mom represented to us that I compiled
for this morning:*

*Everyday she was there as
mother to:*
1) Kim
2) Shelly
3) Jay

Mother-in-law to:
4) Larry
5) Marsha
6) Me

*Grandmother or "Bubbie
Leanore" to:*
7) Shanna
8) Jodie
9) Joshua Herbert
10) Annie
11) Joshua Adam
12) Jamie
13) Peshie
14) Jordie
15) Avi
16) Esti
17) Sari
18) Mindy
19) B.Z.
20) YoYo
21) Zack

She was a loving and cherished:
22) Aunt
23) Sister-in-law
24) Friend
25) Business Partner
26) Supporter

*She was a devoted child to
her own:*
27) Father and
*28) Mother during their lives
and she cherished their memories after they departed*

She taught her children:
29) Courage
30) Dignity
31) Honor
32) Commitment
33) Faith
34) Will
*35) She taught us how to
handle Adversity*
36) How to listen
37) How to guide and advise
*38) How to run and manage a
household*
39) Generosity

40) Charity
41) The value of educating our children
42) The importance of being part of a community
43) Prioritizing
44) Values
45) Integrity
46) Honesty
47) Reliability
48) Sensitivity
49) Order
50) The importance of paying attention to detail
51) She taught the little things that can be so big
52) Courtesy
53) Showing appreciation
54) Consistency
55) Independence
56) She was a model Jewish woman
57) With a strong Jewish identity
58) Who appreciated the specialness of the Yamim Tovim (Jewish holidays)
59) She displayed appropriate modesty
60) She was kind
61) Accepting
62) A gracious and hospitable hostess
63) A good cook
64) She had no airs (don't be confused by her shyness)
65) She treated all people equally
66) She knew how to give love
67) And how to receive it
68) She was willing to get her hands dirty to help
69) She guarded confidences
70) She had and shared sound judgement

71) And common sense
72) She knew when to speak up
73) And how to speak up
74) And when to hold back
75) She knew enough to let us make our own mistakes
76) And was there to help us pick up the pieces
77) She was someone we wanted to please
78) And to make proud
79) And to share successes and good times with
80) She was our reality check
81) And she knew how to keep us in check, when we needed it
82) She was a wellspring of inner beauty
83) And outer beauty
84) She made this world better by being in it
85) She gave life and never stopped nurturing it
86) She showed us how to fight and not give up
87) How to appreciate each day
88) How to appreciate each other
89) How to withstand devastating loss
90) And how to get on with it
91) She also showed us how to preserve, honor, and cherish memory
92) How not to forget the past
93) How to appreciate family
94) How to help
95) How to care
96) How to be a mother/parent
97) How to live fully
98) How to say goodbye
& 99) How to die like a tzaddik (righteous person)

I, too, stop at 99, not because she lacked a blessing , not because we lacked a blessing when we had her— but because we are truly "chaser Aleph" — missing one of the most important people in our lives!

We miss that one today, as we shed tears of sorrow, and we will miss that one, perhaps even more, next week when we will gather, please God, to celebrate my Joshua's upcoming Bar Mitzvah, when our sad tears will mix with some joyful ones, as well.

The juxtaposition of these two events, as well as one of the very events of Mom's last day, reminded me of a story told by Rabbi Krohn:

A young mother of a large family was stricken with a critical illness. She knew that she had only a few days to live. What made matters even worse for the family was the fact that her son was about to celebrate his Bar Mitzvah shortly, a few days after Rosh Hashana (Jewish New Year).

With each passing day life seemed to ebb from her. A few days before Rosh Hashana she called her beloved son into her room and said to him, "Please do me a favor and put on your special Bar Mitzvah suit. I'd like to see how handsome you will look in it."

The child was surprised at the request, but realizing the seriousness of his mother's condition, he hastened to obey. A few minutes later he came into her room wearing the brand-new suit he had never worn before. He stood proudly before his ailing mother so she could see him this one time.

She couldn't help but shed tears as she visualized how wonderful it might have been to share the simchah with her family. The son, too, was moved to tears by this moment. After a few minutes, the boy left the room.

Later that day, the young mother was visited by a friend, to whom she described what had gone on earlier. The friend expressed surprise, "How could you have done that to your son — didn't you think that such an experience might be too painful for him?" "My intention was not for my own benefit," the mother replied, "I did it solely for my son. I wanted him to be able to wear his new suit for his Bar Mitzvah. You see, an avel (mourner) may not put on new clothes, and had he not worn the suit at least once before, he would not be able to wear it for his Bar Mitzvah — and I wanted him to have at least that."

She passed away a few days later.

On the 2nd day of Passover this year, just a few short hours before she passed away, Mom asked Josh to "lain" (read) his Torah reading for her out of his tikkun (a practice book that has pages written in the special Torah script). I know that Josh, like the rest of us, finds it difficult to go on with life, and even to embrace celebration, without his Bubbie Leanore. I would not have blamed him if he would have said his heart is not into it, that he did not want to continue his practice and his Bar Mitzvah preparations. But Mom had him "lain" for her, she asked him near her end. Every time he sings the trop (cantillations) he can picture singing to her. When he will stand on the bimah reading from the Torah he will know that she heard him read and can hope that she hears him then too.

The blessings that she gave us and that she was for us, are with us — they survive her physical life. I have no doubt that she will be an effective advocate for us before the heavenly court to assure that we continue to receive His blessing. I just hope that we can live up to her standards, her teaching, and her example and serve as living tributes to her righteousness.

May her soul be bound by everlasting life and may we all merit to be reunited with the coming of the Messiah.

We stood on a cursed mountain, on a sad day full of pain, and yet could discuss and appreciate the blessings we had and continue to have. The mountain was not cursed, we who stood on it were not cursed, the curses were not even truly curses. We gained from the experience. We gained perspective, appreciation, and some understanding. There may be easier ways to learn these lessons, but few are as effective.

God did not curse *Har Eyval,* or the tribes on it. God, through the words of the *leviim,* was teaching His people about their destiny and history. Sometimes blessing can only be achieved or understood if viewed through *kelalah*. Sometimes the curse is the advance guard of the *berachah*.

SHOFTIM
Bishops and Pawns

As I mentioned last chapter, this week I face a mountain, the mountain of *berachah* (blessing), the celebration of my son's Bar Mitzvah. This is such an important event in our lives that I have been wrestling with how to deal with it, present it, and write about it. I could take the approach I took for my niece's Bat Mitzvah (see, *"Vayishlach:* I would like to thank") and include the remarks I composed for Josh to deliver at the party. I could incorporate my own remarks; essentially praise for my wife and for Josh's many fine rabbis and teachers. I could include the humorous song I wrote about Josh that his siblings and cousins have been rehearsing and will perform at the party. But a funny thing happened on my way to the Bar Mitzvah...

Friday afternoon I left the office and headed for the airport, as has been my routine this summer. I checked in, received my seat assignment, and soon boarded the plane. I had an aisle seat and for quite a while the two inner seats toward the window were vacant.

A few moments before takeoff a gentleman moves down the aisle.

He is wearing a black jacket with black pants, a Christian cleric's collar, and a large and very ornate crucifix, which hangs around his neck by a thick gold chain. Of course, he has the seat right next to me. His traveling companion is a teenaged boy and they are conversing with each other in rapid-fire Italian.

As the stewardess goes down the rows to make sure our seatbelts are on and that our seats and tray tables are in their upright and locked position, he directs some remarks to her in unaccented English. Thus, I am fairly certain that he is either American, or is quite fluent in our language. At this moment, however, I feel no compelling need to make any polite conversation.

As the plane speeds down the runway and into its takeoff, I sit with a small colorful laminated card with the words of the traveler's prayer and I recite it in an undertone. Perhaps not coincidentally, at that same moment, my neighbor is sitting with his eyes shut, one hand clutched around his crucifix, with lips moving in silent prayer. As he finishes, he makes the sign of the cross, and then opens his eyes. We simultaneously and somewhat awkwardly noticed what each of us had just done. I turned to him and say, "Why do I feel like telling a joke about a rabbi, a priest, and a minister on an airplane?" He laughed and proceeded to tell me just such a joke, and I returned favor (the story he told, was one I had heard many times, but the thrust of the punchline was noticeably different).

The flight was nearly full, so this means that there were well over 100 passengers on board. I asked my neighbor what the odds had to be for the airline to randomly place a rabbi (perhaps the only one on board) next to a priest. He said, about the same as a rabbi being seated next to an archbishop. You see, my flight companion was non other than the Archbishop of Sicily, who is the U.S. for a few weeks visiting family (he is an American originally from Queens, in New York City).

I would like to pause here for a moment and reflect on what was happening on that flight. Just a few weeks earlier, we experienced *Tishah B'Av,* a sorrowful day commemorating Jewish tragedies throughout the centuries. While much of the liturgy focused on the destruction of the two Temples and our long and bitter exile, the service included lamentations composed as memorials or testimonials to quite a variety of atrocities committed in the name of the Catholic Church throughout the Middle Ages. Descriptions of Crusades, Inquisitions, and book burnings are punctuated with the spirit and sacrifice of those martyred.

As one delves into Jewish history, one discovers how time and again the Christian clergy incited the lay populace to violence. Many of the infamous blood libels were instigated by the Church leadership. The Church mandated the expulsion of the Jews from Spain near the height of what was otherwise a Golden Age. How many Priests, and Bishops, Archbishops, and Popes have used their positions, their platforms, and their power to violate our people? Centuries of institutionalized, ingrained, anti-Semitism molded a Europe that could engineer, allow, assist, or ignore, a Holocaust. As for the recent acknowledgment by the Pope that the Jews are not responsible for the death of Yeshu — this is a case of too little, too late!

Yet here I was, sitting next to the Archbishop of Sicily, making polite conversation, smiling, joking, and discussing theology. I picture, in my mind, the rabbis, many of whom were giants of our faith, who were forced under threat of death to engage in such discussions, disputations, and debates. I picture men dressed like my neighbor ordering pogroms and executions. I can not help but feel that I somehow violated the honor and memory of generations past. However, as I simply want to believe, perhaps we are witnessing a new era, a change in attitude, which may lead to even greater things.

The Archbishop and I discussed a rather wide variety of issues, albeit in a rather restrained way. I answered his questions in a somewhat circumspect manner so as not to highlight the divisions within Judaism and not to denigrate Christianity (in other words, I kept the gloves on). But I did not pull punches when it came to

295

Church treatment of Jews through the ages.

I did not take notes of, or record this conversation. However, I would like to relate some of the highlights, as I can best recall.

The first question the Archbishop asked was whether it was true that there is a group of Jews in Israel that currently advocate the actual reconstruction of the Temple. He added that Christianity believes that the Temple will not be physically rebuilt but will be subsumed into the persona of Yeshu — "he will be the Third Temple," the Archbishop commented.

I answered that mainstream traditional Jews (a term I did not define, but used to avoid dealing with our own "family" squabbles) believe that the Temple will be rebuilt when the Mashiach comes. I noted that we pray for this several times each day. I added that there is some disagreement among the sources as to whether we will be given the opportunity to physically construct it or whether God will present it to us (lowering it from Heaven). I also explained that the structure of our daily services and a number of our religious practices either parallel, commemorate, or simply stand in the place of Temple rituals.

When I mentioned Temple ritual, the Archbishop observed that one of the best feelings he has is when he puts on his special vestments to lead a mass or other service. It was his understanding that the robe, headgear and other ornaments he uses originated with *Kohanim* (a word he used, and pronounced correctly) in the Temple and that the Church liturgy was based on the Temple service. Thus, he felt a certain purity to his worship of God during his time of service.

I commented that while I did not want to burst his bubble, I could not agree that the garments he described even remotely resembled those worn by the *Kohanim* (and that are described rather completely in our Torah). However to assuage his feelings somewhat, I propounded my theory of the function of those garments, as set out more completely in *"Tetzaveh:* Clothes Make the

Man," complete with the analogy to Avi's hockey experience.

The last topic he broached was an observation regarding what he perceived as the similarity in attitude we (Orthodox Jew and traditional Catholic) shared in adhering to a more classical or traditional form of our respective religious faiths. He criticized the Protestant faiths for veering from the structure and the rituals of the Church and attempted to analogize it to the "rift" between Orthodox Jews and Conservative and Reform Jews. He viewed both Orthodox Judaism and Catholicism as pure forms of religious practice and the others as deviants molded to suit the shifting contemporary mores, attitudes, and needs of their followers.

Again, I basically held my tongue. Although, I could not resist noting that early Christianity was, essentially, just such a movement. I also pointed out that while the Church no longer requires that Mass be led in Latin, in Orthodox congregations the traditional Jewish service, and in fact nearly all spoken liturgy, is still recited in the original Hebrew.

As our conversation waned, I returned to my writing. No, I was not writing an installment of this book, I was composing/polishing my remarks for the Bar Mitzvah. After a few minutes, the Archbishop asked what I was working on. I told him that I was celebrating my son's upcoming Bar Mitzvah this weekend etc. I then turned to him and said that this highlights one of the biggest differences between us and between our faiths. Regardless of whether I happen to be a rabbi or simply just an educated and devout Jew, one of the primary tenets of our belief, recited at least twice daily in the *Shema* is *"Veshinantam levanecha v'dibarta bam"* ("and you shall teach them thoroughly to your children and speak of them"). Ours is a religion of transmission — father to son, mother to daughter.

The *seder* nights of Pesach revolve around teaching our children. The pageantry of Purim, the flags, candy, and apples of Simchat Torah, and the Chanukah presents all reflect our emphasis on bringing our faith alive for the kids — assuring that they learn not by rote but by experience. The words of our forefather Avraham, who had proven his faith in test after test, yet who had not been given an heir, ring through time "What can you give me seeing that I go childless?" (*Bereishit* 15:2). Our offspring and theirs after them, like ourselves, are links in a chain that reaches back to Sinai and that binds us to God as His Chosen People.

Yet the leadership of the Catholic faith — their Priests, Bishops, Cardinals, Popes, Nuns, etc. adhere to vows of celibacy. They violate God's desire that man "be fruitful and multiply." They deny themselves that bond from parent to child that serves as a useful model for understanding aspects of our relationship with G-d. They also miss out on transmitting their personal and deep love of their faith to the ones that would matter most.

The Archbishop admitted that this was not always the Church's path (he mentioned that celibacy for the clergy was first imposed in the 13th century). In fact, he explained that celibacy had more to do with politics, nobility, and control than holiness. Yet, he did try to provide some explanation grounded in reserving oneself for God or being able to do God's work free of the distractions of wife and family. His defense of celibacy seemed somewhat less than whole hearted.

I was quite tempted to follow up by quoting from this week's portion of *Shoftim*. This portion continues what was started in *Re'eh* — a list of laws and commandments that will be of significant importance to the Jewish people once they enter the Land of Israel. The Torah describes a system of courts and the monarchy (the Executive and Judicial branches), laws about making war, and a series of prohibitions relating to idol worship, false prophets, and witchcraft and sorcery. But the section I was alluding to, involves the role of the *kohanim* and *leviim* and their share of the land, or lack thereof.

Devarim 18:1,2 states: "There shall not be for the *Kohanim*, the *Leviim* — the entire tribe of Levi — a portion and an inheritance in

Israel, the fire offerings of God and His inheritance they shall eat. He shall not have an inheritance among his brethren, God is his inheritance, as He spoke to him."

Yes, there is a notion in Judaism of a class of Priests and *Leviim* who are dedicated to His service. These people, in fact, can claim God as their inheritance. However, this is only in the material sense — they get no portion of the land so that they are free to do God's work. "God is his inheritance." Nevertheless, the *Kohanim* and *Leviim* leave a legacy, their children.

My father once told me the story of a man who came to his rabbi and offered the synagogue a $50,000 if the rabbi would make him a *Kohen*. The rabbi said that there was no way to fulfill this request. The man offered $100,000, $500,000, and $1,000,000. When it hit $1 million, the rabbi said, "come back in a week, I will look to see if there are any loopholes."

The man returned in a week and the rabbi said, "I tried, I looked in every book I have, I called every learned colleague — there is simply no way for me to make you a *Kohen*."

The man dejectedly turned to leave the room. The rabbi called him back and asked, "Please tell me, why is it so important to you to be a *Kohen*?" The man replied, "Rabbi, my great-grandfather was a *Kohen*, my grandfather was a *Kohen*, my father was a *Kohen* — I likewise wanted to be a *Kohen!*"

In truth there is only one way to be a *Kohen* or a *Levi* — your father had to have been one. If these functionaries were celibate, there would be none left after the first generation. God may not have wanted them to be involved with the material world — to own property, to work the land, or to be involved economically. But an important aspect of their status was to insure continuity — to raise and educate children that could carry on God's work after them.

One does not have to be Jewish to love Levy's rye bread, and one does not have to be a *Kohen* or *Levi* in order to understand the role our children play in the continuity of our faith. My son's

Bar Mitzvah is certainly a cause to celebrate. Yet, in one sense it may be a greater celebration for my parents than for my wife and me. As they attend the festivities, they feel the pride of knowing that they have raised children that are raising children as observant, knowledgeable Jews. Their commitments and values become a legacy and an inheritance that is more important than anything material that they can pass down.

The words "God is his inheritance," in the verse can thus be read with a slightly different inflection. God is not merely the inheritance he receives, He is the inheritance that is passed to the next generation. His is the only truly meaningful legacy that any of us need concern ourselves with passing on. This type of legacy will never be passed on by the Archbishop and his like.

I was going to end this after the last sentence. However experiencing the preparations for the celebration and watching Josh don his *tefillin* (phylacteries) for the first time triggered a thought on one other aspect of the phrase "God is his inheritance." When we look at our children we sometimes have tunnel vision — we think a lot about what we do for them, what we buy them, how we feed and clothe them, how we educate them. We can rattle off the sacrifices, the late nights, the vacations we couldn't take, etc. We never focus on what we receive — not merely the love, joy, and devotion. I am talking about the "inheritance." God, through our children, gives us the chance to experience things again — as if for the first time. I re-experience the joy I felt putting on *tefillin* for the first time, a feeling twenty-four years in the past, when Josh puts on his.

This is also an inheritance — God giving me, giving all of us the chance to refresh and renew through our children.

KI TEITZEI
Beanie Battle

Summer vacation is over; the family is home and the kids are embarking upon a new school year, with its challenges and growth opportunities. This period of renewal coincides with the winding down of the Jewish year and the "home stretch" of this book.

While I expect to be a little more reflective in the concluding chapter or two, I did pause this week, as we survived Josh's Bar Mitzvah celebration relatively unscathed, to reflect on how fortunate I have been through the weeks since I began writing last October. The Aramaic words *Siyata D'shmaya* (Divine Assistance) stand out in my mind. Week in and week out God has helped me to focus on events, some extraordinary, some routine, with a meaningful perspective. Some weeks, in fact, He presented me with multiple topics and gave me the understanding to choose the most meaningful one.

This exercise in judgement in selecting weekly topics, however, has been skewed, somewhat, by a variety of personal biases and other factors. Some events were simply too intimate or private to discuss. Some topics may have been prone to misunderstanding. Also, I tried to steer away from current events — the progress of the peace negotiations in Israel, terrorist bombings, political scandals, celebrity deaths (i.e., Princess Di), etc. Finally, I avoided recent faddish pop culture so as not to date this work — any references to film, song, or merchandising have stood a certain test of time, at least in my judgement.

Pet rocks, lava lamps, hula-hoops, leisure suits, disco music, and the Macarena have all flashed and burned. Were I to devote time to this year's equivalents, I would be losing the reader of five to ten years hence (or two or three weeks hence). This week, however, I must make an exception. One of this country's most intense (an inexplicable) fads entered my home — and I was even responsible — BEANIE BABIES!

For those of you who are cave dwelling hermits — Beanie Babies are small beanbags, about the size of a clenched fist (I have big hands!), that come in a variety of animal characters. There are dogs, cats, foxes, crabs, tigers, lions, etc. — far in excess of one hundred different models. They retail for between $5 and $6. I underline retail because in that term lies their allure and mystique. They are (or seem to be in) great demand yet they are nearly impossible to find at regular stores at regular price.

The manufacturer, Ty Toys, realizes that it has a monster hit. Rather than saturating the market and going for the big kill, Ty doles out measured quantities of the product. The company has avoided the toy superstores (Toys R Us and Kay Bee), preferring to distribute through specialty toy stores, card and gift shops, and upscale boutiques. The company also varies the mix; retiring some characters, while introducing new ones.

Some examples of the mania created by this product:

• Earlier this year the company did a promotion with McDonalds. A customer could purchase a specially produced mini-Beanie Baby with the purchase of a combination of hamburger, soda, and fries. The promotion was expected to run for several weeks. Not only did the production run of these mini-Beanie Babies sell out in mere days, television news cameras showed images of literally hundreds of hamburgers and other items piled up in garbage bins outside of the restaurants. People were actually buying 5, 10, even 20 hamburger meal combinations that they did not want or need (let's conservatively say for $4 to $5 a piece), simply for the right to purchase one of the toys (again, let's say for $2 or $3) — and these were not even the real full-size Beanie Babies.

• On the Internet there are web-sites dedicated to the buying, selling, and trading of Beanie Babies. Some individual characters are being listed for sale at prices in excess of $1500.

• Burglars recently broke into a home of a young family whose child had a collection of several dozen Beanie Babies. The thieves offered to return the toys for a $10,000 ransom.

• There is a card and gift shop near my office that periodically receives shipments. This past Wednesday they received 1600 of them. Even with an imposed limit of 10 per customer — they sold out in two and a half hours.

And this is just the tip of the iceberg!

My children, like most, have a radar sense that focuses in on the "must have." Beanie Babies blipped on their screens last March, when we were spending time in New Jersey during the last stages of my mother-in-law's illness. In part to distract them and in part to relieve their anxiety, we agreed to purchase some Beanie Babies for them, if we could find any. We were, and have been, unsuccessful in this quest — always seeming to arrive the day before or after a shipment. By April and Passover, their clamoring for Beanies died down. We were resigned to the fact, and the children accepted, that they were too difficult to procure. (To the kids' credit, they did manage to keep it all in perspective. One day this summer we were out shopping in a mall that was hosting a craft show and flea market. One merchant had a locked glass case displaying eight or nine Beanies. He was offering them for sale at $30 a piece. The kids understood, without our saying a word, that the toys were not worth that price, to us). As the months have gone by, their furor has subsided and the kids have a new selection of "must haves."

On Tuesday, this week, I drove to a shopping center near the office during lunch to browse in the bookstore. As I was scanning the new arrivals, I overheard one of the sales girls tell the other that Marshall Field's ("Field's"), a large department store nearby, was expected to receive a shipment of Beanie Babies around noon. It was about 12:20 P.M. on my watch.

I quietly left the store and walked over to Field's. When I entered the store, I asked a clerk where the Beanie Babies were being sold. I was directed to a remote area of an upper floor of the building. Near this area was a large sign that proclaimed that purchases of Beanie Babies were limited to 25 per person. As I approached the sales area, I noticed two sales associates sorting through a large bag of Beanies, separating them by character. By some turn of good fortune, I was second in line. The woman in front of me ordered eight or nine. I stood waiting weighing my options — should a select one or two for each child; should I look at the individual characters to pick out the cute or nice ones; should I simply select 25, the maximum, with full understanding of the value of the toys to the market and to my children; should I, should I, should I?

Let us step away from this for a moment. Here I was, a grown man, with no particular obsession with bean bag toys, who has many other important/financial obligations, who has spent little time contemplating Beanie Babies (in fact I can not recall even having seen or held one before that day) — and not only did I feel compelled or obligated to make a purchase, I was contemplating a not insignificant purchase. In what seemed like hours, but was, in reality, only a minute at most, I ran the gamut of rationalizations and reality checks. Because these items were desired, artificially scarce, and available here and now, I was about to impulsively, without premeditation, planning, or forethought, purchase as many as I could.

I asked the sales associate for one of each — which turned out to be 27, in all (she was kind enough to allow me to purchase all of them, even though this exceeded the limit of 25). For a moment I felt elated — gratified — that I am going to be a hero; I am going to please my children. I can brag about how I beat the system and satisfied the family's Beanie Baby cravings. When I got back to the car, however, I felt stupid — I had just spent $170 on beanbag toys! What possessed me to do this?

In this week's Torah portion of *Ki Teitzei* I found the answer, which lies not in a moment or an action, but in a process.

The portion of *Ki Teitzei,* like *Shoftim,* and perhaps even more like *Mishpatim,* is a compendium of laws of everyday Jewish life. The laws in this portion run the gamut from societal, to sexual, to religious, to ethical. All told, the portion contains 74 commandments. However, my Beanie Baby experience relates most closely to the first three passages.

The portion opens with a description of the commandment relating to the *yephat to'ar* ("woman of beautiful form"). In this section God, in His Torah, responds to the real, rather than the ideal, nature of man. The primary actor is the Jewish soldier engaged in the heat of battle. He notices a beautiful woman among the enemy captives and he lusts after her. The Torah realizes that a man in such circumstances may not be able to control himself; so it gives him a controlled means of satisfying his desires. He may not savagely take her, but he must follow a process. According to some views, he may actually be able to cohabit with her one time even before she undergoes the process, but he must then follow the prescribed steps that may well lead to his marrying her.

(This section, all by itself, may provide some understanding of my Beanie-Mania. We learn from it that there are times when we can get caught up in a pursuit, when we are in the heat of battle, so to speak, to such an extent that passions and irrational urges do get the better of us. While we must certainly strive for control, we sometimes succumb.)

Immediately after describing the *yephat to'ar* process, the Torah presents an interesting legal discussion involving the rights of a first born son. The situation presented is a little unusual. The actor this time has two wives; one identified as beloved, one hated. Both women bear him sons. The one born first is attributed to the hated wife. The Torah directs that the father cannot declare the son born to the beloved wife to be his first born. He must give the rights, consisting primarily of a double portion in the eventual inheritance, to the son of the hated wife.

The very next section, seemingly unconnected to the proceeding one, describes the *ben sorer u'moreh* (the wayward and rebellious son). The Torah directs that if parents have a son who is essentially rotten, a real juvenile delinquent (defined more completely in the Talmud) who fails to respond to their discipline, they must accompany him to the court and proclaim "This son of ours is wayward and rebellious; he does not hearken to our voice; he is a glutton and a drunkard" (*Devarim* 21:20). His crimes are petty theft (from his parents) and gluttony. If various procedural requirements are met, the boy is executed by stoning.

(Two observations from the Talmud about the *ben sorer u'moreh* are worth noting. First, even though his present actions are not capital offenses, he is judged based on a projection of his inevitable behavior. If he steals and is a drunken glutton now, in his parents' home, he will likely be a murdering highway robber when he achieves independence. Thus, it is better in the overall scheme that he dies while still a relative innocent than while culpably guilty. This may seem harsh, but this is the Torah's moral judgement. Second, the Talmud reports that in the history of the Jewish court system, this process was never invoked.)

Rashi, in his commentary, explains that there is, in fact, a connection between the opening three sections of *Ki Tetzei*. He describes a progression: "If you marry her (the *yephat to'ar*), ultimately she will become hated (a likely result considering the circumstances of the marriage and the religious and cultural differences between the spouses), and in the end, she will bear a rebellious child (the *ben sorer u'moreh*)" (Rashi on *Devarim* 21:11). A leads to B, which leads to C. There should be few big surprises in life. Most everything, even those things that are unpleasant or seem out of character, is just the consequence of previous steps and actions.

I could claim that spending $170 on 27 Beanie Babies was the result of a momentary compulsion; temporary insanity. It seemed that way. It felt that way. It was hard to explain afterwards. Yet, as I look back I see that I was a primed pump. The kids had nagged for months; we had been unsuccessful in several trips to the toy store to purchase them; I had read articles in the newspaper describing the mania; I could hear the excitement in the voice of the sales girl at the book store who was privy to the information about the shipment. Without realizing it, I was more than a primed pump, I was a spring wound very tightly — and the scariest part is that I was not even aware of it!

This week also marked the beginning of the Jewish month of *Elul,* the month leading up to the High Holy Days. In *Elul* we concern ourselves with *teshuvah* (repentance). We prepare ourselves to battle our evil inclinations, to resolve to change and improve, and to beg for forgiveness. Part of this process involves acknowledging and recognizing that we have sinned through verbal confession. It is hard to admit wrongdoing especially since it is so easy to make excuses.

Just as I lost this battle with the Beanie Babies, over the past year I lost many battles with my baser inclination. I lost because I did not recognize the strategic importance of the skirmishes along the way. I also did not pay enough attention to the cumulative effect of some of my actions and choices. But as with the Beanie

Babies, and my newly hatched plan to use them effectively as tools to reinforce the positive behavior of my children, I have to make the best of the situation. If I try to engage the enemy during this holy time, with pleas for repentance, prayers to God for assistance, and an eagerness to improve, I may be able to turn the negatives into a final positive — to win the war after losing many battles — and perhaps will merit that "Hashem your God, will deliver them (your enemy) into your hand, and you will capture its captivity" (*Devarim* 21:10).

KI TAVO
Curses — Foiled Again

Anger, especially anger accompanied by loss of control, rarely produces a positive result. In fact, our sages analogize such anger to idol worship. Yet, we are human and anger is a very human emotion. Frustration, impatience, zealousness, retribution, hurt, self-righteousness, and other motivations can trigger it. It is also a method for dealing with stress and for transferring feelings or blame or guilt.

People feel angry with some frequency. However, people with a modicum of self-control rarely express it demonstratively; exhibitions of anger, when they occur, are unflattering, hurtful, and destructive. Our blood pressure goes up. Our faces get red. We raise our voices. We use language that is not usual in tone or content. We use words that are equivalent of verbal bullets — they are intended to damage and pain the target. Sometimes, people resort to forms of physical expression — throwing objects, ripping or breaking things, and unfortunately, even hitting and injuring others.

Most of us are aware how harmful anger can be and we know

that outbursts and tantrums rarely resolve conflicts or solve problems. If we could step back from a situation, we would likely be able to regain control. Often, when we cool down and look back at the incident, we wonder how we could have lost it, especially over something that was, no doubt, rather trivial. Certainly, a videotape of our actions would provide a healthy dose of embarrassment, and, if one possessed the ability to laugh at one's self, a few laughs at how ridiculous we looked and acted.

One of the keys to understanding our own anger, and our ability to control it, is to look back after time has passed, passions subsided, and the fires have cooled. With honest reflection we, hopefully, can take the remedial steps necessary to undo whatever harm was done and can learn to manage ourselves better when faced with the inevitable next provocation.

In this case, I feel that two weeks is sufficient to reach back and analyze a recent and thankfully quite rare occasion, when I lost it. That incident, was unremarkable for its typicalness — it is a situation that many will be able to understand and identify with. However, it was important to me this week because it occurred recently enough, in my memory of experience, to help me avoid a similar conflagration that might have had a more far-reaching consequence.

I will start with this week's trigger.

My children attend a large Jewish day school, with an enrollment of nearly 900. The school has two buildings, each about one mile apart from the other, housing, separately, the boys and the girls divisions. The early childhood classes, the pre-school and kindergarten programs, with nearly 200 children, are divided between the two facilities. In recent years the school has nearly outgrown its available space. The school's governing board appointed a committee to study the problem and to recommend viable solutions. The committee's top suggestion was that the school undertake to build a new early childhood education facility.

This would better serve the needs of the younger children and would free up four to six classrooms worth of space in each building.

I was appointed to a steering committee for the building project. The committee's overall task is 1) to identify and procure a suitable location 2) to select an appropriate design firm and contractor, and 3) to assist in the fund raising for the project. After working with the design and building people to ascertain the space requirements, our top priority was to find land that would be conveniently located, affordable, and appropriately sized and zoned for the school's needs.

At one of our first meetings, a report was given that an ideal parcel had been identified. It was located near one of the other buildings, it was sufficiently large, and it was owned by another Jewish organization — which had acquired it from the Jewish Federation a number of years ago. This organization was not currently using this section of the land (in fact it was temporarily leasing it to a local car dealer, who stores excess inventory on it), which was on the far end of its large lot.

In our minds the project should be able to proceed with little opposition or interference. We would pay the organization fair value for the section of land we needed; the school would anchor a section of the neighborhood that is vital to its long-term stability (for a number of years, members of the community were fleeing to more affluent suburbs), and the school itself is identifiably vital to all of our futures. A no-brainer, right? Wrong!

When we met with representatives of the organization, our eyes were opened to the definition of self-interest — theirs not ours. First, some of their membership did not want to "forfeit" the income stream from the auto dealer. Second, others espoused a desire to retain as much of their land as possible so that they would have a larger parcel of marketable property if and when they ever decided to abandon their own location and to relocate elsewhere. Finally, others simply expressed their disapproval of our desire to spend $1 million, give or take a few dollars, for the project (why don't we send our kids to public school?). In their opinion, we could and should be spending our money more productively.

There was not one person at the meeting who stressed potential expansion or growth of their own organization. Quite the contrary, most of the current membership has moved to further suburbs. Similarly, no one expressed encouragement for our project. It was as if we were a "them," the enemy, an alien group encroaching on their needs, practices, beliefs, and vision.

As the meeting progressed, I began to simmer, then boil, then flame — inwardly. How could they be so shortsighted? How can they fail to see the benefits of the project to the community, to our people, and to our collective futures? I began to interpret their statements, most in reality relatively benign, as dripping with venomous, sectarian bigotry. However, a little voice inside my head started saying — calm down, you do not want to lose it or to say anything you may later regret or which may impede any potential future negotiations — remember what happened two weeks ago!

Yes, it happened two weeks ago and it is still difficult to face.

Two weeks ago we hosted a celebration for Josh's Bar Mitzvah. For us, this event was significant on a number of levels. Since Josh is our oldest, this was the first such major celebration that we had to plan. Additionally, as I have discussed previously, my wife and her family are in mourning following the passing of my mother-in-law. This meant that extra care had to be taken so that the mourners could participate (i.e., no music, no African safari) and that the mix of emotions of the day could be managed. Moreover, because we had so recently experienced a series of family tragedies (see, *Kedoshim:* 'The Delicatessen at the End of the Galaxy"), we felt it extra important to celebrate as a family — for the event inclusively to involve the extended family.

Primarily for this last reason, we arranged to hold the affair in New Jersey. In essence, for this important celebration we decided to sacrifice a gathering of friends in Detroit for a gathering of family in New Jersey (over 90% of the invited family members live in New York and New Jersey. By unscientific means, we determined that fewer than half would incur the cost of travel to Detroit for a week-end, whereas nearly all would drive the 10-45 minutes to the quite centrally located venue we selected). We meticulously tracked down addresses and mailed out the invitations extra early so as that people could avoid scheduling conflicts.

Kim and I, thank God, have relatively large extended families. Thus, we had to establish guidelines for our list of invitees. Essentially, although there were a few exceptions, we invited the following categories of relatives: parents, grandparents, great-grandparents, aunts, uncles, great aunts and uncles, brothers, sisters, nieces, nephews, first cousins, our parent's first cousins, and a few friends who lived in the area. As the day approached and the response cards trickled in, we were glad to see that we would have the kind of meaningful participation we hoped for.

The planning involved coordinating, from long distance, many details over several months. For the most part, we did a decent job of not leaving anything important for the last minute. The night before the party, however, was still hectic (though not frantic). I was reviewing my remarks and listening to Josh practice his. Peshie had the flu and needed our attention. The other kids were bouncing off the walls in the excitement and we tried to keep them occupied and out of our hair. Kim was finalizing the seating arrangements (courtesy of a flurry of last minute responses and our phoning those few who did not respond in a timely manner) and was preparing the place cards.

Realistically, my nieces would have gladly done this last task, but Kim wanted to be busy. She did not want to concentrate on the darkness marring her joy. She was doing what she could to block out the fact that her mother would not be there with us to celebrate the *simchah* (joyous occasion) of the first of her grandsons to

313

reach Bar Mitzvah; a grandson named after her husband, Kim's father.

About 10:30 P.M. the phone rang. It was Kim's first cousin Sarah (not her real name). Kim and Sarah are the same age. They grew up together and went through elementary and high school together (of course these statements are true for at least three or four other cousins, as well). They went to different colleges, married, and settled into their own quite separate lives. However, they do speak on the phone infrequently (making it a point to call each other on their birthdays) and spend some time together in the summer.

Sarah informed Kim that she just had to call — she did not want to face our *simchah* without getting something off her chest. How dare we not invite her children to our party (we did not invite the children of our first cousins, unless they happened to be Josh's friends, kids he regularly spoke to or played or went to camp with). She somewhat frantically blathered that, she thought that she and Kim had a "special" relationship and that due to this closeness her entire family should have received special treatment and consideration. Kim calmly explained how and why we made our decisions.

Sarah's response was to launch into a tirade accusing Kim of all sorts of slights and insensitivities dating back to when the girls were in diapers (all thematically unified by the refrain "you never really liked me"). Kim, to her credit, tried to reel Sarah back in and hold things together. However, the timing of this call was inauspicious at best. As she became frustrated with Sarah's failure to listen to reason, the emotional floodgates literally opened. We wanted nothing more than family unity and healing, a little sunshine after a dark night. Now, less than 12 hours before the festivities, a self-absorbed individual in a desperately selfish act was literally ripping open an emotional wound otherwise being held together by the flimsiest of stitching. Kim was literally shaking and could barely converse, let alone focus. We hung up the phone and tried to regain some calm.

As upset as we were, we still did not want the event to be

marred by petty emotions. Although I was pretty worked up myself as I was forced to witness the damage Sarah inflicted, we decided that I should go to Sarah's parents' house, Kim's aunt and uncle, to ascertain whether things could be smoothed over. As an extra measure, to keep things in perspective and to remind them of the stakes, I brought Josh along. I guess that I expected said aunt and uncle to assume a parental or elder statesman-like posture — to admonish us silly kids to make nice — to kiss and make up.

Instead I encountered rather stern demeanors braced for conflict. As a parent, I can understand the importance of supporting your own child and their decision. A parent also wishes to remedy or avenge any harm or hurt that may befall them. However, one would think that a parent has the maturity and experience to keep things in perspective — what is the situation; what is at stake; who is involved? In a close family one would think that the lines of force creating distinctions between sons and nephews or daughters and nieces are rather thin. Yet, here, inexplicably, the opposite seemed true. The tranquility of our *simchah* was being breached, my wife was being assaulted with a senseless torrent of emotions and while I went over to broker normalization — they were sticking to their guns. As we had decided before I went over, rather than risking further tension the next morning, we uninvited that branch of the family. Needless to say my, personal anxiety level was going higher and higher. At that point, it would have taken very little to set me off.

And very little it was. Kim's uncle rose brusquely to show us to the door and in an indignant tone curtly asked us to leave. By showing diffidence when I expected conciliation, his actions pulled my trigger. As I stepped out the door onto the porch I shouted, "Your children should only know what it's like to celebrate these occasions without parents." Which translated from the Jewish syntax means that I essentially cursed them with the expressed hope for their untimely demise.

This was not one of my prouder moments. I understand the motivation behind my words — a desire to rebuke them for such insensitivity to Kim's emotions and their audacity to rain on our parade — but I do not think that it fully excuses verbalization of such sentiments. Thus, when I was faced this week with a situation that similarly put my control to the test, my inner voice of experience pulled back the reins and I sat quietly.

These two experiences helped me to understand this week's portion of *Ki Tavo* in a new way. The portion begins where the last few have likewise been, providing details for a number of commandments — the bringing of the first fruits and the confession of the tithes. After essentially concluding the *mitzvah* instruction, Moshe gives a brief "pep talk" in *Devarim* 26:16-19, exhorting the people to serve God with a full commitment and with enthusiastic freshness — treating every day as if it were the one on which they received the Torah.

While Ki Tavo contains other material, as well, it is most famous, or in this case infamous, for the *Tochecha* (the rebuke). The portion lists, in quite excruciating detail, the abject horror that would befall the Jewish People if they slid down a slope away from adherence to the commandments of the Torah. Such a litany of curses appears twice in the Torah, once here and once near the end of *Vayikra* in the portion of *Bechukotai.* The curses range from the standard drought, famine, and exile motifs to things like mothers being forced to feast on the flesh of their young. The sages offer a variety of comments on the significance of the two recitations and their differences. Just on a superficial level we notice several variations: Whereas *Bechukotai* contains 49 curses, the list in *Ki Tavo* is 99 curses in length; the former curses are in the plural whereas these are in the singular; the first set were presented in that first year or so after the Exodus, the latter near the end of the forty years; and the first set were declared by God, the second by Moshe.

Sages in later generation had the benefit of hindsight. They could, and have, identified historical periods when God plagued us with most, if not all of the curses. A number of sages seek to align the two sets of curses with the eras of the destruction of the First and Second Temples. Yet there seems to be some disagreement about which set corresponds to which Temple. Moreover, one can certainly find an eerie fulfillment of these curses in the Holocaust era.

As I read and digest the curses, I am overcome with questions — why did the people not understand the consequences of their actions — consequences that were foretold in the Torah? Why did God have to create such a wide variety of curses and punishments? And finally, if we are His Chosen People, what was He really trying to accomplish by presenting our predecessors with these curses — it could not have been to show them how "Bad" (as in awesome and powerful) He can be, it could not have been to cower and intimidate us (He wants love), and it unfortunately has not proven to be a particularly effective deterrent — so why list the curses or, more to the point, why list them twice?

I found the key to understanding these curses by reflecting on what I experienced over the last two weeks. God can exile us and smite us with a catalogue of curses. The consequences are tragic and terrible. Yet, the curses we hurl at each other and the damage we inflict with our words and actions can be far harsher. We are a family, a community. We should support each other, encourage each other, and cherish growth and the good times. Instead we denigrate, impede, criticize, complain and ultimately punish and destroy.

I believe that it is instructive to look at the Talmud's description of the events leading up to the destruction of the Second Temple. The Roman Legions were preparing to lay siege to Jerusalem. Hundreds of thousands of Jews resided within her walls. The full might of Rome was intent on victory, but after three years, it made little progress.

The Talmud (*Gittin* 56a) relates that three wealthy Jewish patrons resided in Jerusalem. The first pledged to provide wheat and barley. The second pledged wine, salt, and oil. The third pledged wood for fuel. All told, they warehoused sufficient provisions for twenty-one years.

As the siege went on, two prevailing philosophies emerged as to a course of action. The Rabbis believed that the stand-off could be ended through treaty negotiations. The radicals, however, wanted a final and direct military confrontation. To force the issue, the radicals burned the stored provisions. As a result of this action, thousands died of famine (a number of representative deaths are graphically described in the text), many of the curses of the *Tochecha* came to fruition, and ultimately Jerusalem and the Temple were destroyed. Our own actions, Jewish action, family conflict, cursed us far worse than it seemed God was willing to. God limited His curses to a list — we can far exceed it. Our cruelty is not tempered with mercy. Our anger is not measured by appropriateness. Our reactions are not balanced by judgement. Our responses are not tempered by Omniscience.

Upon closer examination this message is coded, if you will, in the two *Tochecha* renditions. The version stated in the plural is shorter than that of the singular (the more self absorbed and selfish we are, the worse the consequence). God's Divine version is shorter than Moshe's human one (man is willing to curse himself far more than God is). The version for the humble and still somewhat subservient recently freed slaves is shorter than that of the totally free and independent wanderers (ego brings its own curses).

We can not take back words hurled in anger. We, likewise, can not replay events that have already taken place. The pictures and videos of Josh's Bar Mitzvah will forever be missing uninvited family members. Future *smachot* will be tainted with awkwardness. Why do we do this to ourselves? Why do we replace Divine blessing with self-inflicted curse? I think we know the answers — they are just too painful to honestly confront.

NITZAVIM-VAYEILECH
Standing Room Only

The challenge this week is to avoid writing so much that my prose dwarfs the two portions themselves. You see, the double portions, *Nitzavim* and *Vayeilech,* read this week jointly consist of only seventy verses (*Nitzavim* has forty and *Vayeilech* has thirty). Maybe some enforced discipline will bring about sharper, crisper writing. Maybe this is a convenient excuse for writing less since I have so much to do in order to prepare for the upcoming holidays.

Rosh Hashana is only a week and one-half away, with Yom Kippur close on its heels. These are the Jewish Days of Awe, days on which our actions and character are evaluated in the heavenly court. God judges everyone in order to determine whether they merit reward or punishment, feast or famine, and life or death in the upcoming year. As an attorney, I would never consider walking into a courtroom to represent my client without having first prepared as much as necessary and possible. The stakes in this spiritual courtroom are far higher than anything I ever have encountered or will encounter professionally. Therefore it behooves me to prepare — through study, by reviewing the liturgy, by attending inspirational talks, by thinking about repentance, and simply by heightening my spiritual sensitivity and awareness — to face the Days of Judgement.

There is a lighter or pleasant side to this time of year, as well. Many people send out New Year's cards as a way of touching base and saying, "I am still out here and I occasionally stop to think about you." Although it is somewhat more expensive, I try to phone select relatives and friends (some do beat me to the punch) — to hear their voices and literally to connect with them. In a way it closes the loop on the prayers and meditations of last year's Days of Awe. In synagogue we asked who will live, who will die, who will become rich, who will become impoverished, etc. As I reach out and touch family and friends, I see the answers that were written. I learn about the birth of new children and the death of parents. I learn about job losses and promotions. I hear things that make me happy and some that are quite disturbing.

On the heels of last week's near tirade, I should know better than to venture back into the realm of the disturbing. However, I must share the contents of two of my pre-Rosh Hashana conversations because they have been weighing on my mind and have affected how I expect to approach God with my prayers for the upcoming year.

One of the calls I made was to our friends Ed and Rachel in Chicago. Ed is an attorney who is about ten years older than I am and, when I first started in practice, was a mentor of sorts (he was more than happy to take a fellow religious attorney under his wing). We both moved away to pursue our career paths in later years and it seems as if this call is the only time we take to catch up.

I dialed and Rachel answered. I asked how things were and she answered, "Not so good. Ed and I separated about six months ago and we are in the process of getting a divorce." I groped for something appropriate to say after this real conversation stopper.

I finally managed the composure to ask how she and the kids were handling things. She replied that they moved past the initial denial and were getting on with life. However, she said that one disturbing incident continued to gnaw at her.

It seems that at the time when Ed and Rachel decided to separate, their oldest daughter Chani, then twenty-two and in graduate school, was three months into an engagement, with the wedding looming a scant four months away. When her in-laws to be, caught wind of Ed and Rachel's marital woes, they put the kabosh on the impending nuptials. In their eyes, the smart, beautiful, refined, personable Chani, whom they supposedly adored, was now a leper, a pariah. What was her transgression? Her sin was that her parents had the audacity to live their own lives and end their own twenty-five year marriage.

Rachel explained to me, a babe in the woods whose oldest is only thirteen, just how irrational and exasperating the dating and marriage game is within segments of the Orthodox community. Any defect or fault, any handicap or infirmity, any skeleton in the closet for a descendent or sibling of a perspective mate can render that child untouchable and unmarriageable.

As I was to discover two days later, this was just the tip of the iceberg.

Yes, just two days later I placed a call to Jeremy and Rose in Philadelphia. Jeremy is an old *yeshivah* and college buddy and racquetball partner (King Arthur's courts in Fort Lee, New Jersey during our Y. U. days) who is now the head of Pediatrics in a major hospital and a geneticist. After we exchanged pleasantries and best wishes, Jeremy said that he needed to share with me the account of an incident that took place at his hospital over the weekend. He was home relaxing on Sunday night and he received a page. His presence was requested in the emergency room. This request was strange since he was rarely involved in emergency cases and anything related to his genetics work was typically more laboratory based.

When he arrived at the hospital, he was met by one of the staff doctors who explained that a couple had come in with a deceased two-week-old infant. They claimed that they were out camping when the baby had stopped breathing during the night, while they were asleep with it in their tent. Jeremy still did not know why he was called in. Then he was brought in to meet the parents — who were in a small room with their dead child.

Both parents appeared to be in their early forties and were dressed in what the general public would term Chasidic garb (he with long black coat, black pants, white shirt, and large black hat; she with long skirt, with stockings, blouse with long sleeves, and a kerchief on her head). Jeremy immediately suspected that they were not likely to have been out camping, especially with an infant, but then again, he was not one to judge a book by its cover. Apart from the fact that this matter involved observant Jews like himself, he still did not know why he was called. This was surely a matter for pathology or the medical examiner. However, when he finally looked at the baby, comprehension hit him like a load of bricks. The child showed signs of Down Syndrome, a fact Jeremy con-firmed shortly thereafter in his lab.

The issue now became clear, as clear as mud. Should he refer the matter through channels to the appropriate authorities to con-duct a homicide investigation? Was he required to show a measure of compassion to the parents and not raise an alarm? After consulting with a few of his colleagues and a respected rabbinic authority, he was left with only one choice — to inform on the situation.

Jeremy was present when the investigator came to question the parents. In the glare of accusation, they were unable to stick to their original story very long. They reluctantly admitted to commit-ting the despicable act. When asked for their reasons — was it financial; was it emotional; was it, in some twisted way, religious? they responded that their older children were at or were approach-ing marriageable age. They felt that if "word got out" that they had a younger sibling who was handicapped, their own prospects would be severely limited, if they did not dry up completely.

(Jeremy confided in me that this is not an uncommon attitude within the Jewish community. He has treated other children with obvious and severe handicaps and genetic defects who were brought in by parents who had legally changed the child's name so as to be able to mask the family association. Moreover, he works with several organizations that quietly seek to place such children in homes with adults who will properly care for and appreciate them.)

I thought of these two incidents as I reviewed the opening verses of this week's portions of *Nitzavim* and *Vayeilech:*

> All of you stand today before God, the heads of your tribes, your elders, your officers, every Jewish man. Your children, your wives, and your stranger that dwells in the midst of your camp, from the woodcutter to the water carrier. For you to pass into the covenant of God your God and His oath, that Hashem your God executed with you today. (*Devarim* 29:9-11).

Moshe, in his final day, has been communicating and explaining the contract or covenant between God and the Jewish people. There will be much blessing if we live up to expectations and horrible curses if we stray. God had previously made promises to our forefathers, Avraham, Yitzchak, and Yaacov and He had given the Torah at Sinai signaling His acceptance of our people. Moshe now physically and symbolically united the children of Israel so that they could stand together and accept the covenant and the responsibilities it engendered.

Moshe could have started with a simple "You are all gathered here today to" But no, his introduction is rather verbose. He enumerates every type of Jew — all shapes, sizes, ages, and sexes. He notes political and economic class. He even deals with parental lineage. They all stand together. They were all addressed equally.

They were each crucial to the covenant. They were individually important.

The lame, the children, the divorced, the converts, and the poor were as significant as the strong, powerful and rich. Everyone standing there accepted God's covenant and, in turn, was bound to God and His promises.

Next week we are all likewise going to stand before God. We are all to be judged. The Heavenly Court has its own rules and procedures. One of the most important is the fact, as described by many sages, we are judged the way we judge others. If we are impatient, quick to find fault, intolerant, or severe, we will be extended the same courtesies.

Moshe's words and actions in *Nitzavim* and *Vayeilech* teach us that every fellow Jew, no matter his level of religious observance, or physical appearance, or mental acuity, or genetic imperfection, or marital status, is part of God's covenant. He is as much their God as yours or mine. How dare we judge someone else, let alone an innocent offspring, spouse, or sibling, based on our own fears, prejudice and ignorance.

When I stand before God on Rosh Hashana to offer my prayers and pleas, I will shed tears for Rachel and Chani and for all the children who have parents who think like that couple in Philadelphia. I will also pray that God grant understanding to those who can not comprehend the crippling damage that their attitudes are inflicting on future generations.

Perhaps when we can, if we ever can, stand all together we will merit that each New Year will be sweet, for all of our days and the days of our children.

HAAZINU-VEZOT HABERACHAH
We'll be Coming Around the Mountain

At approximately 11:30 A.M. on a crisp and bright September Sunday morning, my friend Joey pulled into our driveway and honked the horn of his late-model Buick. Upon hearing this eagerly awaited sound, I bounded out the door. I was ready, I was psyched up, and I was geared up in suitable attire, a Detroit Lions hat and matching "Hawaiian blue" team logo sweatshirt. In my hand I held a bag containing all of the necessary provisions: deli meats, rye bread, hot mustard, half-sour pickles, soda, and a chunk of those wonderful oatmeal/chocolate chip brownies that my daughter baked for this past *Shabbat*.

We were on our way to the Silverdome to watch a football game. Actually, we were on our way to watch more than a game. This was "The Game." The Lions' opponents on this football Sunday were to be none other than the defending Superbowl Champion Green Bay Packers — the despised Cheeseheads. What makes this game such an event, aside from the fact that the Packers are a good football team and longtime division rival, is the mix of fans in attendance. Since Wisconsin is relatively nearby and since Packers fans are so fanatical about their team — they descend upon the Silverdome in hoards.

Let me describe the look of a typical Packers fan:

We start with the obligatory officially licensed jersey (the cheapskates wear some form of t-shirt). Next comes the face paint, which is applied in a variety of ways; some paint their faces yellow, some green, some half-and-half, and some apply it in streaks like Indian war paint. Finally, we have the headgear, of which the most common variety is a large yellow triangular piece of foam or polyurethane shaped like a wedge of cheese (hence the appellation Cheeseheads). Some fans, of course, simply dispense with the hat altogether and paint their hair yellow, green, or some combination thereof.

These fans clearly love their Packers. But it seems as if they love something else nearly as much as their Packers — BEER. That's right, many of these people left their homes at 4 or so in the morning to drive 5–8 hours to Detroit for the game, decked out in their costumes. As soon as they arrive in the parking lot, out comes the coolers and pop goes the bottles and cans. These human sponges can't drink it fast enough! By the 1:00 P.M. kickoff, many of these people not only look like clowns, they are acting like them, in their pickled haze.

In the early stages of the game, it seemed as if our Lions Den would be co-oped as a Packer Party Place. The Packers jumped out with two early scores and were manhandling the Motown crew. But, as the game progressed, momentum shifted. The Lions took control and ultimately dominated the game. The moods of the Packer faithful digressed from euphoria, to mild concern, to panic, to deflated despair. These fans and their hangovers would have a long ride home. By Monday, their weekends would be forgotten (as soon as their stomachs settled) and they would simply shift their passions and attentions to next week's game. As Fleetwood Mac would say — "Yesterday's gone."

By midway through the fourth quarter of the game, its outcome was no longer in doubt. Thus, we headed for the parking lot with about five minutes to go on the game clock (fifteen to twenty in real time) in order to beat the traffic home.

Ordinarily, this would not have been so important. However, it was already close to 4:00 P.M. and Joey and I had another "date" scheduled, together with our sons, at 5:30 P.M. Fortunately, we were able to exit the parking lot with only minor delays and we had clear sailing on the roads home. I walked through the door at 5:10 P.M., which gave me just enough time to shower and to change into the appropriate uniform for my evening foray: black suit, white shirt, tie (no sunglasses — I am not one of the "Men in Black"), and BLACK HAT. By 5:30 I was behind the wheel, with Josh in the front seat, on my way to pick up Joey and his son David.

We were hurrying to attend a live satellite broadcast, on a large wall-sized projection screen, of an event taking place at two venues in New York. Those venues were not broadcast studios or theaters. They are actually quite well known in the fields of sports and entertainment — Madison Square Garden and the Nassau Coliseum. The two arenas were sold out — filled to capacity. Viewing locations around the United States and the rest of the world, accommodating tens of thousands (who paid between $18 and $100+ per ticket), were likewise sold out. Were we gathered for a pay-per-view-boxing extravaganza; or Olympic basketball or hockey championships; or a Grateful Dead Reunion? No, believe it or not, approximately 100,000 Jews gathered in person and via video to celebrate the completion of a 7 1/2 year cycle of Talmud study, and the start of a new one (This program is called *Daf Yomi,* literally a folio or page a day. If one were to study one complete page of Talmud per day, one would encounter its entire text over the course of 7 1/2 years.

A number of groups, though primarily Agudath Israel, have promoted coordinated study so that any Jew participating, no matter where he lives, learns from the same portion of text each day).

For nearly 3 1/2 hours, 100,000 Jews sat in formal attire (suits, not tuxedos) to listen to the words of renown scholars and sages, to listen to and to sing songs of praise and congratulation and to participate with dignified joy in a celebration of the ages and for the ages. There were no painted faces or heads and the only intoxicants were fellowship and happiness.

Upon the completion of the Talmud (actually, upon the completion of even a single tractate) the participants recite a variety of prayers. In one we thank God, "For placing our portion among those who sit in the study hall as opposed to those who hang out on the street corner; for we arise early and they arise early — we arise for words of Torah and they arise for worthless matters; we toil and they toil — we toil and receive reward and they toil and do not receive reward; we run and they run — we run to life in the world to come and they run to the well of destruction."

This prayer, like my experiences on Sunday, provides a study in contrasts. Other than, perhaps, the memory of a good time, what have Rangers, Knicks, and Islanders fans ever come away with from their experiences in those venues? What did the Packers fans gain from their junket to Detroit? Vanity, nothingness, momentary gratification. What do we get from studying Torah each day, from celebrating accomplishment, from participating in its transmission? Personal growth, closeness to God, national unity. They run and we run.

This week's portion of *Haazinu* is a song that Moshe transcribed to bear witness to the future responsibilities of our nation — from generation to generation. Songs are not merely written down and placed on a shelf. Songs are sung, they are taught, they are memorized, they are internalized, and they resonate from within.

Haazinu is also the concluding weekly Torah portion. No, I do not have a different Torah text than you do. I am fully aware that there is one more portion to come, *Vezot Haberachah.* However, *Haazinu* is the last portion that we read on a *Shabbat,* it is the last portion that is associated with the ebb and flow of our weekly lives. *Vezot Haberachah* is only read on the holiday of *Simchat Torah,* the concluding day of the Festival Season. This portion is read after seven (in Israel) or eight (outside of Israel) straight days of intense spirituality with our *succah* huts and the other holiday symbols. It is not a portion that can be constrained by or assigned to a natural week, it looms above our lives — a goal — a mountaintop. Yet when we reach that mountain, we merely round it and begin again with *Bereishit.*

How fitting that I merit to complete this journey through our Torah on a week that our people have merited completing a journey through the Talmud. How blessed do I feel that I have been able, with God's assistance, to climb week by week up through the themes of our Torah and to learn so much about how it guides us through life.

I write these words literally hours before Rosh Hashana. The Talmud relates (*Rosh Hashana* 17b) that on the New Year, God sits with three books open before him. He judges and examines our actions in order to determine whether we are to be inscribed for life or death, or whether He must push the issue until Yom Kippur. This may seem irreverent, and it is not intended to be, but in my mind I can picture my spiritual analogue as it stands before God in the heavenly court during the review of my year and hands God a computer disc with this manuscript and says — "Look, I saved you some time, just enter this and save — although it does need some editing." (Our lives, like this book, can certainly use some good editing — and God gives it to us through the process of *teshuvah,* repentance — but that would lead me to another essay, another chapter — and this must wait for another time).

Indeed, *"Vezot Haberachah"* — this year and this project is and

TORAH 24/7

has been a blessing. I thank the Almighty for all the blessings in my life — my family, my friends, my community, my co-workers, and my students. I thank Him for providing all of my material and spiritual needs — anticipating most far in advance of my own realization. I thank Him for leading me on the journey that has provided me with the worldview, education, and experience necessary to attempt the integration of ideas contained in the book. And *acharon, acharon chaviv* — last, but most dear — I thank Him for the blessing that is my wife Kim — my partner, soulmate, love, critic, coach, teacher, best friend — who stood by me and my need to create during what proved to be one of the hardest and most difficult years of her life — the year in which we lost her beloved mother — *Payah Leah Bas Alter Ben Zion Halevi.* May the merit of any Torah study that results from this book be an *aliyah* (a source of spiritual elevation) for Mom's Neshama (soul).